Canadian Acts of Kindness

Chicken Soup for the Soul: Canadian Acts of Kindness
101 Stories of Caring and Compassion
Amy Newmark

Published by Chicken Soup for the Soul, LLC www.chickensoup.com
Copyright ©2018 by Chicken Soup for the Soul, LLC. All Rights Reserved.

The publisher gratefully acknowledges the many publishers and individuals who granted Chicken Soup for the Soul permission to reprint the cited material.

Front cover illustration of bears courtesy of iStockphoto.com/Boszorka (©Boszorka)
Front and back cover illustration of snowy background courtesy of iStockphoto.com/ Relentless_one (©Relentless_one)
Back cover artwork of Canadian flag heart courtesy of iStockphoto.com/Aquir (©Aquir)
Interior photo courtesy of iStockphoto.com/VisualCommunications (©VisualCommunications)
Photo of Amy Newmark courtesy of Susan Morrow at SwickPix

Cover and Interior by Daniel Zaccari

Distributed to the booktrade by Simon & Schuster. SAN: 200-2442

Publisher's Cataloging-In-Publication Data
(Prepared by The Donohue Group, Inc.)

Names: Newmark, Amy, compiler.
Title: Chicken soup for the soul : Canadian acts of kindness : 101 stories
    of caring and compassion / [compiled by] Amy Newmark.
Other Titles: Canadian acts of kindness : 101 stories of caring and
    compassion
Description: [Cos Cob, Connecticut] : Chicken Soup for the Soul, LLC,
    [2018] | Contains stories that were published previously in other
    Chicken Soup for the Soul books.
Identifiers: ISBN 9781611599831 (print) | ISBN 9781611592832 (ebook)
Subjects: LCSH: Canadians--Social life and customs--Literary collections.
    | Canadians--Social life and customs--Anecdotes. | Canada--Social life
    and customs--Literary collections. | Canada--Social life and customs--
    Anecdotes. | Kindness--Canada--Literary collections. | Kindness--
    Canada--Anecdotes. | LCGFT: Anecdotes.
Classification: LCC F1021.2 .C452 2018 (print) | LCC F1021.2 (ebook) | DDC
    971/.07--dc23

Library of Congress Control Number 2018949249

PRINTED IN THE UNITED STATES OF AMERICA
on acid∞free paper

25 24 23 22 21 20 19 18   01 02 03 04 05 06 07 08 09 10 11

Canadian Acts of Kindness

101 Stories of Caring and Compassion

Amy Newmark

Chicken Soup for the Soul, LLC
Cos Cob, CT

Changing the world one story at a time®
www.chickensoup.com

Table of Contents

❸

~There for Each Other~

❹

~The Power of Friendship~

❺

~We Are Family~

❻

~Doggone Kind~

❼

~Purrfect Compassion~

❽

~The Joy of Giving~

❾

~Holiday Helpers~

Introduction

What's the best way to make yourself feel great? Do an act of kindness for someone! Scientific studies have shown that doing good for others is not only good for the recipient of the kindness, but also for the person who is doing it, making that person measurably happier and healthier.

Of course, Canadians are known around the world for their kindness. But even they need some help in letting that kindness shine through. Sometimes you might not know exactly *how* to help, or you feel that you might be interfering, so you hold back and you don't do that kind thing you were contemplating.

What I love about this new collection of stories from Chicken Soup for the Soul, just for Canadians, is that these stories show you that it's okay to follow that impulse! You'll find stories about every kind of kindness in these pages, from the everyday to the extraordinary. And you'll probably come away from this book with some new ideas for ways that you and your family and friends can make a difference in your communities and in your country.

Canada is filled with people who care *for* and *about* each other. One of the ways they help each other is through United Way Centraide Canada, which enables volunteers and donors to become champions of generosity in their communities.

In the pages of this book, you'll read about how volunteering and giving changes the lives of both the givers *and* the recipients. In Chapter 1, for example, which is about "The Power of Community," Laura Whitman tells us how the city of Halifax came together on the

100th anniversary of the historic explosion in the harbour. Laura's United Way decided they would enlist 500 volunteers to do 100 projects for the community on December 6, 2017. They ended up surpassing those numbers and Laura says it "was a citywide display of volunteerism, kindness, gratitude and enthusiasm." When she learned that a businessman named A. H. Whitman had stepped in to help the city right after the explosion 100 years ago, she decided to research whether there was a family connection. Sure enough, Arthur Hanfield Whitman was her husband's cousin.

Canadian kindness comes in many forms, and we made sure to include an ample supply of stories that involve hockey, because this is, after all, Canada! In Chapter 2, which is titled "Kindness from a Stranger," Leigh Anne Saxe tells us that it was the Leafs' last game in the Maple Leaf Gardens and Leigh Anne's whole family wanted to go. But there were *five* of them, and only *four* season tickets. So Leigh Anne and her sister were "sharing" a ticket, until a ticket collector noticed that they kept switching who got to go in and who had to stand outside and wait. He let both girls in. Leigh Anne says, "It might have seemed like a little thing to him, easily forgotten, but it made a huge difference to us, and when I think of that night, I still remember what he did for our family."

I'll bet that kindly ticket collector *did* feel good about his act of kindness. He probably went home with a warm glow in his heart. Because when we reach out and help a stranger, it changes us. Mary Anne Molcan talks about that in Chapter 3, which is called "There for Each Other." She was rushing home for Thanksgiving dinner after work when she encountered a young man who had missed his bus. If he waited for the next bus, he'd miss his curfew and his bed at the Salvation Army. Mary Anne looked into his eyes, and she says, "I saw a person. I saw him. I heard a small voice that quietly said, 'He's someone's son.'" She drove him, and as they chatted he learned that she was missing her own Thanksgiving dinner. That made him cry. Mary Anne says that not everyone should offer a ride to a stranger, but this felt right to her, and she says, "In finding the strength to allow myself to be a little vulnerable, I opened myself up to a life-changing experience."

It's not all about helping strangers, because, of course, "charity starts at home" as the saying goes. Julie Winn has a story about that in Chapter 4, "The Power of Friendship." She describes living in Toronto, in a neighbourhood that feels more like a village where everyone helps each other. Her neighbor acts as a surrogate grandmother to Julie's children, and they in turn do nice things for her, such as shoveling her back stairs. She turns around and delivers homemade cookies the next day. This is how communities are supposed to behave, engaging in that back and forth that makes us all feel like family.

Speaking of family, did you know that Family Day is a uniquely Canadian holiday? In Chapter 5, "We Are Family," I was impressed by Heidi Allen, who actually adopted a forty-year-old man with Down syndrome whom she met when she was working at a school for disabled adults. Heidi ended up raising her baby son with his special big brother, and she says, "He taught us that family doesn't just exist in the DNA. Family is a feeling. Family is love."

Family includes your pets, and they can get in on the kindness act, too! If you have a dog or a cat, you'll love Chapters 6 and 7 of this book — "Doggone Kind" and "Purrfect Compassion." Kimberley Campbell tells us about her rescue dog, a retired racing Greyhound that became a therapy dog and visited a ninety-year-old lady in a nursing home. That lady hadn't spoken in at least a year, until Itssy put her head in the lady's lap.

Our pets really do have an intuitive ability to perform their own acts of kindness, and Shirley Stevenson learned that when her cat started asking to go outside every day at 1 p.m. Shirley decided to spy on her cat one day. She learned that a group of disabled young adults walked past her house every day at that time, and her cat Marmalade had been meeting them outside for months. Petting Marmalade was the highlight of their daily walk, according to their chaperone.

One of the things they see all the time at United Way is that giving is a two-way street. One year you can be the recipient, and the next year you can be back on your feet, sharing with people who are experiencing the same challenges you just overcame. Jennifer Bly shares a story about that in Chapter 8, which is about "The Joy of Giving."

She says that she used a food bank for almost a year when she was going through some medical problems. At first, she was embarrassed, but the staff was so kind and understanding that she didn't feel judged at all. A couple of decades have passed since those tough times, and now Jennifer joyfully donates food and serves as a volunteer at her local food bank.

That joy in giving is described by Niki Card in her story about Conscious Kindness Day, a wonderful annual event conducted by United Way Winnipeg that has been adopted by other United Way Centraides across the country. Niki tells us that her daughter performed acts of kindness for strangers, for the staff at her school, and for family members. And as a teacher, Niki watched her students prepare for the special day, giving up many recesses to do so. She says that the "ripple effect of spreading kindness is very noticeable," and that "Conscious Kindness Day is a real boost to morale for both the giver and the recipient, and the impact lasts much longer than a day."

Winter is the season of giving, with Christmas and Hanukkah and a general sense of sharing in the air, and Chapter 9, about "Holiday Helpers," is a heartwarming look at the ways that Canadians bring light back into those dark months. I loved Danielle Kuhn's story. Her little boy wanted to give toy fire trucks to the local firefighters, who weren't "allowed to play" with the model ones they had in a display case. This desire to give gifts to the firefighters has grown into a massive undertaking by the Kuhn family, in which they take food and sweet treats to uniformed personnel in their town on Christmas Eve. Those firefighters, police officers, paramedics, and associated emergency responders have been their grateful recipients for more than twelve years now, and Danielle says that making the rounds of their town's on-duty first responders is the highlight of their family's Christmas.

When we decided to use this collection of stories about Canadian acts of kindness to support a Canadian nonprofit, we knew that United Way Centraide Canada would be the perfect partner. A portion of proceeds from the book sales will go towards funding all the good work they do to help build stronger communities for everyone. I'm sure the book will have an even larger impact, as it will create thousands of additional volunteers and donors spreading joy and light across Canada.

I want to thank you for picking up this book. I know you will finish it a different person than you were when you started it. The power of Canadians working at the local level to create a better country for all is truly astounding, as you'll discover in these 101 heartwarming and inspirational stories.

—Amy Newmark—
Editor-in-Chief and Publisher
Chicken Soup for the Soul

Chapter 1

The Power of Community

I Came Home for This?

The cat has nine lives: three for playing, three for straying, three for staying.
~English Proverb

We had done it a million times before — leaving the front door open for just a second. But she usually didn't care. We would run in to grab "one more thing," and then scoot out the door, firmly locking it behind us. And she really didn't care. Sure, she might come and investigate, but she had food, water, a comfy blankie — she had it made on the "inside." What was so much better for her outside?

But then, one day, the unthinkable happened.

She got out.

Sam, our indoor-only, seven-year-old, collarless kitty, was gone — like GONE GONE. That kind of gone. She must have seen something really good out there, like another cat, a raccoon or a deer, and when the timing was right, and the door was open — if only for a second — she bolted.

Sam had only ever been outside once before, and at that time she barely got past our front yard, so fearful was she of the great outdoors. But this time, fear meant nothing to her. There was no finding her. We searched high and low — under neighbours' decks, in bushes, in garages — everywhere. Not a fuzzy kitty in sight.

With heavy hearts, my three men slouched around the house. Every sound outside had them running to the windows, scanning the grounds. Every time we drove through the parking area of our townhomes, we scanned the bushes for a fuzzy little kitty.

I know everyone was thinking the worst, not daring to speak dreadful thoughts. I tried to keep their hopes up, but it was hard.

Sam came to us from a local pet store, Pets West, who in turn got her through the local animal control/rescue. As she was a rescue cat, one of my sons wondered — did she have a chip or tattoo that we didn't know about?

So as requested, and only on faint-hope whim, I hustled to the pet store. Maybe they did, by chance, have a record of her being chipped or tattooed. It wouldn't find her, but if someone took her to the animal shelter, it might be easy to identify her. I secretly hoped they had implanted a microscopic GPS somewhere on our feline friend.

The store's sales clerk, Meghan, looked up our kitty's file. She said they didn't have a record of any chips or tattoos, but advised me to call animal control to see what they knew. I later did check, but with no luck.

But… Meghan gave us something more.

A bit of hope.

After handing me Sam's file number and the phone number for animal control, she gave me a few pointers. Meghan suggested I send her a photo and details of our lost kitty, and not only would she set up a "lost kitty" notification on Facebook — lots of "shares" of lost pets had helped in the past — but she said she would also post an ad on the store's website. And she would post a "lost kitty" poster in their store.

Wow!

I raced home and shared the news with my heartbroken men. I recapped the "Find Lost Kitty" plan, but sprinkled it with "no promises." But it gave them hope. The thought that someone was doing something lifted their spirits. They were most surprised that someone would go out of their way to do all that.

So with details sent to the store, and "lost kitty" posters posted around our neighbourhood, all we could do was wait. And hope. And keep our paws crossed.

Two days later, I had two e-mails. One was from Meghan confirming her Facebook/website work, and the other from a concerned animal lover — a total stranger — who saw the advertisements. Not only did she express her concern for our family, but she also gave us a few tips to enhance our "Find Lost Kitty" plan. Pets West's Facebook page was full of "shares" and comments from other concerned folks — folks we didn't know. Two other folks took the time to phone with sympathy and words of encouragement — "Don't worry, she'll come back soon."

When I shared these e-mails and phone calls with my family they, too, were overwhelmed. It amazed us that so much was being done for us, and by people we didn't know. It was a lesson in community, in folks looking out for other folks. It gave us all a bit of hope, that maybe someone would see our furry Sam. We weren't paying anyone to do this; we didn't know any of these people. Everyone's kindness and concern overwhelmed us.

Days went by. On the recommendation of many, I left her favourite blankie outside, in the hope that her smell/homing beacon would kick in. Nothing.

And then, a week and seventeen hours later, there she was. When one of my sons and husband came back from an outing, there she was, sitting in our parking stall, as if waiting for them to come home. With barely any coaxing, Sam willingly came to my husband, and silently, and without excitement for fear of scaring her, we carried her into the house. And locked the door — double-checking it five times.

To this day, Sam is happy and healthy and is wearing her first collar ever, complete with engraved tag and a bell — just in case.

By the way she sulked around those first few days home, the unfamiliar "noose" around her neck tinkling and jingling with every step, I suspected she was thinking, "I came home for THIS?"

— Lisa McManus Lange —

Angel at Our Door

Every house where love abides and friendship is a
guest, is surely home, and home sweet home,
for there the heart can rest.
~Henry Van Dyke

The insistent pounding on the door brought me quickly from my kitchen. With three little ones down for a nap, I hurried to answer before they were all awakened prematurely.

We had just moved into the neighbourhood and I couldn't imagine who it would be. Opening the door a crack revealed an old man dressed in dirty clothing, wearing mud-encrusted rubber boots. From his hand hung a torn plastic bag.

"Can I help you?" I asked, hoping he had the wrong address.

"Would ya like to buy some fresh garden vegetables?" His voice was shaky with age but his faded blue eyes were hopeful.

"Are they from your garden?" Peering inside his shabby bag, I saw mostly dirt, with a hint of carrots.

"Yes." His voice was soft and scratchy. "And I kin get some apples from a tree in my yard. Would ya like some of those too?"

My heart softened at his neglected appearance, and I wondered if he desperately needed the bit of money he was asking for his produce. With a sigh, I gestured him in. "Please step inside and I'll get my purse."

The next day, he knocked at our door again. This time, my gregarious little four-year-old got there first. "Oh, hello. Would you like to come in for tea?" Heidi's high-pitched-voice carried an adult inflection.

Without hesitating, the old man stepped inside and held out a broken basket with several bruised apples resting at the bottom. "From my tree," he said, removing a worn cap that had seen better days. "Thought ya might like to make a pie."

There was no mistaking the wistful look in his eye.

The three of us sat at the kitchen table and sipped our tea, Heidi's cup containing a much weaker version. Sheer delight in hosting a visitor was evident in her never-ending stream of questions. "What is your name? Where do you live? Why are your clothes so dirty? Will your mother be mad at you?"

The homeless-looking man chuckled as he attempted to answer each question. His name was Mr. Locket and he lived around the corner. His wife had passed away several years before, and his children all lived far away. He was lonely. His need for companionship had sent him door to door under the ruse of selling fruit and vegetables. Ours was the only door opened to him that day.

Eventually, the cookies were gone and he struggled to his feet. Shuffling his way to the door, he turned and offered us a cheerful grin and a wave goodbye.

As I watched him limp painfully to an ancient bicycle propped against our house, my heart melted.

Once on his bike, he wobbled back down the road, perhaps a little less lonely than before. He had promised to return tomorrow, and I knew what I wanted to do.

The next day, the children excitedly awaited his visit. The table was set with china and silver, with fancy napkins folded neatly beside each plate. A small bouquet of garden flowers, picked by little hands, adorned the centre of the table. Tantalizing aromas of cinnamon and sugar filled the house as a steaming apple pie beckoned from the table.

As he entered the kitchen, he took in the efforts made on his behalf, and his eyes filled with unshed tears. He focused on the golden-crusted, sugar-topped, apple pie. Pulling up a chair beside my two little girls, he immediately seemed at home, and we watched with amazement as he devoured half the dessert.

Wiping his whiskery lips, he commented, "Yur pies sure taste a lot better'n mine!"

My curiosity was piqued. "How do you make your pies?"

"Well, I just cut up them apples and put 'em in a pan. Then I bake 'em."

I smiled. A few simple tips would help him create at least a better version.

The next day, we found a basket sitting on the step. Inside were several rosy apples.

I slipped another pie into the oven that night.

As the days wore on, Mr. Locket became a daily visitor to our active home. In his quiet and gentle way, he endeared himself to each child. I loved to peek around the kitchen door and watch as he sat in our big comfy chair with one or two little ones curled up on his lap, gazing up at him with rapt attention as he read a children's book or told a story.

Mr. Locket became an honorary member of our family. When the little ones were tucked into their beds for an afternoon nap, he would rest his weary head on the back of the chair and join the babies in slumber. He usually went home when the sun dipped low in the sky, but stayed for dinner if pie was on the menu.

Our lively family antics at the dinner table always brought a smile to his weathered face. Later, as my husband put the children to bed, I'd stand in the doorway watching this dear old friend pedal his way home in the dark.

One day he revealed a hidden passion. "Ya know, I used to go to the library and get books ta read. It helps fill in the long, quiet nights. Don't rightly feel like riding that far anymore, though. S'pose you could lend me a book?"

"That's a wonderful idea!" I couldn't believe we hadn't discussed this sooner. I loved to read, too, and I delighted in sharing books. "What if I put a stack beside your chair for you to read during your visits, and then you can take home anything you want to finish?" His answering smile said it all.

It was fun to see which books he selected and watch him disappear between the pages. He still read to the children each day, and the name "Grandpa Locket" slipped effortlessly into our conversations. Both sets of my children's grandparents lived far away, so the children missed having them attend their Sunday school concerts and Christmas pageants. Although extremely deaf, Mr. Locket was now the grandpa that came to "Ooh" and "Ahh" over each little one's part in the programs.

"Did you hear me, Mr. Locket?" Heidi would chirp.

"Well, I didn't rightly hear ya, but I know it was good!"

Heidi would beam, her tiny hand grasping his old gnarled one. The two had become best friends.

Three years after first meeting Grandpa Locket, we learned we were being moved across the country to Ontario. That night, I tossed and turned. Pink sky began to peek through the window before I'd found a gentle way to break the news to Grandpa Locket.

When he arrived that morning, I took a deep breath and blurted it out. "Mr. Locket," I began, my voice wobbling. "We're going to be moving very soon. We're all very sad. You've become a treasured part of this family and we — we — we'll miss you."

The old man's chin slowly dropped to his chest as reality hit. Moisture glistened in the corners of his eyes.

Swallowing the lump in my throat, I took his worn, calloused hands in mine. "I promise to keep in touch with you and write letters regularly. The kids will send you pictures, and I'll ship as many books as you can read." My throat tightened and I couldn't speak any more.

He nodded and softly said, "Thank you for all your kindnesses to an old man. When I was lonely, ya took me in. When I needed a family, ya included me. My life's bin happy cuz of you." He reached down and rested his free hand on Heidi's head, gazing at her as if memorizing every delicate feature.

During our last visit together, we all hugged him tightly.

Without looking back, the old man limped out the door, straddled his rusty bike, and pedalled down the road.

With heavy hearts, we watched the familiar figure disappear around the corner for the last time. As we closed the door, we knew that a part of our lives was drawing to a close and a new stage was beginning, but no matter where we were, we'd never forget this incredibly precious man.

I kept my word and wrote regularly. The kids made him pictures, and I mailed books every month. We never received a letter in return, but somehow we knew he anxiously checked his mailbox every day to see if anything had arrived from us.

About a year later, a small envelope was delivered to our home — a letter from Mr. Locket's daughter. She informed us that our dear old friend had passed away. She'd found the letters, pictures, and gifts that we had sent, carefully tucked away in one of his dresser drawers. "I'm so grateful for your loving care for my father," she wrote. "I can see how much you meant to him, too."

With tremendous sadness, my husband and I shared this news with the children. Although we grieved the loss of our friend, we also felt a sense of joy. Remembering his gentle spirit and spontaneous chuckle made us smile. And we would never forget his love for apple pie.

We still feel it wasn't just an old man who knocked on our door that day, but an angel in disguise. We're so grateful for the unexpected love that swept into our lives the moment we opened that door.

— Heather Rae Rodin —

The Great Ice Storm

*Love and kindness are never wasted. They always
make a difference. They bless the one who receives
them, and they bless you, the giver.*
~Barbara de Angelis

The Great North American Ice Storm of 1998 affected the lives of millions of people in eastern Canada and the northern United States. The culprit was a stalled low-pressure system that took its sweet time moving out of the area. When the storm hit I was living in Ottawa and I was able to see its devastating effects firsthand.

Things were very difficult in the city, with power outages and shortages of basic essentials. Stores and supermarkets were taken by surprise by the extent of the power cuts. On the positive side, it was an opportunity for the community's spirit to be exhibited. People were checking in on neighbours to make sure they were able to keep warm and fed. Everyone shared their resources. The hospitals and essential services were given priority in having their power restored. Despite the prolonged outages, everyone seemed to wait patiently.

Ontario and Quebec Hydro employees were working full out for days on end to restore power. It would only be a matter of time before they were overcome with exhaustion, given the massive task facing them. After a few days of trying to deal with it locally the call went out to unaffected areas of the two countries for help. In response, electric utilities from all over North America sent workers and equipment to help with the clean-up. The mild temperatures at the root of the weather phenomenon did not last as long as the power outage and, as the weather began to turn colder, other problems began to develop in an icy world without electricity.

At the time of the storm I was working in a paper mill as an electrical technician. The mill was an enormous complex straddling the border between Ottawa and Hull, located on a group of islands in the middle of the Ottawa River. Our whole installation was self-sufficient in electrical power as we had six generators dependent only on the flow of the river. Throughout the storm we remained able to generate enough hydro to supply our papermaking needs. As days passed and the after-effects of the storm worsened, the company made the decision to shut down production and to send our self-generated hydro into the system feeding the city of Hull. This went a long way toward alleviating some of the dire conditions that were developing in the area.

Without much to do at the mill, five friends and I decided to volunteer with the City of Ottawa. Regional administrators had activated a rescue plan and were slowly and steadily coming to the aid of people living in outlying areas, but it was an enormous task. We knew that the people living in the city were having a difficult time, but nothing had prepared us for how bad things were in the countryside. Hydro poles and transmission cables lay in ditches. Abandoned cars and trucks littered side roads and many routes were completely blocked by huge ice-covered tree limbs. Smaller trees were so laden with ice that their topmost branches had bent far enough over to touch the ground and become frozen there. Roads that were clear of debris resembled ice rinks and there was very little salting and sanding. Everything had an ice covering.

Had it not been for the seriousness of the situation I would have described it as visually stunning. Light sparkled like glass decorations from the trees and bushes. Houses and cars were coated with thick ice coverings and huge icicles hung everywhere.

With our toolboxes in the back of the city-loaned trucks, we made up work teams comprising a millwright and an electrician. We headed out into the countryside with a list of the places in direst need.

The main issue we were dealing with was the repair and mainte-nance of faulty generators. City authorities had managed to get their hands on hundreds of generators — some new and working well and others that needed a lot of TLC to get them into working order. In many cases there had been no time to properly evaluate the units before they were sent out, so it fell to our little teams to catch up with on-site maintenance and repairs.

The sights that met us were often heartbreaking. Many farmers had been doing their best with what they had available, but you can imagine trying to keep a fully automated farm running when the power goes out and the standby generators do not work. Often, as we approached up the farm driveway, the farmers would come down the road to meet us and direct us to the generator site in an effort to minimize time before we got to work. Of course, when the units were back in service the farmer would want to show his gratitude by inviting us in for lunch or tea. Being practical individuals they understood when we pointed out that we needed to continue on to help the next farmer down the road. We had to stay on track and get through the dozens of calls for help. The farmers' gratitude was nevertheless appreciated, and inevitably their wives sent us on our way with bags full of sandwiches and soft drinks.

I have to say that I have never worked so hard in my life. Certainly I have never been so cold, so dirty, and yet so happy. We were on the road from sunrise to well beyond sunset. As time passed and the crisis continued, the circumstances for some farmers and their animals became even worse. It was not uncommon to arrive at a farm and to find the farmer reduced to tears after he had tried everything he could think of to save his animals. We were the last hope for many.

Being able to bring some relief to people in these extreme conditions was the best reward I could ever have hoped for. Volunteering during the crisis had immediate and long-lasting effects on the lives of my fellow volunteers and myself. It started me out on a life of working to help others who are in difficult circumstances beyond their control. I have an indelible memory of a big, gruff-looking farmer who, lost for words, took me in his arms and hugged me tightly when we managed to put his generator back into service. To him it meant the difference between life and death for his animals. We were just happy we could be of service.

—James A. Gemmell—

It Takes a Village

We cannot live only for ourselves. A thousand fibers
connect us with our fellow men.
~Herman Melville

Thirteen is an awkward age for anyone, but it proved to be an especially stressful time for me. My family life imploded, and we learned that keeping secrets could be a dangerous, even life-threatening, practice.

My father had always been a heavy drinker. That was nothing new. But when he lost his job, a downward spiral began, with threats of violence against my mother and us kids. I never thought I'd feel so helpless or so afraid. Unfortunately, that was only the beginning.

When my mother went back to work full-time, my father was left to care for my baby sister. The day I came home from school to find my father passed out on the couch and my sister crying in her crib, with a diaper that had obviously been full for hours, was the last straw. My father couldn't be trusted to look after a child, so my mother paid our next-door neighbour to babysit. Of course, she wasn't about to admit the real reason why. She pretended my dad couldn't child-mind because he was looking for another job.

Violence escalated in our household until my mother found the courage to kick my father out and seek divorce. Sounds easy enough. It wasn't. My father refused to leave our family home and my mother had no choice but to take out a restraining order against him. She did what she had to do to protect us.

The police escorted my father from our house, but that didn't keep him away. He phoned so often that we stopped picking up. He filled tape after tape on the answering machine with death threats. He sent us pictures in the mail of all the guns he had access to. He sent photos of himself holding those guns, aiming them at the camera.

My mother took all this to the police, but they shrugged it off. Tapes of death threats and pictures of guns didn't qualify as evidence, they said.

Still, we kids were too ashamed to tell anybody what was going on. My mother talked to our lawyer, the police, and a few family members, but my siblings and I? We had only each other. Keeping secrets is prevalent in households with rampant substance abuse. We were secretive to a heartbreaking degree.

After a while, it wasn't enough for my father to threaten us by phone and through the post. He smashed a window and broke into our home, entering when my mother was at work and we kids were in school. When I came home that day, with my younger siblings in tow, I knew we needed the police. But, in a time before cell phones, how could we make an emergency call? In our suburban neighbourhood, no payphones were close by.

We had to break the silence.

My siblings and I went next door, to the neighbour who babysat our youngest sister. We told her everything — about my father's drinking, his neglect, his death threats and his guns. She helped us call our mother, and Mom phoned the police. My father was taken away in handcuffs for violating his restraining order.

If only the ordeal had ended there.

But that was just the first of many times my father broke into our house. When we put bars on the windows, he broke down the door. We couldn't hide what was going on from the neighbours anymore, not with the noticeable police presence at all hours of the morning. There comes a point where you can't lie any longer. You can't cover for a family member who has wronged you.

When we told our neighbours the truth, something incredible happened.

The next time my father came to "take back his house," he gave us warning. He even gave us a date. My mother called the police right away, but they said he wasn't in violation of his restraining order yet. There was nothing they could do in advance. She'd just have to call them when he got there.

We were all afraid, but my mother, in particular, was beside herself. She'd done everything she could to protect us kids. But if she waited for my father to arrive before calling the police, it could be too late.

This time, when she vented her concerns, it wasn't to my grandmother — who often didn't believe the things Mom told her — but rather to our next-door neighbour, the woman who cared for my baby sister during the day. My neighbour was a loud and opinionated woman, and when she called the neighbourhood to action, the neighbourhood listened.

If my father was afraid of one thing, it was exposure. He trusted us to keep quiet, to keep his secrets. He shouldn't have. Because, on the day he said he'd take back the house, our neighbours came to our rescue. They all joined hands and formed a human barricade across our driveway.

My father drove up the street, and his car slowed almost to a halt when he saw us — the whole neighbourhood standing alongside his kids, showing him they were there to support us, that his threats and behaviours were unacceptable, that he needed to leave.

And he did.

When his car pulled away, my mother thanked the neighbours and told them we'd taken up enough of their time. They were adamant. He wouldn't give up so easily. What if he came back and they were all gone? No, they would stay as long as it took. They'd camp out on our front lawn all night if they needed to. Now that they knew what we'd been through, the neighbours were going to protect us.

They were right, of course. My father circled by the house, again and again, until my mother called in the restraining order violation and the police apprehended him. The neighbourhood, which had never been terribly close or cohesive before that day, worked together to protect us kids and our mom.

Through the whole ordeal, the most terrifying obstacle we faced as a family was an internal one: the fear of admitting the truth, of worrying what others would think. The shame seemed insurmountable.

This horrendous situation was in no way my fault, but it sure didn't feel that way at the time. I thought we were the only ones. I thought no one else could possibly understand.

It took an incredible strain before my mother, my siblings and I cracked the veneer of normalcy. When we told our secrets, we expected the neighbourhood to view our family with contempt. Instead, they became our shield. When the police failed us, our neighbours stepped up. They stood alongside our family, and we finally realized we were not alone.

— Foxglove Lee —

My Brother's Keeper

A part of kindness consists in loving people
more than they deserve.
~Joseph Joubert

Breathing a sigh of relief, I looked in my rear-view mirror, grateful for the distance I was putting between my car and that of the drunk driver as he weaved all over the road. At the same time, I felt guilty.

You can't just drive away. You have to get him off the road! My conscience nagged at me. Or it may have been one of my angels.

"There's nothing I can do. I can't be responsible for his actions," I countered. I was young and slim. A lightweight female does not take on a drunk male driver. And this was before cell phones, so I had no way of alerting the police to come and get this guy off the road.

You're going to look in this mirror and see some poor, unsuspecting family killed because you did nothing. Those thoughts hammered at me relentlessly. I had responsibilities as a human being.

"I'm not my brother's keeper," I said out loud, but without conviction. As the words reverberated, the meaning hit me, and I knew I was. There wasn't anyone else, so the job was mine. I eased up on the gas, realizing I needed to be back behind the drunk. Even then, as I wrestled with the dilemma of getting him off the road, I never paused to think about repercussions. I never thought he might be dangerous.

I had just wanted to get home. I'd been away in the mountains for a few days on an assignment and was excited about seeing my family.

When I'd first noticed the erratic driving of the car in front of me, I had become concerned. He was traveling under the speed limit, but wandering too much. I worried about whether the driver was falling asleep, suffering a heart attack, or drunk at the wheel. I stopped wondering. The driver had crossed the centre line into the oncoming traffic lane. As he swerved back, I saw him toss the brown beer bottle onto the highway.

Oh, balderdash, this guy's smashed, I thought as I watched the bottle explode. My only thought then was to get safely past him. That done, I thought things would be fine, except that inner conversation kicked in.

Now, as the drunk approached again and passed me, the beginning of a plan took root. If I pulled abreast of him, I could honk and motion for him to pull over. That was the theory, but when I put it into practice, he just looked confused and decelerated. After I repeated this two more times, he slowed to the legal speed on a city street, but I was still no closer to getting him to stop. Perplexed and worried that we'd soon have to contend with more traffic, I once again pulled alongside of him, with a silent prayer for this to work. Not comprehending what I wanted, the drunk responded by slowing more and pulling over onto the shoulder. Then I watched in horror as he lost control of his car. The ditches in the area were roomy with gentle slopes. A good driver could drive in and out without mishap. The drunk drove in and stopped, but made no move to get out.

Was he hurt? Sick with worry, I pulled over and ran down to his vehicle. Whether or not I would encounter a mean, enraged drunk had not crossed my mind. He sat slumped, looking as spent as the litter of bags and bottles throughout his car. I rapped on the window. "Are you all right?"

He nodded as he rolled down the window.

"Give me your car keys. I can't allow you to drive." My words, crisp and authoritative, hung in the air and surprised me.

He stared for the briefest of moments, and then reached for his keys and placed them in my outstretched hand.

"If I allowed you to drive in your condition, you could cause an accident." I spoke of how devastated he would be if his actions caused a death. "It would haunt you and walk with you throughout your life."

He seemed to feel an explanation was called for. "I've been up all night. I worked late, and then there was a farewell party. We never stopped. I never thought… I needed to get home… I didn't realize…" He groped for words and then stopped, wilting against the seat, realizing there was no defense.

I opened the door. "Come up to my car, and I'll drive yours out of the ditch."

Minutes later, after getting him settled, I started his car. The impact of the situation hit me. I had a very inebriated man on my hands, and my plan had not gone further than this point. *Okay, angels, what do I do with him?* If I took him with me, that would leave his car stranded an hour from the city. Ideas were examined and tossed.

While I was back up on the highway, listening for a second time to the man explain how he had ended up driving in an unsafe condition, phase two of a plan established itself in my mind. We were on a long, flat stretch of road. That it was not busy had been a blessing up until this point, but now to carry out my plan, I needed traffic. As if on schedule, a car appeared on the horizon. I told the stranger to stay with my car. He offered no arguments as he leaned, using my car to steady and support his body. Like an obedient child, he stood motionless (well, almost) and waited. Placing myself in the pathway of the oncoming car, I began waving my arms like a traffic controller on a runway. The car slowed to show four men looking at me open-mouthed.

"I need one of you to drive this man's car into the city. He is drunk, and I cannot allow him to drive," I explained. Even as I spoke, the passenger in the front was putting on his shoes and nodding.

A slight female, still in her thirties, I stood there in command with a voice that said, "No arguments!"

I gave the men an explanation of the situation and told them to drive the man home. There were no questions. Everyone nodded and said, "Okay."

Returning to my car, I told the drunk of the arrangements, assuring him that both he and his car would arrive home safely. That's when he reached out. He took my hand with one hand and placed his other hand on my arm. I felt no apprehension. He smiled at me and said, "I want to thank you for caring. No one has ever done something like this for me. I just… thank you. You are so… unbelievable."

I took my hand away and squeezed his shoulder. To this day, I have no recollection of what I said to him in response. I remember the wetness in the corners of his eyes. I remember walking him to the car of the Good Samaritans who would take him safely home. And I remember thinking, *Good, now I can go home.* I was relieved that my guardian angels and his were likely doing double time!

— Ellie Braun-Haley —

The Healing
Hand of God

*The prayer that begins with trustfulness and passes on
into waiting will always end in thankfulness,
triumph, and praise.*
~Alexander Maclaren

My husband and I had agreed to a weekend camping trip with our good friends, Doug and Kathy, fellow youth leaders from our church. Our three young children were just as excited about time at the beach as we adults. We had a great time swimming during the day and at night we decided to gather around a campfire.

We edged our lawn chairs closer to the fire pit as a chill settled over the day. While we were talking and roasting hot dogs and marshmallows on long sticks, I realized that our four-year-old daughter, Elizabeth, had wiggled her chair too close to the fire. I opened my mouth to instruct her to move back when the unthinkable happened. The chair tipped forward, dumping her onto the ground at the edge of the pit. She dropped onto a bed of smouldering coals.

All four adults reached for her. My husband and I grabbed her and ran to the nearby water tap. My first thought was to douse her smoking shorts. I hadn't considered the possibility of burns — until I saw her feet. Blisters swelled like balloons filled with water. Our daughter wailed out her pain. Adrenaline took over as we hustled to our vehicle. We covered Elizabeth's burns with a clean towel and, leaving our older children with Doug and Kathy, headed for the hospital in the nearby town.

"She has second- and third-degree burns on her feet and her hip." I wanted to cry for this innocent child who wept out pain she didn't understand. "You'll want to take her to your family doctor to keep an eye on them."

We headed home where Doug and Kathy waited with our other two girls. Elizabeth sat quietly in the car with me, her feet swaddled in white gauze, the burn medicine giving her temporary relief.

The next day we rented a small wheelchair. Our doctor informed us that Elizabeth would be off her feet for a few months and would likely undergo skin grafting. By Wednesday, an infection set in and Elizabeth's temperature soared. That evening, she hallucinated, experiencing an imaginary card game of Go Fish. We headed to the hospital again.

A child should never have to endure debriding. It is a painful process where the burnt skin is removed. Anaesthetic is useless since the nerves in the burned tissue are damaged. For the next week, our little girl underwent the removal of the decaying tissue while I held her and prayed for God to give us a miracle.

I was supposed to go to a women's retreat two weeks after our camping weekend. I called our group organizer and told her why I had to cancel. "Pray for Elizabeth. She's in so much pain. Pray for healing."

Unknown to us, that request went to the retreat leadership team. While the ladies from our church began their adventure in the Muskoka woods, I made daily trips to the doctor to have the bandages changed and new medication applied. Standing behind Elizabeth's chair, I waited patiently while new gauze and tape covered wicked wounds and I prayed. I prayed that God would heal our daughter and that he would use this moment in time to show his love.

Saturday morning came and I headed out into the countryside to our doctor's home. He'd been very concerned about the infection and insisted that the bandages be changed daily. Sunday morning showed no improvement in Elizabeth's feet. We went to church as a family, her little red wheelchair carrying her down the aisle. She played quietly until the service finished and we headed home. That evening, the phone rang and I made my way to the kitchen to answer it.

"The whole group prayed for Elizabeth." Our group organizer's voice hummed with excitement. "It was something. Over 200 women gathered together praying for a miracle. I can't wait to see what God will do."

Monday morning brought a warm September sun and the girls and I climbed into the van and headed to the doctor's house. He'd warned me the day before that he would not be in the office until Tuesday and to come to his house. We pulled up the long drive and parked. Lifting Elizabeth into her wheelchair, I instructed her sisters to remain in their seatbelts until I called them. I turned toward the porch and spied the doctor coming down the walkway.

"And how's my patient today?"

Elizabeth grinned and waited while he squatted before her and unwrapped her feet. I watched from my place behind the chair, the prayer for healing running through my mind. My heart lurched as his expression sobered. What was wrong? Were her feet worse? Had the infection spread?

"I don't understand." The words came out in a slight stutter.

I locked the chair brakes and moved to the front, leaning over the doctor's shoulder. There in his hand rested one of Elizabeth's feet, the skin beautiful and fresh and pink. Not a mark marred the skin that had been a pucker of scorched flesh the day before. I laughed — a single, shocked chuckle — and he glanced up at me, his eyes frightened.

"I guess that's what happens when 200 women ask God for healing." The words slipped from my mouth and I watched the fear turn to confusion.

"If that's what you want to believe."

I laughed again, this time in amazement. "Do you have a better explanation?"

The doctor shook his head and tried to pull on the mantle of professionalism. "I guess we don't need any more bandaging. Bring her in a week from now and I'll check it over again." I thanked him as he turned and headed for his house.

We sang songs as we drove home and then I spent the morning watching Elizabeth chase her sisters around the yard. Two weeks. She had suffered for two weeks and I pondered all that her suffering had accomplished. Because of it, our family's faith grew, a doctor saw the healing hand of God and 200 strangers learned the importance of prayer.

— Donna Fawcett —

7

Nigerian Boys' Village

*The willingness to share does not make
one charitable; it makes one free.*
~Robert Brault

The hot African sun beat down on our vans as we bounced over deeply rutted roads on the outskirts of the city of Kagoro, Nigeria. The sky was a hazy blue and I could feel sweat trickling down my back as we drove.

The road was lined with small plots of land, each home made from mud and concrete blocks. Chickens scurried across the road and goats wandered around the farmyards. Young children played tag on the edge of the road while some of the women pounded yams for the evening meal.

We were on our way to a boys' orphanage to hand out clothes, hats and personal items. Eventually, we slowed down and turned into a narrow entranceway framed by tall bushes. The driveway led to a compound of a dozen cement-block buildings, with corrugated steel roofs that sparkled silver in the bright sunlight.

Several groups of boys gathered as we drove in and parked under a large mango tree for shade. They looked at us curiously because visitors like us — Canadians — never came to this boys' village.

The director of the orphanage came over and greeted us warmly with a handshake. He suggested we sit in the shade where it was marginally cooler. He then had all the boys come over to join us. Somewhat reluctantly, they left their dorms and came toward us, not knowing what to expect.

The director started off. "We want to welcome all of you to our boys' village. We are so pleased you have come. Each of these boys is here because he had nowhere else to go. They all have stories and we're going to tell you some of them."

He called one of the boys to come forward. As he put his hand on this boy's shoulder he said, "Joseph is seven years old and he struggled living with his parents." He then had Joseph turn around. As he lifted up the back of Joseph's shirt we all gasped. There were deep cuts all over his back. "His parents thought he was full of demons so they used a knife to cut his back to let the demons out. Clearly this was very dangerous. Arriving here saved his life." Joseph then rejoined the other boys.

The director motioned for Jakob to come forward. With his hand on Jakob's shoulder the director spoke. "After his father died, he began to get into trouble. Jakob would steal things from the market to help his family. He got caught three times. After the third time one of the men from the market came to his mother. He told her that if he caught him again he would kill him. He was serious. So Jakob's mother searched all over and finally brought him to this place. He is safe here and he feels it's his home." Jakob smiled as he looked at the director and then us.

One after another the boys shared their stories. It was hard to wrap our heads around everything they had been through before getting to the safety of this village.

When the boys had finished talking, we went back to our two vans and unloaded two large cardboard transport boxes, each about six feet long. The boys still had no idea what we were up to. We lined up the boxes so that we would be sure each boy received the exact same items. We started by giving each one a T-shirt, a baseball hat and a tie. After that we handed out toothbrushes, nail clippers, hairbrushes and other personal items. Most of the boys had only the clothes on their backs so we were giving them something very special. Many of them had never even owned a toothbrush before. The boys were excited and immediately put on their new T-shirts and baseball hats.

We had also brought along several soccer balls. The boys posed for photos with these balls before they headed off to play a pickup game.

A couple of the teenagers took me on a tour of the compound. We saw the new pump that went deep enough to bring up clean water for the first time. We walked through the dorms where every boy had his own bed with a net over it to protect against malarial mosquitoes.

They had their own little garden where they grew vegetables and yams. The village also had a few goats that provided milk, and sometimes, meat. Every once in a while a neighbour would give a small donation of food to the boys.

As the sun began to slide down in the afternoon sky and color it orange we knew it was time to leave. We had to get back to where we were staying before dark, when the highways would become dangerous due to bandits.

All the boys came together to say goodbye. Many shook our hands and thanked us.

Then Jakob stepped forward to speak. "Thank you for coming here to our village. Thank you for all your gifts. We are the thankful ones for what you have brought to us."

But Jakob didn't know the larger truth. We were the ones who were thankful for the opportunity to give gifts to these boys. They appreciated everything we gave them. We were the ones who saw the excitement in their eyes as we handed out the T-shirts, hats and towels. And the excited sound of the boys playing soccer with the balls we brought was the greatest reward we could receive.

— Rob Harshman —

8

Class Picture

The true gift of friendship is the gift of yourself.
~Author Unknown

I walked to South School every day with Glen, who lived in a broken-down house — more of a shack really — down the street from me. We'd join up on our way to school, kicking rocks down the sidewalk in the fall, throwing the odd snowball in the winter, floating little matchstick boats down the gutter rivulets in the spring.

We never said much to each other. Glen wasn't much for words. He had been held back a grade or two in school, and he was much taller and bigger than the rest of the kids in our third grade class.

He always seemed to be a bit embarrassed, scrunching to fit into the little desk in Mrs. Lougheed's class. Or sad. Maybe he was just sad. All I know is sometimes when I'd look at him across the room, struggling with his reading or his arithmetic, my heart would hurt a bit.

Glen loved one thing more than anything else — his dog, Blackie. A big old black Lab, as quiet and gentle as Glen himself. Outside of school the two were never apart. Maybe that's why Glen seemed sad in school. He missed Blackie.

Often Blackie would walk Glen and me to school and then make his way back home by himself, and often Blackie would be there all by himself at the end of the school day, waiting to walk us home again. Those were Glen's favourite days. And mine too.

Blackie wasn't supposed to be at the school though. Glen's mom had been told that dogs weren't allowed on the school grounds, and Blackie didn't have a license or even a collar for that matter. I don't think Glen's mom could afford stuff like that, or if she could, she wasn't the kind of person who would worry about dog licenses and such.

One perfect spring Wednesday I looked out the classroom window to the playground when the school bell rang and saw Blackie sitting in the schoolyard, in the shade by the baseball diamond, thumping his tail in the cool grass. Like only elementary school children at recess can, we rode a wave of excitement out the classroom, floating through the boot room, a torrent of goofiness gushing out the school doors, barely touching the ground.

Glen made a beeline for Blackie, me right behind him. We were both instantly rewarded with a woof and a lick, but Glen was worried. He told Blackie to go home, that he wasn't supposed to be there, that he would get in trouble. But the big old black Lab wasn't going anywhere, and when he decided on something, there was no budging him.

By this time, most of our class had gravitated over to see Blackie, to pet him and rub his big old square head, kneeling down for a hug, hoping for a lick on the cheek. The most popular girl in the grade, Penny Bond, was on the receiving end of a mighty slurp when we heard it.

The gravel crunched as a van pulled up right beside us, near the baseball diamond on a narrow driveway behind the old school building. Nobody ever drove on that gravel — except the dogcatcher. He had a bright orange van, and pretty well every single kid at South School hated that van. To this day I don't like that shade of orange.

"I have to take the dog," said the dogcatcher as he got out of the van. "Move away now kids, go play over there."

He gestured with a big pole toward the playground equipment. The pole had a loop of rope on it. It looked like a noose to me.

"Come on now kids, I gotta take the dog. Go play now." He was still keeping his distance, but nobody moved. Blackie woofed. Glen kneeled beside Blackie, hugging him, blinking back tears.

"He's my dog," said Glen. "It's okay, he's my dog, Blackie."

But the dogcatcher just took a step toward us, slowly swinging the pole with the noose on the end. "I don't see a license on this animal. He doesn't even have a collar. I have to take him to the pound, kid. If he's your dog, you can claim him there and pay the fee. He ain't allowed on the school grounds."

"But, we don't even have a car," said Glen, trying really hard now not to cry in front of all of his friends. He didn't want to say that his mom didn't have the money to get Blackie out of the pound. He didn't want to say it, but we all knew what happened to dogs that nobody claimed from the pound.

The dogcatcher wasn't listening. He took another step toward Blackie, and Glen started to cry and suddenly, somehow, we all stood in front of Glen and Blackie. We stood between them and the dogcatcher.

And then Penny Bond grabbed my hand, and I grabbed someone else's hand, and somehow we all linked together, and we were forming a circle — a huge circle of gritty third grade kids, arms outstretched, building a human fence around our friend and his dog.

It was one of those moments. One of those moments you know you'll always remember, even when you're old. Especially when you're old.

We stood there in our circle, Glen and Blackie in the middle of that circle, the dogcatcher outside of the circle, not exactly sure what to do. Nobody said a word. All you could hear was that Glen had stopped crying.

We would have stood there forever if it weren't for Mrs. Lougheed. Somehow she was out the back door of the school and calling to the dogcatcher. They stood over by his ugly orange dogcatcher van, Mrs. Lougheed doing most of the talking.

We hung onto our circle even harder now, and then something amazing happened. The dogcatcher got into his van and drove off. He didn't say anything to us at all; he didn't even look over at us. He just drove away.

When all the cheering and hugging and crying died down, Mrs. Lougheed got us settled down back in our own classroom, Blackie sprawled in the corner at the back of the room, snoozing away contentedly for the rest of the afternoon. I think it was Glen's happiest time in school ever.

Glen and his dog and his mom moved away that summer, and I never saw them again. But if you look at our old black-and-white class picture, beyond all the silly smiles and goofy hairdos of proud and shiny eight-year-olds, if you could look beyond the frame, you'd see what I can see: an old black dog curled up just outside of the class picture not very far from the biggest kid in the class.

—Harley Hay—

9

Neighbour from Hell

Today, give a stranger one of your smiles.
It might be the only sunshine he sees all day.
~H. Jackson Brown, Jr., P.S. I Love You

She was determined to make our lives miserable from the moment we met. Edna Strom looked to be in her late seventies. She had a perpetual squint. Her lips curled sourly, as if she had mistaken a bottle of vinegar for soda.

We'd barely moved one stick of furniture into the lower duplex we'd rented next door to her converted two-story home when Mrs. Strom hobbled onto her upstairs front gallery. She glared down at my twelve-year-old son David and then at me, announcing, "You make sure you keep that child out of my yard!"

Since our buildings shared a communal six-foot-high privacy fence that separated our lots, I couldn't understand her concern or hostility. Nevertheless, I replied curtly, "Don't worry!" as I ducked into my entryway with the box I was carrying.

That encounter set the tone for weeks. The next day, while my son was laughing on the phone, we were stunned to hear a loud pounding from the other side of his bedroom wall, which connected our dwellings and ran the entire length of both houses.

"Stop that racket right this minute!"

Mrs. Strom's furious voice filtered right into the kitchen I was painting. I rushed towards David to find him sitting on the bed, eyes wide with shock, his conversation forgotten.

"Mom, I was just laughing!" he protested.

"I know, honey," I soothed, gulping back my own growing anger. "Listen, let's just let this go until we're a little more settled in. I'll deal with it in a few days if it continues, okay?" I promised.

"Okay," he agreed reluctantly.

That same afternoon, he and a friend went out front to play pitch and catch. Within minutes, they both returned, their expressions clearly indicating that they were upset about something.

"What happened?" I sighed, certain our neighbour had struck again.

"She yelled at us from her balcony to go play in the back yard," David complained.

I handed each of the kids a soda, instructing them go out back. Then, I marched out the front door to confront the cranky old woman. This was our home too and I was going to nip this problem in the bud. There was no way she was going to continue scolding my child, especially since he'd done nothing wrong, nor been excessively loud.

I found her sitting ramrod straight in a rocking chair on her front porch, peering out into the street. Her summer dress was crisply ironed, her polished shoes gleamed, and every hair was in place. She wore a pearl necklace with matching earrings. When she saw me approach, she narrowed her eyes, pursing her lips even tighter.

"Is something wrong?" I asked her.

"My boy is coming to visit," she informed me haughtily. "I didn't want to get hit by your son's baseball while I wait for him."

"I'm sure he was being careful," I told her stonily. "He's not a bad kid, ma'am. In the future, if there's a problem, please come to me so we can solve it instead of shouting at him."

Not waiting for an answer, I turned and went back into the house. As I entered the common foyer, I almost bumped into the upstairs tenant who was checking her mail.

"I see you've met Edna Strom." She smiled. "Pay her no mind. She sits out there every day the minute the weather turns warm and waits for her son to visit. He only comes when he needs money. Even then, he's loud, rude and obnoxious, treating her like dirt!"

The apple doesn't fall far from the tree, I almost muttered, but bit my tongue. "Is she always that crabby?" I asked instead.

"Always. Just ignore her. Everyone does."

Edna didn't let up on her tyrannical behaviour. She hammered on the walls if we so much as dropped a pot cover or raised our stereo or television to a decibel above a whisper. Even adjusting the ring of our phone to accommodate her couldn't please the woman. We could almost feel her scowl sear into us as she kept her ever-present vigil on the balcony in the pathetic hope that her son might drop in.

Two months later, we were finally settled in and decided to have a cookout for friends and family. I prepared for the event, ignoring the persistent banging whenever I closed a cupboard or refrigerator door a little too hard. By that time, Mrs. Strom was becoming background noise.

The day of the barbecue, as people arrived, I noticed that Edna wasn't at her usual post. Her son had dropped in two days earlier and was every bit as vocal and insufferable as I'd been told, belittling his mother and demanding money. I assumed she wouldn't expect him again anytime soon and was taking a break from her lookout.

As the last guest arrived, we moved to the back yard. I was serving appetizers when a movement from her upstairs window caught my eye. I looked up to see her observing a laughing group of my visitors. Unaware that she could be seen, her usual bitter demeanour was absent. Instead, a combination of sad, wistful loneliness seemed to suffuse her features, and I felt a growing sympathy tug at my heart.

Seconds later, I was ringing her bell. She opened the door, shocked to see me.

"Can I help you?" she asked coldly, and I smiled.

"Mrs. Strom, I was wondering if you'd like to join us since we're neighbours. I'm sure my family and friends would love to meet you."

"Well, I — that is — I — I'm not really dressed to — "

I noticed then that she was clothed more casually than I'd ever seen her.

"You look fine," I assured her. "Everyone is in jeans or shorts. You'll fit right in. Please come."

For the first time ever, I saw her smile, catching a glimpse of the beauty that must have been hers when she was younger.

"Well, if you're sure," she said shyly, patting her hair nervously and straightening her blouse. "I have a fresh cheesecake I can bring — my late husband's favourite. I made it this morning."

"Why, that would be wonderful," I gushed. "Come, let's go."

My husband and son hid their shock, welcoming our neighbour with warm smiles when I escorted her into our yard on my arm.

"Everyone," I called out, "I'd like you to meet my friend and neighbour, Edna Strom."

We never heard a harsh word from her again. In fact, we became close friends, forgiving and forgetting our rocky beginning, and embracing our friendship instead. She no longer sat on her balcony waiting tirelessly for her son's sporadic visits. She was far too busy teaching me her favourite recipes, and joining us for family occasions where she was received with love and respect until she died peacefully five years later in her sleep. Only a week before, she had hugged me tightly and thanked me for being the daughter she never had. I mourned her like I would a beloved relative, grateful that I looked past the thorns to see the fragile flower within.

— Marya Morin —

10

No Hostess Gifts Please

Christmas is the season for kindling the fire of
hospitality in the hall, the genial flame
of charity in the heart.
~Washington Irving

For the past eleven years, friends of mine have hosted a Christmas party that for the most part resembles what you might expect at any gathering of friends and family during the holiday season. There is always a wonderful assortment of good food, never an empty glass, and plenty of great company. However, the Trafford Family Christmas Party is one-of-a-kind.

First and foremost the instructions are clear. "Please, do not bring a hostess gift." Not that the hostess doesn't deserve one — it's just that long before hostess gifts were in vogue the Trafford Family asked guests to bring canned goods for the local food bank. The entrance to their home often looks like a small distribution center on the eve of December 23, but once you're past the boxes of canned goods stacked outside it is always warm and inviting inside and filled with the promise of what is still to come.

Secondly, you are encouraged to bring whoever happens to be staying with you during the holidays. The more generations of family you bring, the better. There have been occasions when three generations of a family can be found at the Trafford's Party.

Thirdly, and certainly a key factor contributing to the spirit and joy of the evening, is the music. Along with your canned goods and your relatives you are encouraged to bring an instrument. Many people bring guitars, some bring flutes, mandolins, trumpets, drums, tambourines, maracas — even the occasional penny whistle. Voices are always welcome!

The first time my family attended, December 23, 1997 to be precise, was actually the Second Annual Trafford Party. I'm sure they had no idea they were starting a tradition that continues to bring generations of families and friends together year after year.

I've known my friend Dave, the host, since I was twelve, but we had lost touch with one another for a number of years. In 1997 our families moved into the same neighbourhood and in November we received an invitation to the Second Annual Trafford Party. Having missed the first I didn't quite know what to expect. With my wife and children joining me, I took our donation for the food bank — I had no desire to take my relatives and we would probably leave early anyway — we still had a closet full of presents to wrap. I certainly wasn't going to take my guitar — it had been years since I'd played it.

When we arrived, we deposited our canned goods in the appropriate bin, took the opportunity to catch up with some friends we hadn't seen in a number of years, and were just settling in by the fire when Dave announced it was time to go caroling. While we were initially a little uncertain about what to expect, we decided to bundle everyone up (with three kids under the age of eight, this is no easy task) and accompany him along with many other brave souls who chose to venture out into the cold. That night we stood and sang Christmas carols for people who opened their doors to us. Dave played his heart out; we all sang and anyone who opened his door in our neighbourhood that night over twelve years ago remembers and will tell you how wonderful it made them feel. It was a magical night — one I will never forget.

This year, over a decade later, the invitation arrived late in November and started with the same message as it had in years past: "No Hostess

Gifts Please." The difference this year was there was no request for canned goods. It read: "Let's fill a stable." The Traffords had decided to ask friends and family and their community to help provide a family in some remote part of the world with essential animals that would, in turn, allow that family and their community to sustain itself. As I reread the invitation I couldn't help but recall the story of a baby named Jesus born over two thousand years ago in a stable surrounded by animals. A baby whose birth started a tradition that has lasted just as long and had an incredible influence on history and brought hope throughout the world.

Each year my children, now in their late teens, start asking about the Trafford's Christmas Party sometime just after Halloween. If the invitation for December 23 hasn't arrived by the end of November they start to get a little antsy. Our friends Anne and Dave and their children Erin and David Jr., whether they like it or not, have created a tradition that has become one of the most important parts of my family's and our community's Christmas traditions.

Like a little kid who lies awake in bed waiting for Santa, I can't wait for tomorrow night. It's December 23!

By the way — my mom and dad are really looking forward to the party, a couple of cousins have arrived from Europe and will be joining us and… I'm taking my guitar!

— Tom Knight —

11

Little Free Libraries

I think of life as a good book. The further you
get into it, the more it begins to make sense.
~Harold Kushner

As a professional writer, I can't afford a lot of stuff, so I don't buy a lot of stuff. Anyway, where would I put it? I live in a one-bedroom apartment. I acquire only what is necessary and keep only what I use. There's no space for more.

However, I started my career submitting fiction to short story anthologies, and every time my work was published I received contributor copies of those books. After years of prolific authorship, I amassed boxes of books.

Then I read Stephen King's *On Writing* and it got me thinking. He suggests editing out ten percent of whatever you write — your novel, short story, whatever it may be. Ten percent of what you've written is unnecessary. This may not be true for everyone, but I'd always been a wordy writer. Cuts improve content.

I started looking around my apartment and wondering if the same might be true for books themselves. It's hard to see books as stuff — they're so much more. There are whole other worlds inside their pages.

Even so, my bookshelf was overrun with fiction I'd purchased at library fundraisers or picked out of people's garbage. I kept books I had read. I kept books I hadn't read. I kept books I'd gotten bored with after the first few chapters. I'd kept every book I bought in university, some of which I'd never cracked because the professor changed the course syllabus — and some of which I'd never cracked because, let's face it, I wasn't the world's greatest student.

So, in addition to multiple copies of anthologies that featured my writing, I owned shelves of books I didn't "need," in the strictest sense of the word. Though I'd managed to pare the rest of my life down to just the essentials, I had this ever-growing mountain of books around me.

But that made sense... because I was a writer. Right?

I knew I could donate books to the local library and they would sell them to people like me, so I put together a big bag. I felt pretty darn good about myself because proceeds would help fund the library's important programming. Although, at a dollar a pop, my books were barely a drop in the ocean.

At Christmas, I gave my books as gifts. Friends and family always asked to read my writing, so it seemed like a good idea. Turns out most people consider a book you wrote yourself to be a bit of a cop-out, as a gift — somewhere between self-promotion and free shampoo samples. My grandmother's always happy to receive a book I contributed to, but everyone else seems to prefer homemade jam.

Books kept rolling in — wonderful for my writing career, not so wonderful for my tiny apartment.

And then one day, while walking home from my local community centre, I spotted a tiny house on someone's front lawn. It was propped up on a wooden post, which made it look somewhat like a birdhouse, but right at eye level and right next to the sidewalk.

Instead of birdseed, the tiny house contained books.

It was a Little Free Library: an adorable structure with flowers painted on both sides and a Plexiglas front door that swung open to reveal a world of reading. "Take a book. Return a book." That's what the sign said. No library card necessary. No late fees.

It was for anyone. It was for everyone.

Just a sweet little home for books, continuously stocked by members of the community.

"Hey," I thought. "I'm a member of the community. Why don't

I contribute?"

As soon as I got home, I opened my big boxes of books and selected a few I thought the neighbours might like. The next day, I walked back to the Little Free Library. I'd only gone there to contribute content, but I spotted a novel by an author I'd been meaning to read for years. I came away with a book to devour and return — one that wouldn't add to the clutter of my overstuffed bookshelf.

As the months went by, Little Free Libraries sprang up like flowers across the city. Everywhere I went, I seemed to stumble across one. I started carrying books with me so I'd always have something to contribute.

My collection of short story collections dwindled, and I felt great about getting them out into the world. What good were they doing boxed up in my living room? Books are meant to be read.

Every time I walked by a Little Free Library I'd contributed to, the last book I'd put in there was already snapped up by another eager reader. The libraries seemed to enjoy complete and frequent changeovers. Shelves didn't stagnate. There was always something new.

Little Free Libraries became my go-to spot for book browsing. I still purchase new books by authors I cherish, but now I get the added pleasure of thinking, "When I'm finished, I get to share this with the entire neighbourhood!"

Last summer, I met the owner of that very first Little Free Library I came across. She was sitting on her porch, reading a book, of course. I thanked her for providing this wonderful resource to the community. She asked me if I'd read anything good lately.

At the end of our book chat, to my surprise, my neighbour thanked ME — not for contributing books to her library (I hadn't disclosed that I'd done so), but for borrowing from it. She seemed genuinely overjoyed that the neighbours were using it.

People who live in big cities — and especially people like me, who live in huge apartment buildings — often don't feel a special sense of community. We think that's reserved for small towns. But after donating books I've read and books I've written to Little Free Libraries, I feel like I'm part of something. I felt a sense of belonging. And, unlike boxes of books, a feeling of community is something you can't keep a lid on.

— Tanya Janke —

12

Happiness Is Raising a Roof

Never believe that a few caring people can't change the
world. For, indeed, that's all who ever have.
~Margaret Mead

The picture of my self-indulgent lifestyle sickened me. The speaker's words pierced my heart; I was horrified to discover that I was a middle age, successful and pampered woman. I needed more clarification so I leaned forward with interest as the conference speaker continued: "Many women in other parts of the world cannot get into their SUV and drive to the nearest medical walk-in clinic. They cannot run to the corner store or shopping centre to pick up fresh vegetables, toothpaste or a new outfit for their next social function. These women have time and no stuff. People in North America have stuff but no time."

I sat back in my comfortable chair and was jolted back to reality. I looked around at my beautiful conference room, the women in their exquisite outfits, and I knew in the next few minutes I was going to a local restaurant to enjoy a splendid meal with friends. I cringed when I realized I was one of those self-indulgent women.

Over the years I saw videos and heard numerous pleas for impoverished countries, children dying from AIDS, grandmothers raising their children and grandchildren. I have always done my part by adopting children in Africa and Haiti and sending money when I saw the need. But that part is easy for me. Pull out my chequebook and write a cheque to ease my guilty conscience. I've done my part; what more can I do?

This time I knew it wasn't enough. At the end of the day, as I drove across the bridge to my home in West Kelowna, British Columbia an outrageous idea hit me: *Heidi, until you see your own lifestyle as self-indulgent, you will never understand and experience the plight of these impoverished women. For the next four months don't buy anything for yourself or indulge in any luxury and see how this makes you feel.*

This was the middle of August, so that meant I had to do without any shopping, restaurants and any other indulgences until the middle of December. By the time I arrived at my home I was determined to do it and excited by the prospect. In fact, I was going to take it one step further. Whatever money I would have spent in those four months I would contribute to a worthwhile project.

Over the next two days, as the conference continued, I shared my story with my closest friends and asked if they wanted to join me. I was amazed at their excitement and eagerness to jump on board. Word spread and soon we had twenty-three women ready to sacrifice everything for the next four months and donate the money they saved to a worthy fund. It was interesting for me to hear what other women indulged in and what they had to give up:

"I'm not much of a shopper Heidi, but I do spend about $150 each month on specialty coffees."

"I don't spend money on clothes, but I sure do love to shop for kitchen gadgets."

"Gardening supplies, flowers and tools are my weakness."

"I watch too much TV, I am going to cut off my cable for the next four months."

"I spend way too much money on magazines each month."

We all indulge ourselves in different ways. I have the luxury of buying new outfits for my speaking engagements, and I love the challenge of finding just the right attire for each event. I was just going into my busiest months for speaking engagements and I would have to "make do" with what I already had. For the first time I was shocked and yet very grateful that my closet was already filled with beautiful clothes, scarves and shoes and all I had to do was get creative.

The next few months were a revelation. I discovered I had so much more time to spend on coffee dates with friends instead of stopping off at a mall or a favourite store. And I was able to go right home after work. I also found that I had shampoos, toothpastes and soaps tucked away that I had never used. Eventually when I did go into the mall with a friend, I found the atmosphere to be loud and confusing. I was quite disgusted with the frenzy of people searching for their next purse, shoes or unnecessary trinket. I saw the obsession of our culture with stuff and it saddened me. Finally I was able to "feel" and experience a smidgen of what women from an impoverished country might be feeling.

At the end of four months the twenty-three women handed me the money they would have spent. Some of the women had tears in their eyes when they gave me a cheque and said things like: *"Heidi, this experiment has changed me forever, thank you for allowing us to experience it. I don't know when I have experienced such joy."* When all the money was deposited I was amazed and delighted with the final amount. After some research, and by placing this money into trusted hands, we were all delighted to be able to put a roof on a church in Hermosillo, Mexico.

These four months of walking in someone else's shoes taught me truths that will affect me forever and have changed me. Here's what I learned:

1. Stuff does not bring me happiness.
2. Before I buy anything I re-evaluate the cost and need.
3. Nothing will change until my heart really wants it to change.
4. We are all on this earth to help one another and we all have to do our part.
5. When we pour out our lives for others, we are the ones who experience the happiness and feel fulfilled.

I am so grateful that a speaker had the courage to tackle some tough issues about the overindulgence of my lifestyle. Those words changed my behaviour and put new happiness into my heart.

—Heidi McLaughlin—

13

Honouring Halifax's 100-Year Legacy of Giving

If you light a lamp for somebody,
it will also brighten your path.
~Buddha

On December 6, 1917, the port city of Halifax, Nova Scotia was changed forever. Two ships in the Halifax Harbour collided, sparking a small fire onboard the *SS Mont-Blanc*. The fire spread, sending a huge plume of smoke into the air and attracting the attention of onlookers, most of whom were unaware of the ship's deadly cargo. At 9:04 a.m., the nearly three kilotons of TNT onboard the *Mont-Blanc* exploded. The pressure wave and tsunami that followed devastated the city in every sense of the word.

Now known as the Halifax Explosion, it was the largest man-made disaster in Canadian history. Approximately 2,000 people were killed and 9,000 others were injured, including more than 1,000 people who were blinded by flying debris and shards of glass from shattered windowpanes. Structures were demolished, children were orphaned and families with surviving members lost their homes, jobs and belongings in an instant.

Today, reminders of the disaster can still be found throughout our city. There's a world-renowned exhibit at the Maritime Museum of the Atlantic, a towering monument in a neighbourhood that was completely levelled by the blast, fragments of the *Mont-Blanc* are preserved where they landed kilometres away, and a clock at Halifax's City Hall is frozen at the precise time of the explosion.

The scope of the tragedy is where the story of the Halifax Explosion begins, but that is not where it ends. Within hours, business leaders, neighbours and change-makers began to organize a citywide relief effort. A combined thirty million dollars was raised from local and international contributors, including the city of Boston, which remains a kindred spirit and friend to Halifax to this day.

The large-scale relief effort sparked the first movement of charitable citizenry in Halifax and eventually led to the establishment of United Way Halifax. From the $100,000 relief fund contribution from Scotiabank, to the first United Way Halifax donation from W. A. Black, generations of giving within companies and families have continued ever since.

It is with this legacy of compassion, generosity and community-building in mind that United Way Halifax decided to do something special to commemorate the 100th anniversary of the explosion. After months of research, ideation and discussion, the concept for Wake Up Halifax was born.

We envisioned 500 people completing 100 volunteer projects in one day, proving once again that Halifax is a place where we show up for each other. We chose to host Wake Up Halifax on December 7th because one hundred years earlier, it was the first day that residents would have woken up to their tragic new reality and with the difficult work of rebuilding ahead of them.

We believed wholeheartedly in our vision, but getting there would be no small task.

With less than four months, a small team and a modest budget to work with, we set out trying to identify community needs that volunteers could help with and recruiting hundreds of people willing to be generous with their time. United Way's nearly 100-year history, extensive network of partners in the business and social sector, and well-known reputation for facilitating community volunteerism gave us a running start — and we didn't stop running until it was all over.

To get to 100 projects, our team confirmed every single one personally, by phone. We also sourced the funds and supplies needed to make them happen, from the wrapping paper and bows needed to wrap 200 gifts, to the recipes and ingredients needed to cook 160 meals and the paint, brushes and rollers required to beautify more than fifty community spaces.

To get to 500 volunteers, we reached out to both citizens and businesses, in the same way the explosion relief effort did. We invited people to register as teams of five with their colleagues, family members or friends; then we supported and inspired them in a variety of ways. Wake Up Halifax was an opportunity for them to pull together — and they seized the heck out of it.

Starting as early as 7:00 a.m., nearly 400 volunteers showed up to the Wake Up Halifax kick-off breakfast. They fuelled up on coffee, heard from the Mayor of Halifax, changed into their Wake Up Halifax T-shirts and started posting photos on social media using their unifying hashtag: #todaywewill.

By 9:30 a.m., they had fanned out to project sites all over the city.

One team spent time at an under-supported community centre — painting, cleaning up and completing light construction duties. Another visited a community garden run by neighbourhood youth and helped prepare the garden beds for winter. And several cooked tea biscuits and shepherd's pie for men, women and children in emergency shelters and transitional housing units, to name a few.

In total, 535 Wake Up Halifax participants completed 105 hands-on projects that day. Fifteen neighbourhoods and fifty-seven community organizations benefited from their compassionate action and every major media outlet in the city paid attention.

More than anything the team wanted Wake Up Halifax to be a reminder that each day is a new opportunity to act, give and care. What we got was a citywide display of volunteerism, kindness, gratitude and enthusiasm… and the top trending hashtag on Twitter.

It was one of the most memorable days of my career and our

project team ended the day feeling proud of the way we honoured Halifax's 100-year legacy of giving.

As the renowned composer Leonard Bernstein once said: "To achieve great things, two things are needed; a plan, and not quite enough time." In this spirit, we had the formula for Wake Up Halifax just right.

Between our commitment, teamwork and thorough planning I always trusted we would pull it off, but I couldn't have predicted just how personal the work would become.

During my research in the months leading up to Wake Up Halifax, I came to know about a man known as A. H. Whitman, who was a businessman in Halifax in 1917. After the explosion, he immediately stepped up to help organize the community response.

As president of the Halifax Board of Trade at the time, his innovative thinking and social responsibility sparked the creation of a Community Chest, later named United Way Halifax, which continued to distribute funds to those in need long after the explosion relief effort was done. He is credited with bringing modern ideas and resources to social work and encouraging volunteerism and generosity.

Whitman is my married name, so naturally I was curious to know if there was a connection. As it turns out, there is. Arthur Hanfield Whitman is my husband's cousin. One hundred years after he was mobilizing people to lend their hearts and hands wherever they were needed, I found myself at United Way Halifax leading an eerily similar effort.

For me, this new insight about our family tree serves as a humbling, serendipitous reminder that we can never truly know the impact of our efforts.

Whether we touch one person's life with a small act of kindness or introduce an innovative idea that eventually leads to large-scale change, all of our interactions with others can have a ripple effect. They all have the potential to spread over time and distance in ways that we can't see. Knowing that a shared passion for United Way has tied two distant pieces of family history together has given me new appreciation for this mystery.

With this fresh perspective and in the spirit of Wake Up Halifax, I'm more committed than ever to creating as many heart-warming ripples as I can. Knowing that I can't see where or how far they'll go is half the fun.

—Laura Whitman—

Chapter 2

Kindness from a Stranger

14

Breaking the Ice

A smile is a powerful weapon;
you can even break ice with it.
~Author Unknown

"Can you go into the Calgary Flames dressing room and do a post-game story?" I stared at the phone and cringed because I had been dreading this call for months.

It was make it or break it time. So I did what any enterprising young reporter would do; I lied through my teeth.

"Sure, no problem," I told my assignment editor. "I can do that."

I started shaking in the second period and by the end of the game I was filled with such terror I thought I was going to pass out. The Flames did their part by winning that night, but by the time I met up with my cameraman outside the dressing room door I was a trembling, sweating mess. Being the lone woman in the group I stood out like a sore thumb and more than a few smirks and eye rolls were tossed my way by all the male reporters waiting to get into the dressing room.

The doors swung open and we charged through like a massive cattle drive heading for the barn. Caught up in the wave, I kept my eyes firmly glued to the red rug on the floor. Not daring to look up, I followed the microphone cable that was attached to my camera and it led me to a pair of naked feet. Looking up quickly, I found myself interviewing Jim Peplinski. Once the scrum was over the herd was off again and the microphone cable led me over to another pair of feet.

This time as I glanced up, I looked into the bemused eyes of Lanny McDonald, whose trademark mustache was twitching as he looked at the stressed out woman with the shaking microphone. Soon the herd departed again and glancing wildly around the room I noticed goaltender Mike Vernon in the corner. After collecting a few more good clips I ran out the door. We shot a fast standup extra for the story at ice level and then drove the videotape to the airport to make the last flight to Toronto. My first hockey post-game report was winging its way to TSN and my job prospects were flying along with it.

The mid to late eighties were glory years for hockey in Alberta. Calgary was beginning to make a serious run for the Cup but the spotlight was shining on the Edmonton Oilers. When Gretzky and the boys came to town the Calgary Saddledome exploded like a three ring circus. Everyone wanted to talk to the Great One and heaven help you if you ever missed his pre-game press conference.

But one day, TSN didn't need any extra Gretzky clips. They wanted Mark Messier, the tough guy everyone called The Moose. In the early days of his career Messier was a man of few words and let his fierce, physical play on the ice do the talking. He was 205 pounds of muscle, aggression and to put it bluntly, he scared the living daylights out his opponents — and me. Whenever the media wanted to talk to Messier we were always told he was in the trainer's room. A few of us would try waiting for him but one by one the reporters would disappear and then finally give up all together.

On this night, TSN was willing to wait. My cameraman Brad sat down near an empty player's stall and I hid out in the stick room. One hour passed and no Mark Messier. The team bus left. Messier was still with the trainer. We weren't leaving and neither was he. Finally the weary PR guy came up and yelled, "Get your camera ready — Mark's coming out!" I ran towards Brad and grabbed the microphone. With my eyes fixed on the floor I could hear Messier approaching and you could tell right away that he wasn't happy. The feet were getting closer and I started to panic, praying that Brad would get the camera going before The Moose exploded into the room. As Brad fiddled with the camera and fumbled in his bag for a white balance card, the large pair of irate feet arrived in front of us.

"We'll be right with you Mark."

"Let's just get this over with!" Messier barked.

Finally after what seemed like an eternity we got the camera rolling and I snapped my eyes up from the floor to stare at the seething face of Mark Messier. He was clearly not impressed and I swear I could see steam coming out of his ears. But something had caught my eye and I don't know if it was from nervousness, tension or exhaustion but as I looked into Mark's eyes I suddenly burst into laughter. Not just little snickers but huge embarrassing gasps and guffaws. Now it was obvious Mark was angry. My cameraman looked at me like I was mad, and the PR guy just about had a nervous breakdown.

"What's so funny?" Mark asked through clenched teeth.

I settled down a bit and gasped, "I'm sorry Mark but...."

I pointed down towards his kneecaps. One of the toughest guys in the NHL, the man known as The Moose, was wearing Frosty the Snowman boxer shorts. Mark glanced down at the cartoon figures dancing across his shorts and I watched the sneer change to a smile as he started to chuckle.

"Yep, they're something, aren't they?" he said proudly.

Now everyone was laughing, even Mark. I apologized, pulled myself together and did the interview.

A few weeks later, the Oilers were back in town again. We had just finished our pre-game interviews with the Flames and all the media had gone out to the stands to watch Edmonton's morning skate. One by one the players came out on the ice, stretching and doing slow laps. Messier arrived and began to skate. As he glided by he looked up in the stands, nodded his head and said, "Hi Teresa." My cameraman gasped and all the male reporters sitting near me were in shock. One of the top players in the NHL had acknowledged a rookie female sports reporter. With one simple gesture, I was now part of "the club."

Years later, I was sent to New York to follow one of the Rangers' playoff series. Over time my confidence had grown and I wasn't such a novelty anymore. But the New York media were a tough bunch and this group was acting like a pack of jerks. Mark Messier was now the captain of the Rangers and my cameraman and I waited patiently beside his stall. Finally he burst through the door and strode up to the assembled media. With elbows flying, the pack of New York media hounds physically shoved us to the back of the scrum. Winded and shocked, I pushed back into the fray trying to get my microphone near Mark. As he began answering the first question his eyes scanned the assembled media. To my surprise, he suddenly stopped and yelled, "Hey, Teresa. Get up here!"

His arm shot out through the New York journalists, parting the way like Moses and the Red Sea, allowing my cameraman and me to walk right up to the front. All the reporters had stopped taking notes and were now standing with their mouths open.

"Who is *she*?" I heard one of them mutter.

Satisfied he had things the way he wanted them, Mark looked back at all the reporters and said with a smirk, "Okay, we can start again. Teresa, did you have a question?"

I will always remember the kindness of Mark Messier as I struggled to make my mark as a sports reporter. There were so many times when I questioned my sanity and willpower to keep going. But with a simple gesture, one of the toughest guys ever to lace up a pair of skates validated what I was doing and served notice to the male dominated world of sports that women could do the job and be accepted for their knowledge and skills.

Looking back on fourteen phenomenal years at TSN I still have to laugh. Who knew it would be a pair of Frosty the Snowman boxer shorts that would break the ice?

— Teresa Kruze —

15

The Gloves

The roots of all goodness lie in the soil
of appreciation for goodness.
~The Dalai Lama

I had just returned to Canada after spending almost a month in a warm mountain valley in Mexico. I had gone to spend Christmas with my husband, who was teaching anthropology there. What a change it was being back in freezing cold Alberta.

I was scheduled to work on New Year's Day so I got up at seven and walked outside to assess the weather. The warm Chinook winds assured me that we were in for a good day. I didn't bother to retrieve my winter gloves from our other vehicle.

My first day back at work went well and as night approached I remembered the car needed gas. It felt a lot colder by the time I headed for the only gas station that was open at eight in the evening. I hadn't wanted to use that particular station because it was self-service only and it was starting to get very cold again.

I must have looked pretty funny as I tried to squeeze the gas handle with my hand in my coat pocket. There was a member of the Royal Canadian Mounted Police watching me from one of the other pumps.

I felt that I should provide an explanation. "I know I look silly, but my hands are so cold and I thought if I put my hand in my pocket I could use my coat for protection. Of course, that means I have to stand in this awkward position." I looked as though I was hugging the car.

For a moment, he said nothing. "He probably thinks I'm a real nut case," I thought to myself. Then I heard a voice and saw a pair of gloves sticking out beyond his gas pump. "Could you use a pair of gloves?"

I shut off the pump and walked over. "Oh, yes please." I replied, taking the offering and slipping my hands into the warm leather gloves.

I went back and returned to filling my tank. Then I leaned over, still holding the handle and noticed that the police officer was pumping gas with nothing to protect his own hands from the cold. I had thought he was lending me some spare gloves, not taking off his only pair.

I felt grateful for the kindness of the officer. I also felt a tad embarrassed, then worried. I suggested he take back the gloves. And he declined. "But you need something for your hands, too," I said.

"Oh, I get used to it," he responded. "Don't worry, I'm fine."

In minutes my tank was full and I thanked him, returned his gloves and went in to pay for my purchase. I felt so elated at being the recipient of his thoughtfulness. As the officer came in to pay for his own gas I smiled at him and told him how grateful I was.

He stood there and said, "It was my pleasure."

I knew he meant it. The gift was small but my hands and my heart didn't think so! What a lovely "welcome back" from the country I love.

— Ellie Braun-Haley —

16

Who Was that Man?

He had a face like a benediction.
~Miguel de Cervantes

The temperature in downtown Toronto at noon on Thursday, November 20, 1980 was a chilly four degrees Celsius (39F) and a wet snow was falling as I walked northward on the east side of Yonge Street at 11:55 a.m. Why would I recall such mundane information on a particular date more than three decades ago? Partly because my life changed that day, and I remember it like it was yesterday.

I was working as editor of a high-profile corporate magazine for an international company. I should have been happy in my career, but I was miserable. I felt unfulfilled because my dream was to be a full-time freelance writer, working out of my home, but I did not have the courage to escape from my secure corporate job. I had the love and encouragement of my schoolteacher wife, Kris, but even that wasn't enough to strengthen my resolve to pursue my life's ambition.

On this particularly wintry day I decided to walk the short distance from the King Street office building where I worked, in the heart of Canada's business capital, to enjoy the quiet solitude of the noon-hour Mass at St. Michael's Roman Catholic Cathedral on nearby Church Street.

The sidewalks on this bleak and nippy day were teeming with noonday shoppers and workers on their lunch break. There was also the usual number of panhandlers standing on street corners along this stretch of Yonge Street, known as "the longest street in the world." As

I neared Richmond Street I was lost in my troubled thoughts when a tall, slim, bearded young man thrust something into my hand. I didn't miss a stride. Yet, in my haste, I noticed that he was rather shabbily dressed and wore a long, dark-coloured raincoat that seemed much too flimsy to ward off the November chill. Our eyes met for the briefest of moments and he smiled at me. He neither asked for money nor spoke, but he did hand me something.

I thought no more of this stranger and I soon reached the cathedral just in time for the Mass. The then-150-year-old church in downtown Toronto had served as an oasis for me in the past. During the service I prayed for guidance, strength and the courage to change my career and follow my dream of being a freelance writer. Yet, when the Mass ended, I was no more certain of my future than when I had arrived forty-five minutes earlier.

I stood on the steps of the church and prepared to return to the office when I reached into my pockets for my gloves. My right hand came upon the tiny booklet that had been handed to me by the stranger. For the first time, I saw that it was a miniature, red-covered, thirty-two-page "Personal Bible" measuring a mere two by two-and-a-half inches. I opened the paper booklet to the first page, and my eyes widened as I read aloud the words of John 14:27 that filled the entire page: "Let not your heart be troubled, neither let it be afraid." The verse rang in my ears like the tolling of a bell, and I realized it was tolling for me.

Without hesitation, I ran down the stairs and retraced my steps along Yonge Street to Richmond, but the man who'd given me the little holy booklet was no longer there.

I returned to my office feeling like I had been relieved of a heavy burden. I gathered some personal belongings from my desk, picked up my briefcase and informed my boss that I would not be returning. He was very understanding. He was well aware of my unhappiness in my job.

The next morning I made a cold call to *The Toronto Star* and was connected to Mike Walton, an editor at the paper who is now deceased. I told him that I had a story idea that might interest him. I said I'd like to write a feature article for *The Star* titled "101 Free Activities for

Winter." He said if I could pull it off, he'd pay me $175 for the story and he'd publish it in the new year. I was true to my word and he was true to his: My article appeared on a full page in the country's largest newspaper on Sunday, January 11, 1981.

I was a bona fide freelance writer!

Today, I am an award-winning book author, and several hundred of my newspaper and magazine articles have been published in over sixty-five publications in Canada, the U.S. and Europe.

I have worked out of my home office for over thirty years and I continue to follow my dream.

As I write this, I am looking at that little red "Personal Bible" that is always on my writing desk. I often ask myself, in wonderment: "Who was that man at the corner of Yonge and Richmond Streets on that fateful day in 1980?"

— Dennis McCloskey —

17

It Happened One New Year's Eve

Miracles happen to those who believe in them.
~Bernard Berenson

My eighteen-year-old daughter Olivia and I were dining at a local restaurant for the first time all year, courtesy of a gift card I'd received from work for a performance achievement. We were seated in the corner with only one table as a neighbour. A couple in their sixties came in and were seated there when we were about halfway through our meal.

When we rose to leave, the lady, observing that Olivia was likely a cancer patient, said, "Hello, how are you, dear? How are things coming along for you?"

"I'm doing okay," said Olivia.

"I've been where you are," said the lady.

"Oh?" I asked. Olivia told her that she had osteosarcoma and would have an operation the next week to have a bone in her arm replaced with a metal rod.

The lady tapped her arm. "This one here," she said. "I have two metal rods. Osteosarcoma for me, too."

We had not met anyone with osteosarcoma since we began this journey in September, and here we were on New Year's Eve in a restaurant we hardly ever went to, meeting this beautiful person who was so willing to share.

"Can I ask when you were diagnosed?" I said.

She replied, "Fourteen years ago, and I'm still cancer-free." Olivia's face lit up like a Christmas tree.

We exchanged names, and the lady shared more of her story and wished Olivia much success with her surgery the following week.

"God bless you for taking the time to speak to us and for sharing," I said with a lump in my throat.

"You're so welcome," she replied. "Have a wonderful year."

Olivia and I walked toward the car, both of us in a state of disbelief.

"I will remember this moment for the rest of my life," I said to her.

"Me, too." She said with a smile. "Me, too."

My daughter had surgery on January 6th. The tumour was removed in its entirety. When the pathology was done, it was determined that it was 100% necrosis, meaning it was 100% dead cancer cells. The surgeon and my daughter's oncologist said it was the first time in both their careers that they had ever experienced this in an osteosarcoma patient. Her surgeon proclaimed it a miracle.

— Nancy Barter-Billard —

18

An Angel for Becki

Pay attention to your dreams — God's angels often
speak directly to our hearts when we are asleep.
~The Angels' Little Instruction Book
by Eileen Elias Freeman

The darkness was oppressive as she wobbled in heels along the side of the highway. The car had choked to an unexpected halt, and like a normal teenager she did the only thing she could think of… get out and walk.

It was cold and late, and the young girl shivered as the reality of her situation became clear. Home was far away. This could be a long night. If only someone would stop and offer her a ride — anyone — and preferably soon. She offered up a prayer for help and plodded on.

The lights of a truck shone from behind her as it approached. "Maybe he will stop," she hoped. The brake lights flashed on as it halted. "He's stopping!" Her words were lost in the night.

The transport ground to a screeching halt and the cab door opened. A wordless invitation was extended and she understood. Without hesitation the girl climbed up into the seat and closed the door. Slowly the truck pulled back onto the road and disappeared into the night, never to be seen again.

I bolted upright in my bed, lathered in sweat. Was that a dream or was it a vision? It was unbelievably real, and the girl was my daughter! I jumped from my bed and ran to her room, positive I would see her sleeping soundly under the covers.

Her bed was empty. I stood in horror trying to think why she had not come home. As the mental fog began to lift, I remembered she was visiting with friends that evening. Perhaps she stayed there for the night. It was 1:30 a.m. but I raced to the phone and dialled a number.

"Hello?" The voice was heavy with sleep.

"Hey. Sorry to wake you. Becki didn't come home tonight and I was wondering if she stayed at your place?"

"No, she left here a few hours ago. She should have been home at least by midnight!" The voice on the other end began to reflect my own panic.

I told her about the vision that woke me. She promised to pray, and we hung up.

Instantly I felt a force upon me, a spiritual presence driving me to prayer. Over the next forty-five minutes I alternated between lying prostrate in petition and pacing the floor in praise.

At 2:15 a.m. lights appeared as a car turned up our long driveway. I could tell immediately that it was not my daughter's. Was it a patrol car?

My face pressed against the window. I could not breathe.

A small vehicle pulled in front of the house, and tears stung as I watched my precious daughter emerge from the car and make her way up the steps.

Throwing open the door, I pulled her inside, hugging her tightly while plying her with questions.

"My car stopped on the highway and I decided to walk home." She began to explain. "I knew I was never going to make it in my dress shoes so I prayed that someone would give me a ride. A truck slowed down and was about to stop, then suddenly picked up speed again and carried on. Right after he drove away, a car with a mother and daughter stopped and offered me a ride. They saw the truck begin to stop as they passed me and were concerned, so they turned around and came back."

There were no words to describe the emotions that screamed through me. Her story was an exact parallel to the vision that woke me from deep sleep. God had provided an intercessor for His child in an hour of grave danger.

I don't know why that truck driver decided not to stop, but something tells me it was because of an angel walking beside Becki. All I know is that I am eternally grateful to the mother who stopped to save her, and for the dream that caused me to pray for her.

—Heather Rae Rodin—

19

A Tim Hortons Angel

All God's angels come to us disguised.
~James Russell Lowell

Our minds were reeling. We had just met with the oncologist at the hospital. Cancer. It was definite. Surgery was imminent. There seemed so much to digest, so many questions, so many unknowns. As my husband and I contemplated what lay before us we decided we needed some time before we faced our family. We tried desperately to fathom what God's divine plan might be. How could He allow this to happen? How could I have cancer?

"Why don't we get some lunch?" my husband suggested. "Timmies?"

I agreed. A Tim Hortons coffee shop in the big city where no one knew us sounded like a good place to go. We could grab some lunch, talk, and prepare ourselves before we met with our family. We drove down the busy city street and pulled into the entrance of the first Tim Hortons we saw.

I looked for an empty table while my husband got the order. There was a vacant spot by a window. As I headed for the table, I caught the eye of a grayish-haired woman, probably in her early sixties, seated in the corner. She smiled and nodded at me. I returned the greeting.

I sat down and gazed out the window. I thought about my cancer diagnosis and my impending surgery. The tears swelled. My husband sat down with the food and gave thanks.

No sooner had we said Amen than the woman came over to me

and placed a hand gently on my shoulder. I looked at her.

"I have something I think you need right now," the stranger said.

She pulled a green piece of paper from her jacket pocket. She smiled and I felt a strange warmness.

I quietly took the paper from her outstretched hand.

Both my husband and I read the four-stanza poem on the paper. Our eyes brimmed as we read the final lines:

I asked for happiness for you,
In all things great and small,
But it was for His loving care,
I prayed the most of all…

I turned around to thank her for her incredible timing. I wanted to thank her for sensing my sadness and for being so compassionate. I wanted to tell her about my cancer. But she was gone. I searched the sea of faces at the counter. I looked at the doorway. She was nowhere to be found.

God worked in a magnificent way that day. He placed a perfect stranger in our path to let us know that all would be well and that we were assured of His loving care. God's love washed over us in that moment and we felt the glorious peace that passes all understanding.

"An angel?" I said to my husband through tear-filled eyes.

"A Tim Hortons angel." He smiled, and took a sip of his double-double.

— Glynis M. Belec —

20

Angels Among Us

Knowledge is knowing that we cannot know.
~Ralph Waldo Emerson

Piles of dirty, crusted snow lingered in the shade of the hospital as my daughter Nicole laboured to deliver her twins. She had been in labour for eighteen hours but those stubborn babies refused to come out. The two nurses assigned for her double-birth had tried everything to get the babies to drop into the birth canal but nothing worked.

Nicole anxiously watched the heart monitor. The babies were getting tired and their heartbeats were slowing. She pleaded with the nurses and the OB/GYN to do something.

The doctor was used to a birth turning sour. He quietly told the nurses to prepare Nicole for an emergency caesarean.

But the operating room was busy with another woman and her baby; Nicole would have to wait. Nicole's husband, Ian, took her hand. The large twenty-four-hour clock ticked silently as they stared at the green iridescent blips of the labouring hearts.

Nicole was just about to be transferred to surgery when a nurse in blue flowered scrubs entered the room. She was a stranger, unknown to the doctor and his team, but she offered to help. The nurse explained she had just finished a practicum in London, England. The British were using a new method that was successful in helping mothers in this situation. Everyone moved back, making room near the bed. The nurse told Nicole to grab hold of the iron rail above her head and twist her body until her belly was on its side; then she was to push. Nicole grabbed the rail, twisted and bore down. With the first push, Keira slipped into position in the birth canal. A few more hard pushes and she slid out and was whisked away.

Sometimes with twins, the mother labours for the first child and the second flows through the opened door. That didn't happen in this case. The second baby, Brynn, still didn't move. Nicole kept staring at the heart monitor by the bed. The blips were further apart and fainter. Frantic, she yelled to the doctor, "Get the baby out! Now!"

The doctor found the head, grabbed on with forceps and pulled Brynn out.

The ordeal was over. It was quiet in the room and the babies lay cocooned in flannelette and pink knitted tuques. Ian remembered the mystery nurse and said, "I should go find her and thank her."

He went to the maternity wing's nursing station. "Do you know of a nurse who's just returned from a practicum in England? She helped my wife deliver our twins."

The nurses in pink, yellow and red flowered scrubs looked up from their files and shook their heads. He searched the halls, enquiring of all the doctors and staff if they knew of a nurse who had just returned from England. No one had seen or heard of such a person.

In 1993, the American country music band Alabama recorded their hit, "Angels Among Us." The refrain says: I believe there are angels among us, sent down to us from somewhere up above.

It seems that an angel in a nurse's blue scrubs helped Nicole birth her twins that day in early spring.

— Jeannette Richter —

21

How Did He Know?

While we are mourning the loss of our friend,
others are rejoicing to meet him behind the veil.
~John Taylor

I was on a cruise in another land, far from the accident, when it happened. My cousin and I had just disembarked at our second port of call and stood waiting on the dock for my father and brother. They were right behind us, but were not permitted to disembark. An overseas phone call had been placed to our room. My father had to collect the message from the front desk before he could go ashore so my cousin and I waited on the dock for them to return.

We sat down and chatted about the places we would visit that day. Twenty minutes passed and still my father and brother did not return. My cousin asked, "Do you think something is wrong? They've been gone a long time." I didn't hesitate in saying, "Of course not. It is probably something to do with Dad's work." My cousin nodded and we continued chatting. Five more minutes passed. At last we spotted them coming off the ship.

I knew by the looks on their faces that something had happened. My brother and father emerged wearing the same expression, one of worry and disbelief. I ran to them and asked with fear mounting, "What's happened? What's wrong?" My brother pulled me aside. Dad went to Jenny and took her in his arms. We begged to know what was wrong, panic in our voices.

"You're scaring me. What is it?" I asked.

My brother lowered his voice and said, "It's Terry. He's been killed."
I looked at Jenny. She was still pleading with my father to tell her what
had happened. He was trying to gently lead her back inside the ship,
to a private room where we could tell her what had happened to her
brother. I looked at my own brother and neither of us knew what to
say or do.

We got Jenny to a private area, sat her down, and told her that her
brother had been killed. He had been a young police officer, thirty-two
years old, with a wife, a three-year-old boy and a newborn baby girl.
I assumed, at first, that he had been killed while on duty, but then we
learned it was a car accident that had happened early in the morning
on his way to work, just down the road from his home. Jenny's cries
filled the room. I held her and tried to calm her.

What do you say to somebody who has been told such horrible
news? So we sat in silence, her crying and my arm around her, giving
her what human warmth I could.

We left the cruise and flew home on the next flight out. As the
plane began its descent, Jenny, who had been silent the entire flight,
began to quietly sob to herself. I looked at my cousin and wanted to
help her, but didn't know how. I learned that sometimes words are not
needed. I hugged her close and cried silently with her.

Our arrival in Toronto made the tragedy suddenly real. Being
told about the accident while so far away made it seem like a horrible
nightmare. Landing in Toronto brought us back to reality. We were no
longer on a cruise, enjoying the weather and eating wonderful food,
instead we had returned home for a funeral.

Several months later, I was traveling in England. The tragedy was
still with me and I often found myself thinking of the day we were
told about Terry's death. On the streets of Windsor I recalled my last
conversation with him. Terry was quite a bit older than me, so we
hadn't spoken much growing up. The one lengthy conversation I had
ever had with Terry happened just a few days before the accident.
I was at Jenny's house. Jenny was busy in the kitchen cooking, and
Terry and I were deep in conversation in the living room. Our topic of

discussion was the afterlife. Terry believed in it. He believed that there was a place we would go after death. We would see loved ones there once more. He firmly believed this, although I expressed my doubts. Some days I believed and some days I didn't. I found it chilling that Terry's last conversation with me was about the afterlife and his belief in its existence.

Still thinking about Terry and our conversation, I found myself in front of a church. I entered and sat down in one of the pews. As I sat with my thoughts, a man approached me. He was an elderly man, perhaps in his seventies, named Stan. He asked if he might sit with me. I smiled and nodded. He began to tell me stories of the church and the spirits that were believed to haunt it. When he finished, he looked earnestly into my eyes and said, "Forgive me, but I can see that you are sad. Someone has died in your family?" I was a bit taken aback at this blunt question, but I answered in the affirmative.

"It was a man and he died young, in a car accident, didn't he?"

I looked at this man and wondered how he knew what he did. Confused, I nodded and said nothing, unnerved at how much this stranger knew.

"You wish you had said more to him the day you last saw him and you wish you had let him know that you loved him," he said.

I started to cry. The stranger took my hands gently and said, "Your cousin knows you loved him and he wants you to know that he is happy and is working with children who have entered heaven. He loves the children and is very content where he is now."

I sat there, holding the hands of a stranger, and cried. I am not a person who cries easily. I'm always the "strong one" for others to lean on, but that day I was leaning on a complete stranger for emotional support. I left Stan that day only knowing his first name.

Months later Jenny was telling me about a dream Terry's wife had had. It had been so vivid that she felt as though Terry truly visited her. Terry told her not to be sad anymore, that he was happy because he was doing something he loved. He was working with children in heaven.

I had not told anyone about the conversation I'd had in Windsor, England, in a quiet church, with an old man named Stan. I had kept everything to myself and this is the first time that I am writing of it. It was as though Stan had truly spoken with Terry. How else could he have known what he did? The eerie coincidence of the dream and Stan's reassuring words about Terry's "new life" chilled me.

Years have passed since that day, yet I still find myself thinking about Stan. Was he an angel? I wish I could meet him again and let him know how much his words consoled me.

—Laurie Ann Mangru—

22

Coffee Shop Angel

Likewise I say to you, there is joy in the
presence of the angels of God...
~Luke 15:10

The day started out well. My husband was at work and my daughter Sarah, usually prone to grumpiness, was unusually quiet and content. It was about a year and half since she had been born. Adjusting to being a new stay-at-home mom had been difficult, but I had made it through the hump. Yet, I was troubled.

I had suspected something was different about Sarah for a while now. Incessant crying fits lasting for hours were one indication. Resisting body and eye contact was another. Multiple visits to the Children's Hospital in the middle of the night to diagnose the problem only resulted in perplexed, disinterested ER doctors shrugging their shoulders and dismissing my concern with the standard, "She's fine. It must be a behavioural problem."

Then, one Wednesday, we were out for our usual Baby Chat session run by a local medical center. Women would get together and chat while their babies under the age of two played and interacted on the floor.

The nurse running the program at the center pulled me aside and suggested that I have Sarah examined by a specialist in developmental disorders.

"She is exhibiting signs of autism," she told me gently. "I'm not a doctor so I can't say for sure, but maybe you should see someone." Then she hugged me when the tears started to spill down my face. I was oddly relieved. Someone else had noticed. It wasn't just me. Now I was going to use all my strength to help my family and daughter get through a possible autism diagnosis.

With all these thoughts running through my mind, I decided to put Sarah in the stroller and go for a walk to the neighbourhood coffee shop. The birds were singing and the sun was shining — a typical cheesy start one would see in a happy novel or romantic comedy.

Then the crying started. I was used to the crying. I tried everything — a bottle, walking, rocking, singing — it just wouldn't stop. It was especially hard for me because of the people, the ones who whisper and stare. We all know them.

Mostly they had disapproval on their faces. I could almost read their minds as they speculated about what kind of mother I was: "Why is her child so bad? Why doesn't she discipline her?"

Their sanctimonious sneers and cold stares affected me deeply, yet I could understand them. Before I had my own child, I reacted the same way. I vividly remembered one incident in a mall parking lot, where I observed a mom negotiating with her son, begging him to get into the car so they could go home. I recalled how I shook my head and thought, "Just pick him up and put him in the car!"

Now I was on the receiving end of the judgmental stares. Now, I was the flustered mother constantly holding back tears, pleading with my baby, and trying to find every way possible to calm her irrational behaviour. Now I, who had never understood those mothers, pleaded for understanding through watery eyes.

Standing helplessly in the entryway of the coffee shop, I didn't know what to do. Standing still made her cry. Moving the stroller made her cry more. Picking her up made her scream. I felt frozen with frustration, indecision and exhaustion. I avoided the stares as more tears welled up in my eyes.

Then, suddenly, I felt a presence at my back. I turned around to see the friendly smile and gentle eyes of a woman. She was dressed in a coffee shop uniform. Her nametag said "Joy."

"Here, you need this more than I do," she said, handing me a coffee card. I looked down at the gift card in my hands. I couldn't possibly take this! I started to protest but she dismissed my objections. "Employees get one coffee card a month as a bonus, so don't worry about the cost." I thanked her profusely. She cooed at Sarah, who had miraculously stopped crying.

I looked up again when I felt her hand on my shoulder. She smiled.

"Hang in there," she whispered, before turning to clear tables.

Taking advantage of Sarah's sudden quiet mood, I rushed to the counter and purchased a much-needed coffee and donut. I shared the pastry with my little girl, smiling at her intense examination of the donut pieces I had placed on her stroller tray.

I had thirty minutes of blessed relief. Sarah had nodded off with a bottle, and I felt so relaxed that I could have dozed myself. Reluctantly, I rose from my table, discarded my garbage and looked around for my coffee angel. She was nowhere in sight.

I grabbed the stroller and walked over to the counter inquiring about where I could find Joy. The young woman behind the counter furrowed her brows in confusion.

"We don't have anyone by that name working here."

I protested, but she just shook her head. She had no idea who I was talking about.

I have visited that coffee shop many times over the last few years, and have never seen the woman again. Not long after that day, Sarah was given a diagnosis of autism. When I have a stressful day, or feel lost and overwhelmed, I think of Joy and the strength and support she gave me. I believe in my heart someone is watching over me and my little girl and that we are never alone.

— Christine Pincombe-DeCaen —

23

It Was Not Our Time

We all have a guardian angel, sent down from above.
To keep us safe from harm and surround
us with their love.
~Author Unknown

It was a dark, snowy and icy Saturday evening in December a number of years ago when my husband Richard and I were driving our SUV along Highway 53 in Ancaster, Ontario. We were on our way to his brother David's house for the evening. Our three children were with their friends and we were on our own for the night.

The traffic moved slowly due to the slippery conditions, hampered by blowing snow. A good amount of icy snow was on the ground and it kept coming. It was a terrible stretch of road that was often a tricky drive in bad weather.

Suddenly a large transport truck left its lane and headed straight toward us. It was going to hit us head-on. The only thing we could do was drive off the road, so we veered to our right to avoid the truck. We were out of control and travelled into and out of a large gulley right toward a very large and old tree. It had a huge trunk. I was looking right at it and yelled, "Oh God, help us!" Something would have to happen or we were going to smash our car right into that enormous tree trunk. I could see it all coming at my face. Richard was trying to control the car and turn it away from the tree trunk, but it was coming way too fast. To make matters worse, we also needed to avoid a big red fire hydrant just to our left.

I am not sure what happened next, but I felt us climbing the tree trunk with our front wheels and then jerking to the left very hard. So much was going through my mind. Were we going to roll the car or land on our roof? Would we survive? It was all very crazy and it happened in seconds, but it appeared to be happening in slow motion.

Richard grabbed me and I grabbed onto him, so we were both leaning into the middle of the front seat together. Just as we were leaning in, the windows broke on either side of us. We then violently and miraculously landed on all four wheels. The front window then shattered all over us from the force. Fortunately, we had on winter coats, hats and gloves, but our faces were still exposed. After checking ourselves quickly, we didn't find a single scratch, although we were both shaken and traumatized from our very close call.

We just sat for a couple of minutes to collect ourselves. We were shaking and I was in shock. I guess someone must have called the police, as they soon arrived. The officers looked around at our car and wondered how we survived being in a car with that much damage. They noticed the fire hydrant on the left and the huge old oak tree on the right and commented that it was impossible for a car to pass through the small space between them. We said we knew that and that is why we huddled in the middle of the car in case both sides of the car were sheered off. Our side windows certainly did shatter to pieces and our doors were smashed in on both sides.

The police officers saw bark missing from the tree trunk and also noticed a red paint streak along our roof from the front to the back. One officer pointed out that it matched the colour of the fire hydrant. Our roof must have scratched up against the hydrant when our vehicle was shooting by on its side, with two wheels in the air. We were so lucky that we landed upright on all four wheels instead of on the roof or side of the car.

Since we were only a few blocks from David's house, we limped our car over there (amazingly it still drove slowly) on that snowy cold night, with all of the cold air coming through our broken windows. We just wanted to get to the closest home and pretty much collapse.

We were immediately so thankful to God that we were alive and not hurt in any obvious way.

David and Francine opened their front door to find us getting out of a very battered vehicle. They were shocked at the sight of our car and could not believe we survived.

I tried to explain to them what happened, and could not really explain why we were not hurt given what we had just been through. I had seen that tree coming right at us, and for a moment I thought our lives were over. Sharing the story made me realize how lucky we were to survive and I thanked God over and over for taking care of us.

On the Monday after that awful Saturday night, Richard, a family physician, went to work at his medical office. One of his patients who made crafts of all kinds and had a beautiful store in a neighbouring town came in that day. She said that she did not know why, but a strong feeling had prompted her to bring Richard two white guardian angels to place on our Christmas tree for the upcoming holidays.

When Richard came through the front door of our house that evening, he pulled out those two guardian angels from inside some white tissue. He told me what his patient said and I cried tears of joy, thankfulness and gratitude. We did not say a word at that special moment, because we both knew! We had been saved by our guardian angels because it was not our time. And this gift of two beautiful angels from a patient who knew nothing of our accident was a sign that we are never alone in this world. I had screamed "Oh God, help us!" and He had. It was not our time.

— Karen Vincent Zizzo —

24

Subway Rules

Let us go singing as far as we go:
the road will be less tedious.
~Virgil

We were just outside the Toronto subway. I couldn't believe what I was hearing from my stepson. "People are in their own world, and they don't want you interrupting their day. Folks on the subway don't talk."

Josh knew I was friendly wherever I went, and he felt it important to let me know about subway rules. I was raised on the prairies, in a small town called Taber, which is known for its sweet corn. Everyone talked to everyone.

As we climbed on the subway, there was only one seat. My husband nodded at me to take it. I scrunched into the space beside a grey-haired woman, and immediately she muttered in a disgruntled manner, "Oh, yeah, she had to sit here. Make me all uncomfortable. I shoulda known."

"I'm sorry," I told her. "Do you want me to move?"

With a huge sigh, she muttered back, "I suppose you can stay."

The words were okay, but the tone of her voice told me I was not welcome in the seat.

"I'll move if you would like me to. I don't mind, especially if it is bothering you," I told her.

Another sigh. "No, it's okay. You can stay."

Since we were already talking and she had started it, I felt challenged to change her negative perspective. I asked her if she had ever been out to Alberta. She waited all of two seconds, and then responded, "No, but we've been through on the way to Vancouver."

"I love Vancouver," I told her and went on to mention the great weather, friendly people and beautiful plants. "Where are you from originally?" I asked her.

Now here was a topic she wanted to talk about, and soon I heard about her life in the old country. She talked until it was time for her to get off, smiled warmly and bid me goodbye.

I wondered if there might be more people who break the subway rules.

At a station the following day, my husband and son went to buy tickets, and I stood watching people. The ticket taker caught me watching him, and he frowned. I smiled at him, and he glared back at me. I kept on smiling and would not turn away. He strode over to me with a stern look.

"Did you want to sing a song for me?" he asked.

Surprised, yet pleased he was talking, I responded, "I would sing you a song, except my husband is with me, and it would make him feel uncomfortable. If I was alone, I would sing you a song in a minute."

"Did you want me to sing you a song?" he asked. Oh my, he had a twinkle in his eyes, and there was a hint of a smile.

"Yes, please, I'd like that," I told him.

Then he sang "Strangers in the Night." I gasped at his beautiful, deep voice. It was exceptional. I felt I was receiving a special subway gift.

Soon, my husband and son joined me, but I would not take my eyes off the man with the magnificent voice.

When he finished, I said, "Your voice is exquisite. You need to share it."

"I did. I was an opera singer."

"You must continue to share this lovely voice with others," I told him.

"This I can no longer do," he told me. "You see, I am ill and cannot be counted on for bookings. I never know when the illness will flare up."

I thanked him for this special performance. By now, I was wondering what else could happen on the subway. My stepson must also have been puzzling over these two events. I hadn't really believed him — that I couldn't talk to people on the subway. I decided to keep breaking the rules.

That night, returning on yet another subway train, I found a seat next to a couple. I turned to them and said, "I know I'm not supposed to talk to you."

"Why ever not?" the man asked.

"I am told people on the subway do not want anyone to speak with them," I explained, "but have you seen *Crocodile Dundee*?" I paused for them to remember this movie character, and then I stuck out my hand. "Hi, my name is Ellie, and I'm from Alberta." With that, they began to laugh as they took turns shaking my hand.

We chatted like old friends, drawing the attention of a gentleman two seats away.

When the couple stood, they said they were sorry to end the conversation, but their stop was coming up. They turned again as they left, smiling, waving, and bidding goodbye.

As soon as they were gone and the subway train pulled out again, the gentleman who had turned to look at me earlier got up and came over. Apologizing, he said, "I could not help overhearing a bit of your conversation and…" We were soon in conversation.

He stepped off with us as we pulled into our station, speaking in an animated fashion. He said he was thrilled for the opportunity to chat on the ride. Who on earth made up those silly no-talking rules?

As we stood out on the platform, he grinned at us and said, "Thank you. I enjoyed our chat and want to sing a song for you."

It was more of a question, and pleased to have two songs in one day, I responded, "Great!"

Then, with a most pleasant voice, he began to sing, and I gasped at the coincidence for his choice of songs was "Strangers in the Night."

I had the distinct feeling that the universe was trying to tell me something, and I agree: People should chat, even on the subway.

Canadians are friendly in the large cities — so much so that not only do they want to talk to you, but they want to sing for you! And if perchance someone tells you otherwise, for heaven's sake, tune out that person.

— Ellie Braun-Haley —

25

Our Last Game

Having a place to go — is a home. Having someone to
love — is a family. Having both — is a blessing.
~Donna Hedges

Our family loves hockey... and we are huge fans of the Toronto Maple Leafs. We have watched them on television since I was a little kid. But the most exciting part of hockey for my family was travelling from our home in the country to Toronto to watch them play live at Maple Leaf Gardens!

My mom's dad died when she was a teenager. My grandpa had season tickets to the Gardens. The tickets were given to my grandma and eventually they were passed on to my mom. Four seats. First Row Green, centre ice. Perfect. My dad, mom, twin sister and I used to go to the Gardens and cheer ourselves hoarse. We would drive from our home in Georgetown into the big city and excitement would build as we travelled along Highway 401. We would guess the score and see who would be the closest, as the anticipation built up for the game.

My younger sister Aynsley was born in 1978. Now our family had grown to five. As she grew up, she also began to watch hockey and travel to Toronto to Maple Leaf Gardens. Because there were only four seats, many times my mom would stay home as the four of us — my dad, two sisters and I — went to see the Leafs. We always wished it could have been the five of us going together.

Sadly, the Maple Leaf Gardens announced they were closing their doors and the last game would be on February 13, 1999. The Leafs would host the Chicago Blackhawks for the last historic game in the Gardens.

A very special thing happened that night for our family of five. We all wanted to go to the last game so we decided that the best thing to do would be to have all five of us travel to the game. We would rotate ourselves through the three periods of play — that way we would all have a turn to see the Leafs play their last game in the Gardens. My sister Susan volunteered to be the first to sit out for part of the first period. Then I was set to change places with her so that she could see the game too.

As we all arrived at the Gardens that night, Susan made her way to a spot near the entry gate as the four of us went up to our seats in the Green section. After the national anthems played, I was overcome with a feeling that my sister should be sitting up there and I left my seat to go and change places with her earlier than planned. As I walked downstairs, heading towards the gate, a Maple Leaf Gardens ticket collector asked me where I was going. I explained that I was going to let my sister watch the game. He asked to see my ticket. "So you have a ticket?" he asked. "Yes I do," was my reply. I walked a little farther and saw Susan waiting there, wondering why I had come down so early. I handed her my ticket and said, "You are missing out. Go up and we'll change places later on." The same ticket collector had followed me and listened to what I said. With a twinkle in his eye he then asked Susan, "So you have a ticket too?" Now, he had clearly seen me give my ticket to Susan. He smiled at us. Susan said, "Yes." After a moment's pause, the ticket collector said, "Well as far as I can see, you both have a ticket, so what are you waiting for? In you two go!" gesturing us into the rink by waving his arms. And in we went!

This man's kindness, understanding and willingness to overlook the "rules" for this special night are something I will never forget.

"Thank you" is all we could think of saying at the time, and we shouted it to him as we ran up the wooden stairs. As it happened, our seats were located right beside the stairs at centre ice. As Susan and I smiled and joyfully descended the stairs, my parents saw the two of us coming to watch the game together and were speechless. Excitedly, we told them about the amazing gift we had just experienced. My dad moved over to sit on the edge of the stair, so that the five of us could sit and watch the game in a row, all together. We were so happy and felt so lucky. The last game at the historic Gardens and the first game we all watched our beloved Leafs together as a family!

I often have thought so fondly about the man who allowed us both in that night. It might have seemed like a little thing to him, easily forgotten, but it made a huge difference to us, and when I think of that night, I still remember what he did for our family.

If he is reading this story now, I want him to know how grateful I am.

—Leigh Anne Saxe—

Chapter 3

There for Each Other

26

The Little Ways

We are each made for goodness, love and compassion.
Our lives are transformed as much as the world is,
when we live with these truths.
~Desmond Tutu

W hen you are a young active person with a clean bill of health, you never really expect to be hospitalized for two weeks. And you certainly never expect you will like it.

I was put in the hospital after I learned I had flesh-eating bacteria. I had been in a motorcycle accident a week prior and after getting twenty-six stitches I thought it was normal for my thigh to be sore, swollen and oozing blood. I was eighteen and didn't have any experience with serious injuries, so I didn't realize that the black spots around the stitches weren't normal.

I went to the hospital to get more gauze. It didn't take the nurse long to realize something was wrong. I was transferred to a bigger hospital and then into surgery that night. The surgeon cut a large chunk of my thigh right down to the muscle. I didn't know how deep it was for a few days because it had a huge bandage and a VAC machine.

I was on all sorts of painkillers and antibiotics, and I didn't know too much about what was going on for quite some time. I had to have a second surgery, but I still didn't know why. At that point, a few thoughts had entered my mind about possibly losing my leg, but the staff was all so positive around me, I didn't think about it too much.

My surgeon had encouraged me to go walking so I wouldn't lose my strength, and I didn't want to disobey him, so I walked a couple of times a day. During one walk late in the evening, I saw my surgeon sitting at the desk talking to another doctor. He gave me a big smile, so I stopped to talk to him. Since none of the nurses told me what was going on, I figured it would be a good time to ask him.

"You have necrotizing fasciitis," he said. From his tone, I could tell he figured I wouldn't understand his medical terminology.

"What does that mean?" I asked.

He chuckled, but then with a more serious look, said, "It means you're lucky that your wound was an open wound." I didn't understand, but didn't want to bother him with any other questions, so I continued my walk.

After almost a week at that hospital, I got transferred back to the little hospital where I had gone to get more gauze.

The nurses there weren't nearly as busy as the ones in the city and so they had more time to stay and chat. Right away, one of them commented on how lucky I was to have learned about the infection when I did. It probably wasn't good for me to know, but I couldn't resist asking her what would have happened if I'd found out later.

"You could have lost your leg," she said, "or worse."

Most of the time, I really did enjoy the hospital. I was the only young person there, so the nurses gave me special attention. On top of that, members from my church made multiple visits to see me and I got to sleep all the time.

The bad times usually happened when nobody was around and I couldn't sleep. I would be alone with the thoughts of how I could have died, and the irrational thoughts of how the antibiotics wouldn't work and my leg would be chopped off.

One night, when most of the patients were sleeping, I couldn't. My leg was sore, hot and puffy and I was on my cell phone looking up stuff about necrotizing fasciitis. I knew it wasn't a good idea, but I did it anyway. The more I read, the more certain I became that the bacteria would never go away and I would lose my leg. It was illogical, but in my defense I was drugged up and had a big chunk of my leg missing.

I got out of bed, trying to hold back my tears, and walked to the nurse's desk. I was going to ask if I could have something to help me sleep, but when the first nurse saw me she just gave me a hug and asked what was wrong.

"I'm scared," I said quietly. She held me as I cried. I told her what I was thinking about and she listened. Then she made me a banana split and invited me to sit at the desk with the nurses there. One of them talked to me about University, where I was starting my first year in the fall. It wasn't something I really wanted to focus on right then, but I stopped crying eventually, and ended up going to bed with a smile. Nobody had said anything in particular that calmed me down, or solved the problem, but those two nurses treated me with such kindness and love, it made me forget for a while why I was so upset.

It took four rounds of antibiotics, a month with the VAC machine, and lots and lots of waiting for my leg to heal, but it did. If it hadn't, I know there would've been nurses who held my hand through it.

I have quite a large scar on my leg and I love it. It reminds me of the goodness in people. No, it wasn't anything big; everyone at the hospital was there because it was their job to be there. In little ways though, they went above and beyond. That extra made a huge difference to this dumb kid who went looking for ways to scare herself.

— Emily Linegar —

27

Restored Faith

Wherever we travel to, the wonderful people we meet
become our family.
~Lailah Gifty Akita, Think Great: Be Great!

eturning from a family holiday to England, we had a twenty-hour layover in Paris. Determined to make the most of our short stay, we decided to see the Eiffel Tower. Armed with only a map and a few phrases of high school French, we left the airport by train, heading to our first stop, Notre Dame.

We were to switch to a different line of the Metro once we reached the cathedral stop, but instead, we exited through the turnstiles. Once we realized that we made a mistake and that we would have to pay again to get back on the subway, we decided to find our way above ground. Standing in a huddle, we opened our map to figure out where we needed to go.

"Excuse me, but do you require assistance?" I turned to see a fashionably dressed man, perhaps in his mid-forties. His English was excellent but spoken with the most exquisite French accent I'd ever heard.

I answered for the family. "Well, we were trying to take the train to the Eiffel Tower but we left the station by accident.

"Oh, it is no problem. If you like, I can show you the way."

We eagerly accepted his gracious offer, anticipating that he would lead us to the top of the stairs and then simply point us in the correct direction. Wrong.

When we reached the street above, our guide, who introduced himself simply as Thierry, said, "Come, it is this way."

I looked at my husband and my daughter and shrugged. They shrugged back. Surprised, but grateful, I said, "Thank you," and we introduced ourselves. I asked, "Are you sure you have the time to do this? You don't have any other commitments?"

He responded, "Oh, no. I have the afternoon free. It is a beautiful day and it would be my pleasure to show you my city."

Thierry crossed the street and we followed along like ducklings. We walked down alleyways sprinkled with adorable cafés, by patisseries, whose luscious pastries sent the smells of heaven wafting through the air, and into cathedrals and courtyards that were so far off the beaten track we would never have otherwise found them. In one such church, Thierry told us. "There are more kings and queens buried here than in all of Notre Dame. But Notre Dame has Napoléon and therefore the fame and the money. Also, all the tourists."

The entire time we walked, our impromptu guide gave us the history of his beautiful city. It was a spectacular day in Paris. The sun was shining, the sky a saturated cerulean. The sights and sounds and scents of that day are indelibly etched in all of our memories.

In total, Thierry spent three hours walking with us through the streets of Paris. We found out he was married with two girls, one in her second year of medical school, and the other still in high school. He was a businessman but also a published author.

When we reached the tower, he said, "Well, I must leave you now. I hope that you will return to our city when you have more time. There is much to see here in Paris."

We thanked him profusely but he brushed aside our gratitude, saying only, "It was my pleasure. It is good for the universe to give back."

After a picture, hugs, and kisses on both cheeks for all of us, this gracious stranger walked out of our lives — but never out of our memories.

I truly thought this was to be a once in a lifetime experience, but this May I was proven wrong.

We were headed to Halifax to visit my husband's family, in particular his ailing mother who was dying of cancer. We wanted our girls to have one last visit with their nana.

My older daughter, Sarah, had ankle surgery two weeks prior to our flight. She was unable to bear weight and required crutches.

I booked a seat with extra legroom for Sarah so that she could keep her foot up during the flight. On the flight to Halifax we were all sitting close enough together for me to help her with her crutches, and to provide assistance as needed. Our return flight, however, proved to be more challenging.

Sarah was sitting at the front of the plane, in the premium seats. The rest of us were in the back of the plane, in the squished seats. I boarded early, with Sarah, to help her store her crutches and get settled. I struggled to stuff the crutches into the overhead bin, but they were too long. A voice spoke from my right. I turned to see a man, possibly in his mid-forties, who said, "Here, let me help you. There is more room back here."

He took the crutches from me and easily stored them away. I offered my thanks and turned to Sarah. "Okay, sweetie. You should be fine. I'll come back and check on you once we're underway."

The gracious stranger asked, "Oh, where are you sitting?"

I pointed to the back of the plane. Laughing, I said, "Oh, way back there, in the bowels of the plane."

"What is your seat number?"

Curious as to why he wanted to know, I said, "56B."

He smiled and stood to pull his briefcase from the overhead bin. "Fine. I will sit there and you take my seat so you can help your girl."

I tried to refuse. After all, he had paid extra for his lovely, roomy seat, but he refused to take no for an answer. "Please, I insist. It would be my pleasure."

Somewhat bemused, I watched him walk to the back of the plane where he would sit next to my husband. I wondered how we could be so fortunate as to meet another incredibly kind and gracious stranger.

He wasn't finished with us yet, though.

We landed in Montreal only to discover our flight to Vancouver was delayed by an hour. During the trip to Montreal, my husband and our kind stranger had chatted. He was a businessman who lived in North Vancouver and would be on the same flight as us. As we exited the plane, he said, "It seems we are stuck here for a while. If you like, I would be honoured to have you as my guests in the Air Canada lounge." None of us had ever been in the lounge before.

Concerned, I asked, "Are you sure that's allowed?"

He replied, "Please, don't worry. It is fine." He led the three of us, all obviously Caucasian, to the lounge and when asked who we were, this dark-skinned man with a lovely Middle-Eastern accent replied without hesitation, "They are my family."

It's unlikely we will get the chance to enjoy such luxury again, but thanks to this stranger's generosity, we certainly enjoyed the experience.

These two different men, complete strangers from two different continents, have restored my faith in the innate goodness of humanity.

— Leslie Anne Wibberley —

28

Zeal for Teal

In helping others, we shall help ourselves,
for whatever good we give out completes
the circle and comes back to us.
~Flora Edwards

I had two choices. Wallow in self-pity or put on my big girl sneakers and start walking. One part of me opted for self-pity — it was easier. After all a cancer diagnosis does knock the wind out of a person's sails. It was easy to justify defeatism given the nature of the verdict. Others would understand.

But during my journey through the valley of cancer I had a thorn in my side and she was determined not to let me wallow in self-pity. My daughter Amanda responded to my ovarian cancer diagnosis by stepping into a new role — sergeant major!

While my body battled the bittersweet chemotherapy poison, Amanda got busy finding ways to help and encourage me. She contacted Ovarian Cancer Canada and learned there was a Walk of Hope taking place in Barrie. She signed us up, and before I knew it we were fundraising with fury in preparation for the five-mile trek the following September.

Chemotherapy exhausted me, so it was important that I rest, but I found myself occasionally wanting to withdraw and cut myself off from others. I did not want people feeling sorry for me. Out of sight, out of mind. But the more I tried to keep out of sight, the more Amanda was determined to keep me active and involved.

"Mom, I have an idea," Amanda said one day between treatments. "What if we did a special fundraising event that would help raise both funds for the Walk of Hope and awareness for women in the community?"

My daughter, an avid scrapbooker, wanted to invite women to get together for a day of scrapbooking and crafting for the cause. I did a lot of thinking and praying and enjoyed some pensive moments. But I found myself loving her idea and before I knew it I jumped on the bandwagon.

Teal was the awareness ribbon colour for ovarian cancer and Amanda's zeal was contagious. Zeal for Teal seemed a perfect moniker. I started to love our new name. I also started to realize the importance of focusing on the positive and using any excess energy to be a light to others.

The more I helped plan and prepare for the first Zeal for Teal event, the more I found myself thinking less about my cancer journey and more about how I might just be able to help other sisters not yet diagnosed. The idea of doing my part to find an early detection test motivated me.

The first Zeal for Teal event started out in the fellowship hall of our church. Our theme for the inaugural occasion — Pajama Day — was a big hit. So we decided to create a theme for each year. The second year we had a beach theme. The following year was The 50s; last year was The Wild West and this year we are doing Alice in Wonderland. A group of very cool people have been helping, and because our committee has grown so large, we meet at the local hockey arena.

Soon, we will be celebrating our fifth anniversary. Our themed Zeal for Teal event draws women from near and far, with ladies returning year after year and bringing their friends.

Every so often, in between the busyness of the moments, I sit back and reflect. Never would I choose to be diagnosed with cancer. The rigors of chemotherapy and the toll it took on my mind and body were far from pleasant. Yet I am glad that, with a little help from my darling daughter, who really is more a beautiful rose than a thorn, I was able to use my experience to help inform other women. And, with all the money we raise from Zeal for Teal, Amanda and I participate each year in the annual Ovarian Cancer Canada Walk of Hope.

Zeal for Teal helped me see the good in the not so good, find hope in the hopeless, and experience a great deal of love from family, friends, and my community. We have created some mighty sweet lemonade from some very bitter lemons.

— Glynis M. Belec —

29

Eighty-Year-Old Volunteer

I am only one, but I am one. I cannot do everything,
but I can do something. And I will not let what I
cannot do interfere with what I can do.
~Edward Everett Hale

My mother is eighty years old, and every Wednesday for the past fifteen years — except for a couple of months after she had her hip replaced and several weeks after a subsequent knee replacement — she has driven twenty minutes to volunteer at the "old folks home" where she spent many years employed as a healthcare aide.

She was forced to retire when the Ontario government decided to make retirement at age sixty-five mandatory. She swears she would still be working at the nursing home if they hadn't made her quit. The government saw the error in their ways and a few years later mandatory retirement was revoked, but it was too late for my mother. Though she had loved the job and the old people who lived at the nursing home, she was already retired. So she started her stint as a volunteer.

Every Wednesday, even though she is now older than many of the nursing home residents, she volunteers her time to help "the dear old souls" just as she did when she was an employee and being paid for her services.

Mom was, and is, old school. When she worked, she really worked.

No sitting around and shirking responsibilities for her. No letting someone else do what needed to be done. As a farmer's wife she raised five children, kept house, helped with the farm work, and canned and preserved the yield from a huge garden that she planted and tended annually. When she got the full-time job at the nursing home she added night school to her many responsibilities and graduated as a healthcare aide in her middle age.

She worked hard during her career. She helped residents with their meals, helped them in and out of bed and the bathtub, even cleaned up the messes resulting from incontinence. One of her favourite stories is how an older woman, totally embarrassed because she had messed herself, couldn't believe that Mom was singing as she calmly and cheerfully cleaned things up.

"You can sing while you do that?" the old lady, who was known for not saying much of anything, said as Mom worked away. After having so many children and looking after her mother-in-law during the final years of her life, it wasn't a big deal to her. She had changed lots of diapers and cleaned up lots of messes in her lifetime.

A second favourite story is how a supervisor remarked on Mom's "handy-bag" of knitting projects, which she always had with her when she arrived for overnight shifts. While many of the overnight staff took catnaps once the residents were safely in their beds, Mom would work on her projects, ever alert and vigilant in case the residents needed her help — or just a reassuring voice after a bad dream. Night terrors aren't strictly for the young.

Nowadays Mom isn't responsible for the same work she did as a member of the paid staff. In her volunteer role she mainly visits with the residents. Most of the ones who lived at the home when she was employed there, including her own father, have passed away. But she makes new friends each week. She gets to know the new residents, many her age or younger, and is quick with a smile or a pat on the back. She has the time to listen to their life stories and reminisce with those who, like her, grew up in the community. There are lots of stories to tell when someone has the time to listen.

She has taken it upon herself, during her Wednesday afternoon volunteer stints, to make sure people aren't sitting alone in their rooms feeling sorry for themselves or pining for company. It is her personal mission to talk each and every one of the residents into taking part in church services and musical entertainment programs in the common area.

"A lot of them would just sit in their rooms being lonely," she says. "I don't give them a choice. I just tell them that there's a lovely program going on and they should attend and before they can say no, there we are."

Some she walks with arm in arm, others she helps into their wheelchairs and then pushes to their destination. She is proud the Wednesday afternoon events, when she's volunteering, have the largest attendance of any of the special events held at the nursing home.

Mom is there over the lunch hour and often helps those who need assistance eating their meals, coercing some without appetites to have just one more bite, the same as she did with her children when they were little. She has helped residents with knitting projects, taught some the nearly forgotten art of tatting, which she herself learned from her mother, and taught others how to play euchre, crazy eights, solitaire and other card games. There's very little Mom likes better than a good game of cards.

"Solitaire is wonderful for someone who is alone," she says. "It keeps them occupied and it's great for the brain. Anything to keep a person thinking."

Up until a couple of years ago Mom hosted a barbecue for the residents who were mobile enough to visit the home she shares with my dad. She would supply the lemonade and her famous homemade butter tarts and everyone would sit on the front lawn, in the shade of the stately old trees, reminiscing about their lives before "the home."

Also until just a few years ago, she would drive carloads of residents to neighbouring towns for shopping expeditions or lunch out at a local restaurant. When she turned eighty she took a Wednesday afternoon off from her volunteer duties and took the mandatory training course to have her driver's license renewed. Now, though, she usually gets a ride with a younger volunteer or takes the bus when excursions are planned during her Wednesday volunteer time.

Mom swears that she is going to live at the nursing home "when she gets old." We tease her and remind her that she is older than a lot of residents living there now and that if she lives as long as her father, who was at the nursing home for a brief period of time before his death at age ninety-eight, she still has a lot of volunteer years left.

Mom transitioned from hardworking farm wife and mother of five to healthcare aide to hard-working volunteer. She will continue to think of herself that way, and when she moves in she will surely help the staff members with the other residents. That's just the kind of inspirational woman she is.

—Lynne Turner—

30

The Spirit of Giving

Christmas is not a time or a season but a state of
mind. To cherish peace and good will, to be plenteous
in mercy, is to have the real spirit of Christmas.
~Calvin Coolidge

C hristmas at the bookstore was a mixed bag. On the one hand, the days flew by. It was busy all day, and I never stopped. I arrived, started working, and then someone told me it was time for my lunch break. I ate as fast as possible, got back on the sales floor, and suddenly it was time to go home. The list of things I'd wanted to accomplish was about as long as when I got there; I'd just manage tomorrow.

On the other hand, that list was important. The stock barrelled in. We could never quite get everything in its place fast enough. The reality was someone was going to ask for that one item the computer said we had — but was still in the back room, awaiting stocking.

Christmas was a balancing act of off-hours tasking, constant shelving, and running all day. It was exhausting, but also exciting. It also unfortunately robbed me of the joy of the season, even on some of the best days. I'd go home, and all I wanted was to eat something, take a bath, and sleep.

As a manager, I worked Christmas Eve and Boxing Day — December 26th. Often that meant staying until an hour after close on Christmas Eve to make sure set-up for Boxing Day was ready, and arriving very early on Boxing Day to get stickering and signage placed. It was not uncommon for me, since I take the bus, to get home as late as 8:00 p.m. on Christmas Eve, and rise at 5:30 a.m. on Boxing Day to make it back to the mall on time.

Thus, Christmas Day was a chore — a day off in the middle of a busy period. I didn't want to participate, but I forced myself to entertain family and be surrounded by loved ones when — honestly — I just wanted to wear my pyjamas and read a book on my one day off.

Customers, too, were a mixed bag. Regular customers I saw all year showed up in mid-December with Christmas cards, or — the ultimate good day — trays of coffee or tea they'd brought down from Tim Hortons as a treat for the staff.

Other customers weren't big readers, but instead were buying for readers. These customers we only saw once a year or so (maybe twice or three times if you include Mother's Day and Father's Day), and often they were frustrated. The bookstore wasn't a place they felt comfortable. They were unsure which book might be right in the vast sea of titles, and — given time was short until Christmas — they were in a rush. They said things I'm sure they didn't mean. Certainly, Christmas brought out some of the most impatient and sharp commentary from customers of any time of year.

But, sometimes, it also did the opposite.

One year, I found the kind of customer we often dreaded standing in the kids section. He was a man of about thirty-five, holding a piece of paper, and looking completely lost. He had only one bag in his hand from another store, and there wasn't much in it — just candy, I think. He looked tired, and it was just a couple of days until Christmas — he was definitely running out of time, and looked like he'd barely begun.

Bracing myself for "I don't really know what I'm looking for," I asked if I might help him.

When he turned to me, he looked like he was on the edge of tears. He didn't reply to my question, he just stared, and I did something I had never done before — I touched his shoulder.

"Are you okay?" I asked.

"Sorry," he said. He seemed to snap out of it, and took a deep breath. "I need presents for my nieces, my nephew, my brother-in-law, and my parents." He took another breath. "I don't really know what they like, but I know they all like to read. I just need…" He nearly lost his words again, and I could tell he was working hard not to cry. "I just want to make sure there's something to open."

He turned back to the shelves. I could tell he wasn't seeing anything.

It was controlled chaos all around me — people were shopping, I could hear the registers going non-stop, and I knew at any moment the phone could ring.

"Let me help," I said. "Is that your list? How old are your nieces and nephew?"

He handed me the list. I learned the twin nieces were eight, and the nephew was six. I asked him a few questions about what sorts of things they enjoyed, and was starting to get some ideas when his entire body shook.

"Are you okay?" I asked again.

"My sister just died," he said. He was barely holding himself together. "Cancer. She always did Christmas, you know? I figured…" He exhaled, slowly.

I have always kept a pre-loaded gift card for Tim Hortons in my pocket at Christmas. Sometimes, a staff member really needed a few seconds to calm down after a really bad moment with a customer who maybe had a terrible day and took it out on him or her.

"Here," I said, and gave him the gift card. "Go upstairs. Have a coffee, get a donut. Have you eaten today?"

He shook his head.

"I've been there," I said. "My father died around Christmas. It's awful. Tell me about your folks and your brother-in-law. Then go, take your time. We'll have something ready for you when you get back."

He told me about his family, and left.

I went to the cash desk, and while the staff rang through customers, we brainstormed. I explained the man's situation, and what we needed to gather. I asked the staff if they'd mind if I put the last of the "staff treats" budget into paying for some of the items. Everyone agreed.

While I was explaining the situation, some of the customers in line did something I'd never seen before. One by one, some offered up a little bit of money — five or ten dollars — one woman offered fifty.

We found books, toys, some mugs with hot chocolate and a few other small touches. We managed to find enough that everyone would have three items to open. Another staff member and I skipped our break to crouch low behind the cash desk and wrap the items, figuring any chore we could take off the man's plate would help. What wasn't covered by the unexpected donations from the other customers, we covered ourselves.

When the man returned, the gifts were wrapped and tagged. He stared at me when I said it was fine, that it had all been taken care of, gift receipts included, just in case. He gave me back my Tim Hortons gift card, and then gave me a hug.

That year, Christmas Day didn't seem like a burden at all. I was exhausted, and knew I had to get up before dawn the next morning, but I gathered with my friends and loved ones and felt incredibly lucky to spend the day with them.

— Nathan Burgoine —

It's Not What You Lose

A thousand words will not leave so deep
an impression as one deed.
~Henrik Ibsen

My husband, Jude, suffered his first heart attack when he was thirty-eight years old. He had been sailing on Lake Huron with our seven-year-old son, who miraculously followed my husband's instructions and brought the boat safely into harbour.

Jude changed his diet, began exercising regularly, and valiantly attempted to stop smoking. He purchased a filter for the cigarettes and then tried a pipe and then added a highly touted filter for the pipe, all to no avail. The tobacco and its additives had him in its grip.

There were two more heart operations — both of them bypasses. Then five years later, the dreaded but predictable diabetes, awaiting many heart patients, set in.

Panic gripped both of us as one doctor after another made the diagnosis that his left leg from below the knee down needed to be amputated.

The evening before the slated operation, I sat on the side of his hospital bed and held him in my arms as he cried. "I won't be able to live like this," he told me. "A walker. Crutches. A cane. Hobbling along behind you and the boys. Nothing to do but sit. Nowhere to go. I'm too young for this." He truly believed he no longer had a life worth living. I had never before seen him in such a state of absolute despair, so thoroughly and wretchedly defeated.

We sat facing the far side of the private room and hadn't noticed the nurse quietly pausing in the doorway. The tentative clearing of a throat alerted us to his presence. "If I may?" he spoke with gentle respect. "I couldn't help but overhear." He held up the stack of linen and hospital robes in his arms. "I was just coming in to stash these and… well, I heard… and…" He looked both abashed and determined. "I'm going to do something I've never done before. If I may?" he repeated.

And then, perhaps fearing that his courage would wane if he waited for our consent, which might or might not be given, he placed his bundle on a vacant chair and, taking one of the blue gowns, stepped into the bathroom. Moments later, the door opened. "It was a motorcycle accident," he said softly but clearly as he looked into Jude's swollen, startled eyes. "I was twenty-one."

There stood our nurse, his gown wrapped demurely just below his underwear line. His soft-soled shoes and sports socks defined in sharp contrast to the flesh colour of his prosthetics. "Both legs," he said. "One above the knee. One below."

Jude sat, stunned, blinking back his tears.

"It's taken me a few years," the nurse continued shyly. "I'm twenty-six now. But while I healed my body and my mind, while I did session after session of therapy, I also went to school… maybe something I otherwise never would have done. Who knows? But as it was, I received a degree in nursing. I still play soccer — granted not as well as I would have in the Coast League where I played before, but I still play. I'm getting married next month and when I have kids, well…" He pointed to his prosthetic legs. "I guess what I've learned through all of this is that it's not what we lose, like in our cases our legs, but what we do with what we've still got that really decides the outcome of…" He paused to draw a heavy breath, "…the rest of our lives."

And at that, he turned back to the washroom, one leg of his bright red boxers showing below the unassuming blue hospital gown.

Jude slipped back against his pillow. "That young nurse..." He paused to shake his head. "After the operation, tomorrow, we'll get started on our new future. I'm ready."

— Robyn Gerland —

32

Chocolate Comfort

*When Jesus spoke again to the people, he said, "I am
the light of the world. Whoever follows me will never
walk in darkness, but will have the light of life."*
~John 8:12

On a warm June evening, our lives were devastated by
tragedy. Our eighteen-year-old son was killed cycling
home from work in a bicycle-traffic accident. It happened several days after his high-school graduation,
when plans and dreams for his life had seemed limitless. We asked
ourselves, "Will we survive without him?"

An African proverb says, "It takes a village to raise a child." It also
takes a village to bury a child. God, in His abundant faithfulness and
mercy, surrounded us with caring community. We came to understand
that He uses people to be His hands and feet.

Returning home from a road trip, I was overcome with sorrow.
Our once-happy home had become a place of grieving; the walls cried
out for Davis. His warm hugs and bright smile wouldn't be there to
greet me, and I dreaded stepping inside.

Upon arrival, we noticed a brightly decorated box on our doorstep.
We discovered freshly baked chocolate-chip cookies inside, still warm.
Tucked alongside the cookies was a heartfelt note of encouragement
from friends. With a cookie in each hand, I sat on my kitchen floor
and wept. I was overcome with a sense of gratitude. God had provided
a very tangible gift of love through their thoughtful gesture. We found

such comfort in those cookies.

Nothing can diminish the enormity of our loss. It cuts like a knife. But we soon realized after Davis's passing that it was the small acts of kindness from others that helped us reclaim joy in our brokenness. Blessings come through giving. When we stop giving, we stop loving.

I now bake cookies to comfort those with heavy hearts. I appreciate that God wants to use my hands to share the joy of His love with others — even love in a chocolate-chip cookie.

— Sally Walls —

33

Give 'em the Knuckles

It is time for us all to stand and cheer for the doer, the achiever—the one who recognizes the challenges and does something about it.
~Vince Lombardi

Remember that scene from *Forrest Gump* when he's trying to find a seat on the bus and at each row someone says "seat's taken" or "you can't sit here." It's a pretty extreme example of how not to treat an outsider, but it is probably still pretty uncomfortable to watch for just about everyone, because we've all been there. Maybe we haven't been openly rejected like that, but certainly we've been in that spot where you're new to a club or a town or a group or something, and unless you're completely cold-blooded, you've always got at least a little desire to fit in somewhere, find where you belong. Sometimes we don't make the effort with the new guy because we don't have the time or energy to do the whole "welcome to the club, my name is so-and-so, did you find everything alright…." But it doesn't have to be that formal.

We learned that when we joined Juventus, our current bike club. We were new, nervous, excited about taking a chance at leaving the comfort of our old club. There were elite athletes around; people who knew real racing, how to dress, what to ride, how to win. We were just recreational riders and it was intimidating at first.

Now, right from the start we got a lot of help. We were fully welcomed by the established riders and coaches. I remember getting advice from one of the fastest racers around right before a big race, even though he had to prepare for his own race and take care of the rest of the team, and it meant a lot. Another coach invited us to train with the juniors when it fit our schedule better, even though he was busy getting the kids going. All of these gestures made a huge difference for us, but one really stuck out for us because it was at the very beginning, even though it was something pretty small.

At training in the winter, in the very beginning, there was always this one fast guy who trained with the elites. He knew everyone and was part of the main group. After each hard workout, he'd saunter over to his buddies and stick out his fist and they'd clank their knuckles on his, as if to say, "nice work." They "got the knuckles" is what we started calling it. Now, I don't need someone else's approval to feel good: I get what I want out of things, and we didn't view him as some sort of hero or anything, just a fast dude in the club, but we couldn't help wondering if we'd ever be part of the group like that.

Then one day, my wife came home from the workout. It had been a hard one and she was spent. She hadn't felt very strong and she might normally have been a bit down, but she was pumped. She was grinning from ear to ear. "So how'd it go?" I asked.

"I got the knuckles tonight," she said.

Then one night I got them. No grand gesture, no formal welcome, not even a word or anything. Just suddenly one night the fist was pointed at me. It made my week.

We joked about how "getting the knuckles" was some sort of secret handshake at the club and it was the only way to know you were in. We have a friend new to riding and she joined us at the club. Last week my wife came home and said, "Shauna's pretty excited; she got the knuckles tonight."

It really showed us how it doesn't take a lot of time or a big formal effort to make someone's day. So maybe next time you see someone new, maybe the new guy at work, or the new guy at your club, you don't have to take a lot of time to make them feel welcome.

Just go over and give 'em the knuckles.

— Tim Brewster —

34

The Strength of Vulnerability

Nothing is so strong as gentleness,
nothing so gentle as real strength.
~St. Francis de Sales

I have never used the words strength and vulnerability together before. Strength essentially means great power, and vulnerability is about being open or exposed. Somehow I had not thought the two words could go together, but recently I felt the strength of vulnerability through one simple act of kindness.

It was Thanksgiving weekend and my family had decided to have our turkey dinner on the Saturday night. I had to work until 7:00 p.m. so the plan was that my mother and husband would have the dinner timed for around 7:30 p.m. The mall was quiet that evening and I was able to lock the store right at 7:00 p.m. I gathered the garbage and as I looked forward to our family gathering, I did not even notice I had not taken my usual route to the garbage bins.

An agitated young man who had missed his bus stopped me. He needed a ride and if he waited for the next bus, he'd miss his curfew and his bed at the Salvation Army. He'd be forced to sleep outside and he didn't have a sleeping bag. He needed to get there before they locked the door.

The voice inside my head got very loud as the survival instinct kicked in and quickly reminded me of all the reasons why giving this man a ride was a very bad idea. My family was waiting, my cell phone had a 2 percent charge left on it, I might get mugged or raped and on and on. I asked him a few questions and even wished I had some cash on me, to send him off in a cab so that this problem would go away.

As these thoughts whirled through my mind, I looked into his eyes. I saw desperation, but more importantly, I saw a person. I saw him. I heard a small voice that quietly said, "He's someone's son." In that moment, I just knew I had to give him a ride. The embarrassing thing was that I couldn't even remember where the Salvation Army was.

He promised directions and offered to take the garbage bag I still held, while I called home to say I'd be another hour. As we drove downtown we chatted. He was trying to get clean and turn his life around. He got kicked out of the house he was living in. I told him to look into going back to school, unsure of what other motherly advice I could give him.

Eventually, he asked about me and found out that I was missing my Thanksgiving dinner in order to drive him. He began to cry. Perhaps his faith in humanity was restored in that moment; I don't know. All I could think of to say was "Don't cry for me, my dinner will be there when I get home and it's more important that you get your bed. If I was in your position, I'd want someone to help me."

Somehow I knew our roles could easily be reversed. His name was James. We made it to the Salvation Army on time and he had a place to sleep that night. I felt alive and our dinner was made more beautiful by sharing this story. Interestingly enough, if I had taken my usual route to the garbage, I wouldn't have this story to share.

I am not saying we should all run out and give strangers a ride. In this case, however, in finding the strength to allow myself to be a little vulnerable, I opened myself up to a life-changing experience. I made an important human connection that I wouldn't have made if I had taken the safe and fearful route.

— Mary Anne Molcan —

35

Our Guardian Angels

The guardian angels of life fly so high as to be beyond
our sight, but they are always looking down upon us.
~Jean Paul Richter

It had been a year of heartache. My father and my aunt died, and then I got laid off, followed soon thereafter by the hospitalization of my elderly mother. And then there was my divorce, too, and the sale of my house in a bad market.

And yet, the strange thing is, each day I felt like I was being helped.

Rentals were scarce in my neighbourhood but one became available just when I needed it, and it was right around the corner from my sons' school.

The day the three of us moved into that rather dilapidated house, I realized the stove was not working, and while I was wondering what to do, there was a knock on the front door. A truck was parked on the road and its driver now stood in front of me. He was at the wrong address, but he was in the refurbished appliance business. I recall with clarity what I said to him: "You've got to be kidding me." I had a stove the next day.

My old car needed some work. My new neighbour turned out to be a mechanic who helped me very much, yet asked for very little.

With uncanny regularity, spaces in the crammed parking lots of the hospital, the lawyer's office and the stores became available exactly when and where I needed them.

And so it went, day after day, occurrences that singularly could be dispelled as coincidence, but collectively made me awestruck with wonder.

Christmas was coming, and my sons and I had decorated a tree, but there was no money for gifts. And even though I had recently turned forty and was indisputably an adult, I longed for the guidance of my mother, my father and my aunt.

As I was thinking about them, I prepared lunch for my boys, who would be home at any moment. Suddenly, a simple envelope with a law firm's name inscribed on the upper left corner flew through the mail slot and floated like a paper airplane over the scratched wooden floorboards of the tiny foyer. I didn't open it right away; I wasn't ready for negative news. I had had enough.

Later that day, the letter was still sitting on the counter. I stared it down for a moment as if I were accepting a challenge. I held it up to the light of the kitchen window to try to see inside it without actually opening it. Finally, I got up my nerve and sliced open the envelope with a knife from the kitchen drawer. A thick piece of paper came out — a letter. And a check!

The letter said it was a distribution from my aunt's estate, and that there would be more after this. I sat down on a kitchen chair and I cried. I cried for all the losses and I cried for all the undeniable wins.

I was quite aware that this check had come just in time to save our Christmas. The letter was dated December 17th. I can see that date whenever I want because it is hanging on my wall. I had the letter framed to honour my aunt and always remind me to never take for granted the help I received.

After I got that check, I was off to the mall, where the carols blaring from loudspeakers and the noise of shoppers in long lines were all music to my ears. Everything felt magical.

My older son wanted nothing but a puppy. That was it. No other toys or gifts; I had worried over how I would explain that we could not afford a dog, but now that problem was behind us. My son's one wish could come true.

He named her Merry, for Merry Christmas, and that Jack Russell

Terrier was his companion for the next fifteen years.

Ever since that magical time, when everything and everyone seemed to conspire to help us through a difficult time, I have believed in guardian angels. I have felt them all around me.

— Nancy Thorne —

36

Angel at My Bedside

Thy purpose firm is equal to the deed. Who does the
best his circumstance allows, does well, acts nobly;
angels could do no more.
~Edward Young

The subdued lights and muted voices frightened me. I could sense the tension and worry in the room. Something was wrong. Women had babies every day and I'd never heard of any of my friends being whisked away into a dark, isolated area filled with strange intimidating monitors.

I was three weeks past my due date, and although my labour was induced, I suspected the dull ache I'd been feeling in my lower back all day heralded my child's intent to finally enter the world. The dripping tube connected to my arm was simply speeding up the process. Hushed whispers, the worry on my husband Don's ashen face and his weak assurances that everything was all right only increased my anxiety.

Despite the epidural I'd been given, my discomfort grew. A roaring pressure reverberated in my head. I heard moaning, then screams of pain. As they grew louder, I realized they were coming from me.

A cool palm touched my feverish forehead and I glanced up to see gentle eyes behind a masked face. "I'm Debbie, your nurse. I know you're frightened and you're hurting, but we're taking good care of you. Trust us, okay?"

I nodded, and then groaned as another cramp ripped through me. When it dissipated, I became aware of a doctor at the foot of my bed. He examined me while Debbie grasped my hand, positioning herself so she blocked him from my view. A tilt of my head, however, exposed his worried face.

"I want you to breathe with me," the nurse instructed, distracting me. "I understand it's difficult, but we need you relaxed and calm, so follow what I do." She proceeded to inhale and slowly exhale. I tried to imitate her, but all I could do was pant. "Focus" she crooned. "Close your eyes and count to ten with each breath."

I attempted to follow her example, but another agonizing contraction tore at me. My husband gripped my hand, urging me to squeeze as hard as I could. I heard voices emanating from a dark corner of the room. Doctors conferring. The grim, barely audible way they spoke terrified me. "Severe toxemia." "Danger of stroke." "High blood pressure." "Not rotating properly." "C-section."

Staff tiptoed in and out. The dim lights were finally turned off altogether, replaced by flashlights when my vital signs were checked. Eventually, even my husband was asked to leave. I began to cry and protest.

"Shh," Debbie soothed hypnotically. "He'll be in the waiting room, but I'll stay. I'm not going anywhere." Her voice had a mesmerizing effect on me, lulling me through my haze of agony.

As promised, she didn't leave my side, asking me questions about myself, showing genuine interest, and amusing me with anecdotes about her job. As she chattered, her eyes darted to the various monitors and machines. She illuminated my chart with the weak rays of her penlight to jot down the information she read.

I don't know how much time elapsed. Pain and fear mingled together. Every time I became too distressed or incoherent, Debbie managed to pacify me by stroking my hair, wiping my face with a cool cloth, murmuring quietly, or asking questions.

Doctors continued to enter and exit the room, conferring with each other out of my earshot, but their grave expressions were impossible to ignore. Finally, after what seemed like an eternity, one of them approached my bed, where I was balled up in a fetal position.

"We're going to take you into the delivery room, now," he announced.

"You're fully dilated."

"My husband," I croaked, clamping on to Debbie's arm. "I told him I didn't want him in the delivery room, but now I do. Please, can you ask him to come?"

"He'll be there," she promised.

I was wheeled down a long hallway. Debbie walked briskly beside my gurney, continuously soothing me with soft-spoken words and reassuring smiles.

"You're coming in too!" I demanded rather than asked.

"Of course!" she grinned. "After I wash up and get a gown on."

"My husband?"

"He'll be right behind me."

After that, everything became a blur. I thrashed and cried as I was pushed through swinging doors, only relaxing when I recognized familiar eyes behind masks — both my husband's and my nurse's. Then suddenly my world went black.

I woke to the sounds of a baby's lusty cries. Turning my head weakly, I saw a small bundle in Don's arms.

"You have a beautiful, healthy son," someone told me, as my eyes closed again.

The next time I opened them, I was in another darkened room. I groaned and heard some movement at my right. From the dim glow of the hall lights, I could make out a human form sitting in a chair beside me.

"Don?" I called, through parched lips.

"It's me — Debbie," came the response. "We sent your hubby home. But I'm still here."

She stood and approached me, reaching for a small carafe of water. She poured some into a glass and raised my head to take a sip.

"I wanted to make sure you were okay," she told me, adjusting my pillow. "Drink this and try to sleep some more. You've had a rough time."

"My baby?"

"He's perfect," she assured me. "He weighed in at eight pounds ten ounces. You'll see him in the morning. Right now he's screaming down in the nursery with those strong lungs of his."

I drifted off again. Every time I awoke, it was to find that dedicated nurse right beside me, seeing to my every need.

Finally, sunlight streamed through the drawn blinds of the quiet room. I opened my eyes to see Don sitting in the chair Debbie had vacated, relief evident on his face.

"Welcome back," he whispered, wrapping his arms around me. "You had us all scared for a while, but you're going to be okay."

I stared at him, puzzled.

He explained that I had preeclampsia, and that I almost died. My obstetrician had missed the warning signs of toxemia. Luckily, both my baby and I were fine.

That afternoon, I walked a little and stopped at the nurse's station to ask where I could find Debbie.

"She left on vacation as soon as she was sure you'd recover," the head nurse told me. "She was terribly worried about you and changed her flight because she didn't want to leave you."

Stunned, I asked, "Why on earth would she do that?"

"That's Debbie," she replied.

Although I never saw that wonderful, dedicated nurse again, several weeks later, I called to thank her. Her voice on the phone was as caring and kind as I remembered, and I could almost see her shrug humbly when I babbled my thanks for her devotion and care.

Over the years, I've learned one universal truth. Nurses are angels at the bedside.

— Marya Morin —

Chapter
4

The Power of
Friendship

37

Preschool Peer Mentoring

*Perseverance is failing nineteen times
and succeeding the twentieth.*
~Julie Andrews

I heard my name being called and turned just as the young boy crashed into me. With a big bear hug and a smiling face, he said once more, "Whhhhhhhen-D!"

"Michael, how are you?"

Before he could answer, another voice spoke. "Michael, why are you in the hallway?"

Then she turned to me. "May I help you?"

I introduced myself. I was from the childcare center down the street and had an appointment with the kindergarten teacher. Michael had been in my preschool and then Junior Kindergarten three years ago.

She visibly relaxed. I was about to say goodbye when she asked, "Do you have time to visit our classroom?" I accepted the invitation.

The second grade children were busy at various tables. "In the afternoon, they do group work."

"Whhhhhen-D, look, look!" Michael grabbed my hand and pulled me over to his group's table.

I spent a few minutes with him, viewed all of the students' projects, shared one last bear hug, and then thanked his teacher before leaving. I couldn't help but smile — he'd come such a long way.

Before Michael came to us, his assigned specialist advised us that Michael's long-term prognosis was still uncertain. Michael was six months old when an accident had occurred. The resulting injuries caused significant brain damage.

There were delays in all areas of development, but the most significant one was that he could not walk. He scooted around by crawling. The specialist felt that although there was no certainty of success, Michael should aim to stand independently and then move on to walking. She also specified that he should wear a white helmet during the days to protect him from any further head injury.

By the end of his first year with us, Michael showed improvement in all developmental areas, the most dramatic one being able to walk independently. He had an uneven gait, but it was improving.

The following spring, it was suggested that we encourage him to pedal a tricycle. This would strengthen his legs and help him with his walking. Initially, Michael resisted our attempts to encourage him to use the pedals on the tricycle. He preferred to use his feet to propel himself forward. By mid-June, though, he started to use the tricycle pedals.

Unfortunately, one of the other children crashed into Michael. His tricycle tipped over, and although he was not hurt, he refused to go near the tricycle after that. Michael became interested in something else.

The playground slide had steps that led up to a twelve-foot walk-way and then to the slide itself. Michael wanted to make it up those steps. Each day, he returned to the steps to practice. Then one day, it happened. First step, second step, third, fourth, and up he went. The girl who had been in front of him and was now at the top of the steps looked back at him and said, "Come on, it's easy!" There were claps and cheers when he made it to the top.

Then, as Michael faltered and considered whether he should try the slide as well, the little girl said, "Here, let me go first. I'll sit down, and you sit behind me. That's what we do with my little brother."

She sat down, spread her legs so they each touched the inside edge of the slide, and held onto the slide's edge. With Michael sitting behind her, they went very slowly down the slide. When they reached the bottom, Michael turned around with the biggest smile that could ever be on a child's face, looked at me, and said, "WHHHHHHHEN-D, I did it!"

Although this story is about Michael, it is also about that little girl named Shelby. Michael's determination to succeed did propel him forward on that day, but it also happened because Shelby recognized his hesitation, encouraged him, and competently used her own past experience to support him as he successfully achieved his goal. She had stepped into the role of mentor and, in doing so, reminded me that we are all teachers — and we are all learners.

— Wendy Poole —

38

Good Neighbours

*Great opportunities to help others seldom come,
but small ones surround us every day.*
~Sally Koch

I agree with the proverb that says "it takes a village to raise a child." The trick is finding that village when you live in the metropolis of Toronto in 2013. Sure, there are communities within the city, but not the type of small, cohesive group that is required for this purpose. Several years into the mayhem of motherhood, I concluded that you really must create your own village, wherever you are, in order to do this job properly.

I have managed to do this by forming some special relationships with neighbours on my street. Paula is one of these neighbours, and I have been grateful for her presence since my children were small. In the summer, Paula was always the first to admire the chalk artwork on my driveway. When the kids drew roads, she walked on them. When they drew stores, she pretended to buy things, and when they wrote cryptic messages in pre-school handwriting, she tried valiantly to read them. She always made time to talk to the kids, and seemed to know just what to ask to prompt an animated conversation — she had a knack. She gave all of them their first jobs too — walking her dog, Max, giving them clear instructions, a true sense of responsibility, the requisite plastic bag, and probably too much money.

As they grew, my children appreciated Paula's surrogate grandmotherly attitude towards them, and were always happy to lend a hand if she needed help with something.

One snowy winter evening, as we were finishing dinner, Paula phoned. She was feeling under the weather and wondered if our son Jason would mind coming over to shovel her back deck—just a little—so Max could go outside to do his business.

Jason had recently moved past the point of thinking shovelling was fun, but had adopted a stoic, typically Canadian attitude towards the task. Knowing that Max is a diminutive white dog, easily lost in a snow bank (and admittedly, a bit of a princess), Jason knew Max would be reluctant to obey Paula and go out if there was more than a centimetre of snow on the deck.

Jason said he'd be right over. Heading out the door, shovel in hand, he called, "I'll be back in a few!"

About a half an hour later, a figure closely resembling the yeti arrived on our doorstep. Apparently, the snow was still falling thickly; Jason was covered with it.

"How was it out there?" I asked, taking his jacket and wet mitts as he stepped carefully onto the mat in the hall.

"Icy—not too cold," he replied. "I wiped out and fell down Paula's back stairs when I was shovelling. I guess she heard the thump—she poked her head out the door, looking all concerned."

I looked him up and down. "You all right? Any major damage?"

"Just a little cut on my hand from the edge of the shovel." He held up his hand to show me. "Paula felt really bad so she ran in for a Band-Aid. It was kind of embarrassing; she insisted on putting this on for me."

I smiled. "Once a mom, always a mom. Looks like you'll survive. Had you finished the job by that point or should I pop over?"

"No, it was pretty clear—Max can get out, no problem," he responded. After I thanked him for helping out, he headed upstairs to change.

In the past, Paula had hired one or both of my boys to do the full driveway-clearing job. I was happy that she felt comfortable enough to call for a little casual help every now and then. Give the kids a chance to do something nice for someone they know and trust—a chance to learn how to be good neighbours.

A few minutes later Jason arrived in the laundry room and tossed an armful of wet clothing onto the floor.

"Paula tried to pay me, you know," he said. "It wasn't a big deal or anything — the job, I mean — but I think she felt bad that I fell down the stairs. I just slipped; it was my own fault, and I'm totally fine."

"How'd you handle it?" I asked him, stuffing his things into the dryer.

"I told her it was okay, she didn't need to pay me, and it was just a quick job. I was happy to do it for free. She sort of insisted, though. It was one of those awkward times, you know, where you say, 'No, it's okay, thanks' and the other guy says, 'No, really, I insist.' And you go around in circles for a while… I finally caved."

"What, she wore you down?"

"Yeah, but I got her," Jason replied, with a twinkle in his eye.

"What do you mean?" I asked, tiny parental alarm bells starting to jingle in the distance. "How exactly did you 'get her'?"

"She finally just asked me to name a fair price for the job. I told her my fee was one Band-Aid."

He held up his injured hand, wiggled his fingers, and with a self-satisfied grin, loped up the stairs. I stood in the foyer, rather at a loss for words. When had my self-absorbed little kid turned into a thoughtful, helpful, and maybe just a little devious adolescent?

Paula enjoyed being outmaneuvered by Jason that evening. She said as much, when she came by the next day to drop off some warm homemade cookies for him. I thanked her for the baking, and then I thanked her for helping us show the kids how it's done — how to be a good neighbour. We may not have a whole village, exactly, but I think a few wonderful friends may just do the trick.

— Julie Winn —

39

Fourteen Angels

We are each of us angels with only one wing, and we
can only fly by embracing one another.
~Luciano de Crescenzo

My grandma was diagnosed with lung cancer when I was only ten, but I didn't really understand her illness until three years later, when I was thirteen and thought I had it rough. Between big crushes, massive amounts of homework, and arguments with my parents, I felt like I might just explode. I knew Grandma was sick, but it was merely a small thought in the back of my mind. At thirteen, I had enough to keep me occupied.

I'd been playing hockey since I was nine years old, and I loved it. When I was thirteen I played my first year of Bantam hockey. From the very beginning of the season in December, my team and I wanted nothing more than to win the championship, which would mean getting a banner hung up in the rink with our team name on it. We would become a part of hockey history in our small town. That's what we worked for all year, and why we went out every game and played until we gave everything we had.

Finally, at the end of our season, we were close to winning it all. I was pumped for this game; we were playing the team that had been first in our league all year. We'd won our first playoff game against them, and if we won one more game, we'd win the banner. We'd be the top dogs. I was grabbing my equipment and my team jacket when

I heard a familiar voice from the other room.

"What's wrong with Mom?" I heard my mother ask. I walked down the steps to see my teary-eyed mother on the phone. As soon as I saw her in that state, I knew something was wrong. My mom's been in the military her whole life, so trust me — she learned how to mask her emotions early on and she doesn't show them easily.

"Rachael! Time to go!" Dad called to me and I scurried up the stairs, grabbing my hockey bag and sticks and heading out the door.

On our way to the rink, I asked what exactly was wrong with Grandma, since I figured that's who Mom was talking about. He seemed reluctant to tell me, but I weaseled it out of him. Grandma was in the hospital, coughing up blood and having a hard time breathing. I wanted to be told that everything would be fine, that Grandma would be okay. When I asked if she'd come out of the hospital, my dad said what I didn't want to hear: "I don't think so."

I knew I needed to focus, but after waving half-heartedly at the few girls who were already at the rink, I found an empty hallway and sat down on the ground. I tucked my knees up to my chest and soaked the knees of my jeans with tears. "God I hope she's okay," I prayed out loud in that hallway by myself. Somewhere inside of me, I didn't think that my grandma was coming out of the hospital. Somehow I thought this was the last time she'd go in.

My legs were starting to cramp up from being curled into such a little ball in the hallway. I stood, and three of my teammates saw me and ran over to where I was. They asked in worried voices what was wrong, and I realized I needed someone to talk to.

I let my sorrow flow over as I told them how scared and worried I was. Part of me figured they'd probably just turn away; they needed to focus on the hockey game, not my personal misery. These girls weren't my absolute best friends — we didn't have sleepovers every Saturday. They were teammates, girls who knew me because we had similar skill levels at a sport we all enjoyed. I finished my story. I expected them to say they felt sorry for me, but I didn't expect what was coming next.

Our team captain, with whom I'd had a number of spats, pulled me into a comforting hug. "I'm sorry," she whispered. I have no idea how long it was, but each of those three girls helped to comfort me, gave me hugs, and surprised me with their warmth. We went to meet up with the rest of the team for the warm-up.

Even though I knew that I needed to focus on my game, I was still acting melancholy as we walked into the dressing room to change into our equipment. Apparently, my feelings were obvious because a lot of girls asked me what was wrong. Our team captain asked me if I felt comfortable telling the team what had happened. When I agreed to do so, she turned off the music and I stood in the middle of the room, all eyes on me.

"You all may have noticed that I'm... not quite myself," I began. "Just before this game, I found out that my grandma's in the hospital. She probably won't be coming out." Tears welled up in my eyes and rolled down my cheeks. I recalled a conversation I'd had with my grandmother over the phone a few weeks ago. "She told me she couldn't wait to hear that we'd won the banner." I was crying quite heavily now. The reality of the situation hadn't hit me until that moment.

Every single girl hugged me. Lots of them were in tears as well, some because of their own experiences with cancer, some simply from compassion.

"We're going to win this for your grandma," the team captain said, and all the girls nodded in agreement. I was bawling. Their caring touched me more than anything else had.

When we started the game, I saw girls who were killing themselves trying to get the puck, and perfectly controlled shots hitting the back of the net. I saw girls who normally worked hard working even harder. I saw the numbers on the scoreboard for us go up. Even I felt the difference — when I felt too tired, or didn't think I had the energy, I thought of my grandma and how every breath was a struggle for her. I found extra strength.

The buzzer sounded at the end of the third period and I basically tackled my goalie. Tears were streaming down my face. "We won for her," I cried. "We won for her." My teammates cheered with me.

"Your grandma is the most proud grandmother in the world," one of my teary-eyed teammates said as she hugged me. I was the first girl to bring home the banner and I sent a picture of it to my grandmother.

My grandma died the day after we won the banner. From what I hear, it was only seconds after she received my picture that God took her away. My mom was with her and told her the story of what I'd done with my hockey team. She said she was proud of me.

After that day, I believe that love and friendship can help you accomplish anything. My teammates' compassion and love for my grandma and me was the most amazing thing I've ever experienced. That day, God sent me angels in the form of fourteen Bantam hockey players.

— Rachael Robitaille —

40

A Second Second Chance

To give and not expect return,
that is what lies at the heart of love.
~Oscar Wilde

It was early October 2003. I was exhausted, my body filled with excess fluid and my mind focused on worst-case scenarios as we drove past a blur of scenery. Henry gripped the steering wheel, knuckles pale, and turned to gaze at me with a look that — for a moment — washed all my fears and doubts away. I knew by the look in his eyes that his love would see us safely to the hospital despite the twenty-odd staples down his front from the bypass surgery he'd had barely a week earlier. As I touched his forearm, he grinned and stepped on the gas.

In a whirlwind, we arrived at the hospital, an emergency catheter was inserted into a vein in my neck and I started on dialysis. Again.

Henry and I had faced more challenges than most. We'd both grown up with Type 1 diabetes. We'd both experienced kidney failure and had gone on dialysis and the kidney-pancreas waiting list. This was how we met. Only a couple of months apart in 1997, we each had our prayers answered for a second chance at a better future.

And now, here I was, seven years later in need of another kidney transplant. I reached out to family members, a number of whom were tested. None were a match. I reached out to friends. Again, testing was done, but no match was found. My hope dwindled. And the usual sparkle in my spirit faded to barely a flicker.

As always, throughout that winter and spring, Henry stood by me. He drove me to dialysis and eagerly went for any possible type of take-out I thought I might try to eat to keep up my strength. He even helped do chores around the house. He did admit feeling helpless to do anything "to really make a difference." How I wished he knew what a big deal it was.

That summer Henry went on a mission. He recorded a video message at a booth set up by a local news station. With his usual charm, he pleaded into the camera's microphone for someone to come forward to help me.

He phoned the news station and repeatedly left messages. At fifty I lost track but at last he found an editor who would listen. Henry's message appeared on television late one night. My heart swelled as I watched and listened to the man I loved reach out for help. "Consider donating a kidney to my wife," he said through a smile, but on the verge of tears. "She's my world. I need her to be here, healthy, and with me for as long as possible." As he flashed a boyish grin at the end of the clip, tears filled my eyes, although I held onto little hope that it would bring me the kind of help I needed.

Then a news reporter called. She wanted our story. It ran as the second top story of the evening news. The station called us to say that they'd never had such an overwhelming response to a story. Their phones wouldn't stop ringing. By the end of the night, they had compiled a list of over five hundred names of people interested in being tested to see if they were a match to give me a kidney. I couldn't believe it! It was too good to be true.

During a meeting with the transplant co-ordinator, I was told that unless a willing donor was a relative or a close friend prior to my needing a kidney, not one of the thoughtful souls who offered would be allowed to donate one to me. At that time, it was against protocol. Crushed by disappointment, it was all I could do to get up and go through the motions.

In the meantime, our story continued to run for nearly a week.

That Friday the phone rang. Reluctantly I answered it and a voice from my past declared, "Susan? Remember me? It's Tracey…"

Although a grade apart, Tracey and I had gone through public and high school together. During that time, her dad had suffered kidney failure. Unbeknownst to me back then, Tracey had hoped to donate her kidney to him, but wasn't able to do so before he passed away. Because of this, she had vowed — if the opportunity ever arose — to donate one for someone else. By chance her children had left the television on the channel that ran our story. By chance she'd caught one of the broadcasts out of the corner of her eye and recognized me.

She was eager, and determined. "I'm on my way this minute to get tested. Where do I need to go?" And so our journey began.

As we sat side by side in the stalls having our blood drawn, Eric Clapton's "Tears in Heaven" played softly on the radio. "Please," I silently begged the universe. "Please let us be a match." After we left the lab, Tracey pressed the fresh bandage into the crook of her elbow, eyes wide. Flooded with panic that she'd changed her mind and wanted to back out, I asked, "What's wrong?"

"That was the song played at my dad's service," Tracey whispered. "He was there with us, Susan. It'll all work out just fine. I just know it."

The shiver that ran through me left me breathless.

A short while later we received news that "we couldn't have been a better match if we'd been twin sisters," which may or may not have been a slight exaggeration.

And so, in the fall of 2004 — nearly a year to the day after Henry's heart surgery — Tracey and I underwent surgery with the reporter and her cameraman who'd followed my story from the start in tow. Afterward, I awoke feeling strong, filled with energy and somehow "cleansed" from the inside out.

A day or so later, I was told how the cameraman zoomed in on my innards just as the surgeon declared that, "the new kidney produced urine right then and there."

According to Mom, as the family watched the news coverage, Dad proudly declared to anyone who would listen, "That's my girl! She peed on TV!"

Watching Dad as he stood at the end of my hospital bed recounting his tale again, this time to Henry—who gazed at me with the same look of reassurance as the day he'd first taken me to the hospital to have the dialysis catheter installed—I hoped with all my heart that Tracey's dad would shed no more "Tears in Heaven. I hoped that instead he was grinning with relief and pride for the gift of a better, healthier and longer life his daughter had given to me because of him, and because of a husband whose love was, and is, boundless.

—Susan Blakeney—

41

A Cup of Comfort

*Friends are those rare people who ask how you
are and then wait for the answer.*
~Author Unknown

I n my early college years, I worked at a little Starbucks coffee shop in my community. I loved the feeling of pulling my hair up into a high bun and putting my focus and care into creating each cup of joy. When the nights were slow, I would make myself tea and review my notes behind the bar. It was comforting to look out over the steamer and see one or two students enjoying their lattes and focusing passionately on their homework. When we closed up for the night, I would take a hot chocolate home with me and sit at my desk into the late hours, feeling comforted and encouraged to focus on my writing.

On lonely nights, I would indulge in steamers—steamed milk with flavoured syrup—a beverage I learned about from a customer. One night, the shop was empty, and I was just getting ready to close when that same customer came rushing in.

"Are you still open?" Her eyes were red as if she had been crying and her long hair was caught in her sweater as if she had just pulled it on.

I couldn't say no.

"We just closed down the espresso machine, but I could still steam milk if you want a hot chocolate or steamer," I offered.

The girl didn't hesitate. "I need two raspberry steamers please."

"No problem," I said. "They are on us today."

I felt compelled to steam the milk as quickly as I could. She could tell.

"My best friend had a bad day," she explained.

When the girl left the store, I remember feeling numb. I couldn't think of one person in my life who would go through that much trouble to bring comfort to me. I can't remember if I took home a raspberry steamer that night because I was in the mood for a hot beverage or because I wanted to feel included.

It was hard to leave the comfort that I had found in Starbucks. The baristas whom I had grown close to were all following different career routes as they finished their college years. I remember watching them move onto new experiences and deciding that it might be time for me to move on too.

I was hired at a restaurant in the same community as my Starbucks a few months after applying. I loved serving from the start. I felt a sense of pride when I picked up a tray of drinks and would stride down my aisle smiling and assigning them to the right tables.

When Cathleen showed up for her shift at the restaurant, I was excited to see her. We had worked together at Starbucks and were familiar with each other. I was more than happy to share some appetizers with her after work.

I don't remember when small talk over appetizers turned into late night bonding sessions over chick flicks and a bottle of wine, but by the time summer rolled around, Cathleen and I had become inseparable. We got along well with each other's friends and shared a lot of the same quirks, such as our love of wearing new dresses and a terrible sense of direction.

Cathleen helped me through a lot of hard times that summer. I had experienced a bad break-up and found out that a childhood friend was really ill. Just when I thought I was pulling through my grandpa got cancer and dementia. It was Cathleen who kept me going. She never tried to play psychologist with me or to make me forget about it by dragging me out of the house. We kept hanging out in our free time as usual. On the hard nights, Cathleen would share noodles and wine with me as we caught up on the television series that had hooked me.

I had been having a particularly rough week that summer, and I remember looking forward to plans with Cathleen. We decided that it would be nice to sit out on a patio and let our skin bronze as we caught up with all the gossip that had been going on at work and the previous weekend's party. We decided that it would be fitting to bond over Starbucks coffees since we had originally met there.

When we had chosen the perfect table in the sun, Cathleen offered to buy the drinks. I was indecisive on what to order and told her that I would be happy with whatever she chose. It wasn't long before my best friend returned, two raspberry steamers in hand.

— Crysta Windsor —

42

Unrequested and Unexpected

He who sows courtesy reaps friendship,
and he who plants kindness gathers love.
~Saint Basil

O nce upon a time, before six-lane highways and faceless, voiceless, text messages — you know, in the Good Old Days when our parents were asking what the world was coming to — it seemed like we were more connected as people. At least that's what I thought.

Then, in early winter of last year, I underwent surgery to have my left foot re-constructed. I was discharged from hospital on a blustering snowy afternoon. We turned the corner and… "Look at the driveway! Our walk! Who could have? Who would have?" It was fully shovelled. Our twenty-foot long, double width driveway and our walk had been cleared of snow by our elderly neighbour, who, himself, was awaiting a hip operation.

Within the next few days, the phone began to ring and e-mails to arrive — inquiries about my wellbeing. Flowers arrived. Friends dropped by to chat or play *Scrabble* but mainly to ease my serious case of Sititis — no, not an infection, just plain, old too much sitting. I was confined to my chair on wheels for six inching-along, very tedious weeks.

Rides to the hospital were provided when needed and a large, substantial vehicle was loaned to us when we had to make our way to the outpatient clinic on yet another snowy day. All this was offered — not asked for.

And then, two months later and just three days before I was to collect my new orthotics, my partner, going down our back steps to the beach, slipped and broke her ankle. It was a clearly audible snap — a very bad break in five places. There was surgery and a cast and crutches and, again, the chair on wheels.

Once more, when we returned from hospital, when Cecily took her turn at invalidism, our friends and neighbours were immediately on the scene to assist wherever possible. Again, flowers and phone calls and offers of help arrived.

"Would you like us to come by and make dinner?"

"We're going into town. Do you have a grocery list?"

"Shall we come over with a bottle of wine?"

"We'll do the daily dog walks. We love Farlie." And, without fail, they took her for far longer and far better walks than she had previously enjoyed.

And then there was a knock on the door. "We've been away for several weeks, visiting our grandchildren, and just heard Cecily's bad news." In a thermal case, a neighbour was carrying a casserole large enough to feed us several times, a Caesar salad, homemade cheese scones ready for the oven, and freshly baked cookies for dessert.

This outpouring left us staggering with surprise and gratitude. To our neighbours and friends we could not say thank you loudly or often enough.

And as to my concerns about living in a time of faceless disconnection? It took almost a year of the unexpected and the unfortunate; but that year, and the people who stepped in to assist and to encourage, their simple acts of caring and kindness, unrequested and unexpected, made me realize my good fortune in having a home in a small-town community which still inspired such random acts of humanity.

— Robyn Gerland —

43

Feeling Full

Recovery is remembering who you are and using your
strengths to become all that you were meant to be.
~Recovery Innovations

Anxious, obsessive compulsive, and anorexic — had you asked me months ago, I would have told you I was all three. I don't know why then it came as such a shock when the doctor stated I wouldn't be leaving the hospital that morning.

I recognized that I had a problem. But when a medical professional looked at me and said, "You're an anorexic. Your heart, in fact your whole body, is going into failure. You could die," it all suddenly became very real. That diagnosis meant that I couldn't run from it anymore.

I had admitted to my parents that I was suffering from an eating disorder towards the end of tenth grade. What had started as a desire to improve my health rapidly snowballed into a drastically unhealthy change in habits and alarming weight loss. I limited my caloric intake to about 800 calories a day and exercised up to four hours a day. I was consumed with thoughts about my body and how to maintain the "perfect" and completely unattainable goal I had in my mind.

All of this left me with intense emotional distress, physical damage, and a 101-pound devastated body. I had withdrawn and disconnected from my social life. I felt completely hollow and starved of everything in life. I was dying, inside and out.

At the beginning of the summer, after having told the truth about my struggle, my parents immediately did all that they could to help. Sadly, the reality of the matter was that help would be months away. I was put on a waiting list for an eating disorders recovery program, so we were left to face my anorexia as best as we could on our own. Though I still failed to consume an appropriate amount, I did will myself to eat more. And although the constant thoughts of exercise prevented me from concentrating, I did cut my workouts in half. Summer was an uphill battle, but come the end of July, my saving grace was just around the corner.

Camp Kintail was a Presbyterian summer camp near Goderich, Ontario, right off Lake Huron, and also known as my home away from home. That summer was my fifth year at camp, and one of my most profound. Kintail had always been my sanctuary. It was the one place that I could truly be my open and honest self. Every summer, I was graced with beautiful people, scenery, and opportunities to grow as an individual. As a result, I learned that no matter what life threw at me, I could be sure that my time at Kintail could get me through it. That summer I was to spend a month in their leadership program, which ultimately saved my life.

It was my intent to reveal my issue once I got to camp. However, that proved more difficult than I had anticipated. While I had many friends at camp, I felt we'd grown apart. Though I tried, I couldn't bring myself to share my problem. Three days passed and I hadn't told a soul. Then one morning in the lodge, for no reason other than a gut feeling, I approached one of my fellow leaders in training. I knew little more than her name.

"Hayley, can I talk to you?"

Within minutes, tears were pouring down my face as I choked out the truth. To my surprise, she began crying too. She patiently listened to me as I expressed how I felt, but she already knew. When I finished, she looked me in the eyes and said, "One year ago, I was exactly where you are now." Hayley explained that she had overcome her eating disorder the prior summer and firmly believed camp had saved her life. I honestly believe in that very moment she saved mine.

For the rest of camp, Hayley was like my guardian angel. No matter how stressful things got or how difficult I became, she did everything in her power to keep me happy, safe, eating, and feeling supported.

Going home was the hard part, because it meant tests and evaluations, and then waiting until late October for my meeting for the recovery program. But on the third day of school, my stepmom told me that my evaluation had been bumped up. "They saw the result of your preliminary ECG, and they're concerned. They want to see you tomorrow."

With this urgent evaluation came the possibility of admittance into the hospital. It's funny how the world works, because that morning, Hayley (whom I hadn't talked to since camp) contacted me and asked how I was doing. I told her the truth, and she did the same with me. "This is when you have to get better. You're slowly committing suicide. Think about how much you have ahead of you." I honoured her words.

I went to my appointment that morning wearing my kilt and collared top, my hair done, my make-up on. I thought I would be going to school that afternoon. But there I was, sitting in that box of a room, the doctor's words still ringing in my ears. I would not go home for a month.

For quite some time, I blamed myself for this — for the inability to just eat a piece of cake or skip a run. People had reacted strongly upon discovering my illness: "I thought you were smarter than that" and "You've just got to eat." These responses only furthered my self-hatred, and I believed them. Until I started hearing the response from people uncovering the truth: "It's a disease."

It took a lot for me to finally understand that it is a disease. Lying in my hospital bed, devastated and sobbing, I recalled apologizing to my parents for all of the stress I had caused and that I couldn't just be better. They would have none of that. "Would you just tell a cancer patient to get better?" No, I suppose you wouldn't. Thinking that over, I finally accepted that I was sick, and not by my doing. However, getting better would be through my own doing.

My month in that hospital was hands down the hardest month of my life, but I got through it. And I still continue to recover from my disorder. Some days I feel unstoppable, and some days I feel stopped dead in my tracks. Each day, however, I continue to heal and recover, because I have an infinite will to do so.

"I eat. I'm still anorexic."

A friend recovering from her disorder once told me that. It's a statement that explains a lot and holds much truth. I eat, but I still struggle. I'm still ill, and I'm still a long way from being completely better, but that's okay.

It's okay because I have people like Hayley in my life, an incredibly supportive and understanding family, places like Kintail, and a strong drive to recover.

With all of that in mind, I know I'm finally on my way to feeling full again.

— Samantha Molinaro —

44

The Maintenance Man

Each person has an ideal, a hope, a dream which
represents the soul. We must give to it the warmth
of love, the light of understanding and
the essence of encouragement.
~Colby Dorr Dam

I was wary of him. He hung around, repeatedly cleaning the kitchen area of the staff room as my students gathered their belongings at the end of their shifts. I worried he was checking out "my girls." His head was usually down, but it seemed he was eavesdropping on their conversations.

As a clinical instructor, I worked with nursing students on a medical floor on the evening shifts. We wrapped up around 9:30 p.m. and then the students convened in a crowded staff room for a bit of their own de-briefing, joking around, exchanging e-mail addresses, or taking group selfies. As they'd pack up their backpacks, notes, and various electronic devices, laughter emanated from the small group.

I suppose it's natural that we instructors watch out for our little flocks when students might be oblivious to who's watching them. There was no reason to expect anything suspicious; the man had appropriate identification, but I tended to be on the cautious side.

The students were unique in that they comprised a group of Internationally Educated Nurses (IENs), all of whom had studied and qualified for nursing in their home countries and had immigrated to Canada with the intent to refresh their skills and practice here. They were a joy to teach, as most were extremely eager to complete this clinical portion, the last of the requirements that would allow them to write the Canadian RN exams and apply for positions.

One of my star students was a tall outgoing woman from South Africa who had recently immigrated. She'd decided to resuscitate her nursing career after spending a number of years raising her children. Her goal was to polish her skills and return to emergency nursing, which was her specialty in South Africa. Since that was my first career, we had a common bond.

She was a white woman with an unusual streak of vibrantly dyed red hair in her otherwise ordinary head of sandy brown. Joyfully, she sung out her friendly greeting of, "Good morning, M'lady," at the beginning of every shift in her lilting Afrikaans accent. She soaked up everything I could possibly offer. She helped the other students on the computers at the hospital and shared her clinical experiences. She got the most out of her clinical rotation because she gave as much or more than anyone else.

Our end-of-shift ritual continued and the dark-skinned maintenance man still hung about. I noted his sad gaze and felt a sense of loss coming from him.

Finally, one evening he approached me after the students had departed. In heavily accented English, he asked, "What program these students in?"

I told him, but wondered where he was going with this. He related how he and his wife had immigrated to Canada just a few years earlier. They had both been RNs in Africa. For eighteen years he was in charge of HIV/AIDS education programs throughout Kenya and other parts of Africa. He had hoped to practice nursing in Canada, but language was a barrier. He was taking English classes. He had heard a bit about the IEN program and was thinking of applying, but admitted his work and study schedule was already taxing. Once he qualified, if he did, his wife was going to try to regain her RN qualifications too.

I smiled at my own misconceptions about this experienced African nurse who had obviously made a huge impact in his homeland. Ever the ambassador for the college, I told him more about the IEN program and how to apply. I encouraged him to continue with his studies and I wished him the best in resuming his nursing career.

After that conversation, he seemed to relax a little more when the students were finishing their shifts, his eyes occasionally lighting up, although often wistful.

My group continued to expand their skills and share many successes. You could feel the excitement in the air as they neared completion of the clinical rotations and anticipated writing their exams.

On one shift in the final week I came in early to find my South African student deep in conversation with the maintenance man in a side conference room, her clear and encouraging voice melding with his quiet responses, his head eventually nodding in comprehension. He looked up to acknowledge me with a shy smile.

"I accepted into the IEN program," he said with a smile. He held his head higher, his eyes lit up, and he carried himself tall with obvious pride.

He had sought out a fellow African upon realizing the first course was on medication. She was conducting a mini-teaching session on IV therapy calculations.

My heart swelled with pride to see the South African woman sharing her knowledge with the Kenyan maintenance man, proving that the language of nursing transcends race, colour, creed, and gender.

— Colleen Stewart Haynes —

45

Giving Kids the World

When someone tells you that you can't do something,
perhaps you should consider that they are only
telling you what they can't do.
~Sheldon Cahoon

"**W**hat would you wish for if you could have any wish in the whole wide world?" I asked, in what I hoped was an ethereal and magical voice. The child I was interviewing didn't care about the tone of my voice — she already knew exactly what she wanted.

"To visit the Mickey Mouse Clubhouse!"

I'm not a regular viewer of the Disney Junior channel, but I knew enough to know that Mickey's colourful clubhouse existed only in the cartoon world.

"How about a trip to the Walt Disney World Resort?" I enthused. "At Disney you can explore Mickey Mouse's house! And Minnie's house too!"

The little girl batted her eyelashes and looked up at me expectantly. "No. The Mickey Mouse Clubhouse, the one on TV. I really want to go there. To the real one on TV."

"Right. Silly me." How was I going to make this happen?

I am a volunteer Wish Grantor with Make-A-Wish® British Columbia and Yukon — a non-profit organization that grants the wishes of children with life-threatening medical conditions to enrich the human experience with hope, strength and joy.

This means that as a Wish Grantor I am often required to get creative to find ways to fulfill the unique wishes of children.

We joke amongst ourselves that the only limitation to a wish is the limits of a child's imagination — which we all know can be endless!

I sometimes say that I'm a "jaded" Wish Grantor after so many years, but I still tear up at those magical moments that can't help but restore my faith in humanity.

Like when firefighters or police officers take time out to deliver a laptop to a child in the hospital. Or when an entire restaurant staff decorates a booth, buys gifts, and dresses up in costume in anticipation of a wish kid's visit. Or the time I took a family out to a pricey dinner to celebrate their child's wish and when the time came to ask for the bill, we were told an anonymous stranger had already paid it. Or when a celebrity learned that the teenaged boy who wished to meet him was too sick to travel and called him at home, only to be told "No way. I'm still coming. I'm hanging in there."

We get to see inspiring stories play out regularly, and I think all of us volunteers are better people because of it. We get to see the good in the world, every day.

In *Chicken Soup for the Soul: The Cancer Book* (2009) I shared a story about a significant experience that helped shape my life — volunteering as a camp counsellor at a pediatric oncology camp in British Columbia, Canada, called Camp Goodtimes. That experience touched my soul so much, but I don't think I could fully relate to what those kids were going through until years later, when my nine-year-old cousin was diagnosed with a malignant brain tumour and we were told she might not survive the night.

When things seemed at their most hopeless, a fairy godmother from Make-A-Wish entered our lives. The timing was perfect because Paige was already physically, mentally, and emotionally drained from the first part of her treatment. Her wish — for a baby grand piano — gave her the strength she needed to push through the second half.

In her words, "Playing my piano took me to a world of my own. A world that held no pain; a world that held only beauty; a world that was filled with hope; a world that brought me comfort: a world that gave me strength."

Shortly after seeing how this experience changed her life, I contacted Make-A-Wish to find out how I could get involved in this incredible organization. The first wish I was assigned was a celebrity escort — accompanying a wish child onto a movie set to meet her favourite star. I was stoked to say the least.

Visions of hunky heartthrobs danced through my head, so I was naturally surprised to learn that the celebrity guest we'd be meeting wasn't exactly a conventional human movie star. A five-year-old girl from North Dakota had wished her most heartfelt wish — to meet the canine stars of the *Air Buddies* movies — an adorable quintet of Golden Retriever puppies who always seemed to find themselves on unique adventures.

When Ellen's limo rolled up on set, we were immediately escorted to a trailer where the Buddies were eagerly waiting to meet her. I can't even begin to describe the adorably cute chaos that followed but it involved lots of puppy hugs and squeals of glee from a spunky little girl dressed in head-to-toe pink who defined the phrase Bald Is Beautiful. We spent a full day on set. Ellen got to play with the puppies, watch them film stunts, and sit in her own pint-sized director's chair with her favourite puppy — Rosebud — curled up in her lap. When the film wrapped, we were all stunned when the producer decided to put Rosebud on a plane and send her to live with Ellen in North Dakota!

Years later, I still get e-mailed updates from Ellen's family with photos of Ellen and Rosebud growing up together. Rosebud even helps give back to Ellen's cause — people donate to cancer fundraisers to get their photo taken with Rosebud the celebrity dog! Ellen's story, my first wish-granting experience, resonates with me to this day.

Since then, I have granted dozens of wishes — Disney parks, cruises, celebrity-meet-and-greets, shopping sprees and even a gym membership. Sure I've met some of the "heartthrob celebrities" I'd signed on hoping to meet, but in every case they were overshadowed by the true star — the joyful child whose dream was coming true.

My full circle moment was when I recently granted the wish of a little girl named Paige — just like my cousin — who also had a malignant brain tumour. Instead of a piano, this Paige wished to spend time on the beach stomping sand castles with her grandma, so we whisked her off to Mexico to stomp to her heart's content.

Some people mistakenly refer to these special joyful moments, like stomping sand castles, as "final dying wishes," but in most cases I have witnessed, they are instead actually life-affirming wishes that give sick children the strength to continue to fight and survive.

It shows them that miracles can happen and that many people are wishing them well. Out of dozens of wishes, two wish kids have sadly passed away, one almost immediately following his wish to visit a popular television show. But I feel so fortunate to have gotten to know him, and truly believe he held on an extra month and a half and created so many more priceless memories with his family until his wish could come true.

I have heard similar stories of other kids — whose doctors advised they might be too sick to travel — who suddenly perked up as soon as they arrived at their destination and enjoyed a carefree week with family before returning to the realities of their lives.

Call it karma, or just plain luck, but a few years ago I received a phone call from the Orlando Tourism Bureau, informing me I had won a trip to Orlando! I was stoked to visit Disney and Universal Studios, but I was most looking forward to the opportunity to visit a very special place called Give Kids The World Village® where so many wish kids had visited.

It's a magical fairy-tale seventy-acre resort that accommodates kids (and their families) who wish to visit theme parks in the Orlando area. I spent an afternoon there as a "Volunteer Angel" where I had the opportunity to meet wish kids from around the world and hear their inspirational stories.

The most inspirational story I heard that day though, was about how this magical village came to be. The founder, a man named Henri Landwirth, did not spend his childhood in a fairy-tale village.

He grew up, instead, as a prisoner of Auschwitz concentration camp, and lost both his parents before the war ended. Henri worked his way to America on a ship with only twenty dollars in his pocket, but through hard work and perseverance, eventually became a hotel manager.

Henri heard about a little girl named Amy with leukemia who sadly passed away before the arrangements could be made to organize her dream trip to Orlando, and Henri was determined that other kids have the opportunity to fulfill their wishes in time. He felt his own childhood had been ripped away from him too soon, and he didn't want that to happen to any other child.

Through his efforts, an astonishing 138,000 wish families have stayed at Give Kids The World Village since it opened in 1989 and have enjoyed all-inclusive experiences while making day trips to ride roller coasters and meet Mickey Mouse.

My volunteer work with children with life-threatening medical conditions has truly opened the world to me, helped me uncover my passions, and helped mold me into the person of purpose I am today. I feel so fortunate that these brave kids have invited me into their lives and into their imaginations and I have learned to live life to the fullest and fulfill my own dreams, by asking myself regularly: "What would you wish for if you could have any wish in the whole wide world? Then attempting to make it a reality."

— Cassie Silva —

46

Lunch Mentor

If we all did the things we are capable of doing,
we would literally astound ourselves.
~Thomas Alva Edison

I couldn't wait for school to begin, knowing that meant Mrs. Brennan would be my new fourth grade teacher! Loved by all, she was gentle, encouraging and kind, rarely raising her voice. When she did, it was always for good reason.

I adored her from the first day I attended elementary school. She always greeted me with a warm hug when no one was around to witness her favouritism, addressing me as "Little Mary," a nickname that made me smile.

Like many others in our impoverished neighbourhood, both my parents worked out of necessity. Mama started cleaning houses the year before. She couldn't afford to have someone watch me at lunchtime, so I became a latchkey kid. Because I was scared to be alone at home, I would eat quickly and run back to hide in an outside stairwell in the schoolyard to wait until afternoon classes resumed.

No one had ever found me there, but a week into that September, Mrs. Brennan did while retrieving her sweater that had fallen out a window. That same afternoon, she sent a message to Mama requesting that I stay at school every lunchtime to help with some small chores, instead of going home for lunch. The note stated that she would provide a meal for me as "payment." Relieved that I'd be under adult supervision, Mama signed the permission slip.

My duties started the next afternoon. One minute before the dismissal bell rang, I would quietly leave my seat in the back row and exit the room. No one noticed me leaving as they slammed books into their desks, restlessly waiting to leave.

I would race up to the third-floor teachers' room and pull out a paper bag with Mrs. Brennan's initials on it from the fridge. I knew that it held at least two delicious sliced-meat sandwiches garnished with fresh tomatoes and lettuce, along with a large piece of cheese, some cake or cookies, and a small container of milk. Although Mama was an excellent cook, deli meat was a rarity in our home. Cheese was almost unheard of. There was never enough money.

As we ate, Mrs. Brennan listened intently to my trivial childish chatter, drawing me out of my timid shell with her genuine interest. After lunch, I would tidy up, wipe the blackboard and chalk tray, and take the erasers to the central vacuum to clean in preparation for afternoon class. Then I would sneak out the side door and join the other students as if I was coming from home myself. My "job" was over, but never without a tight hug and a whispered "You're a good girl, Little Mary."

That year, we were introduced to creative writing, and I loved it. Mrs. Brennan quickly noticed my aptitude for writing, urging me to do more of it during our meal, and supplying me with extra notebooks to jot down my thoughts and stories. Over time, she encouraged me to try poetry, raving over my crude, silly rhymes as if I were Emily Dickinson.

While I scribbled down my dreams and verses, time seemed to stop. It was only when I heard Mrs. Brennan at the vacuum, cleaning her own brushes, that I realized I was neglecting my duties. Instead of scolding me, she merely grinned.

"It was never about the blackboards, Little Mary," she told me softly. "It was about making you feel safe."

In fifth and sixth grade, Mama made arrangements to send me elsewhere for lunch, but I continued to see Mrs. Brennan and share my creative writing with her every chance I could, never tiring of her excited praise and warm embraces. On the last day of sixth grade, she hugged me as always, but her grip was tighter, longer and somehow more desperate. When we broke apart, I was stunned to see she was crying.

"Are you okay, Mrs. Brennan?" I asked worriedly.

"Don't worry about me, Little Mary," she soothed, wiping her eyes. "I'm just saying goodbye. You have a good holiday and remember to keep writing."

Summer vacation flew by. That September, I rushed to school, eager to see her again, but when the bell rang, a stranger stood in the schoolyard facing the line of fourth grade students. Mrs. Brennan was nowhere to be seen. I asked my new teacher, Mrs. Kondracki, where she was.

"Marya, I know how close the two of you were, so I'll be honest. Mrs. Brennan had cancer in the past, and it's come back. She's dying, dear. I'm sorry."

I had subconsciously known something was terribly wrong but this was still a shock. I swallowed back tears and tried to find my voice.

"C-can I visit her?"

"I'm afraid not. No one under eighteen is allowed, but I see her at least once a week. I'll tell her you asked about her."

"Thank you," I whispered, turning to go back to my desk in a haze. Mrs. Kondracki was considerate and did not call on me for any answers for the rest of the day.

A week later, I approached her again, this time with a meticulously folded piece of paper I'd carefully torn out of my copybook. In my best penmanship, I'd written Mrs. Brennan a poem, telling her how much I missed her, loved her, and wished she was well again.

"Could you give her this?" I asked, my eyes tearing up. "It's something I wrote for her."

"Of course," she replied, tucking it into her purse. "I'll make sure she gets it."

Mrs. Brennan died several months later. I was finally allowed to see her. There was no age limit at funeral parlours.

I stood at the casket, hating that my last memory of her would be this still, lifeless, pale shell of the vibrant woman I'd known.

"Are you Marya?" a voice asked behind me, and I turned around to see a woman about Mrs. Brennan's age.

"Yes," I choked.

"My sister talked about you. She cared about you very much. I want you to know how happy she was that you sent her that poem. She loved it. She asked me to give you this if you came," she added, handing me a note and a little bottle of cheap hand lotion I'd given Mrs. Brennan one Christmas when I had nothing else to offer in return for her kindness. I grinned through my tears at the memory.

"She also said to tell you something else."

"What?" I croaked.

She said, "Remember to keep writing, Little Mary."

I nodded my thanks. I couldn't speak anymore. I placed the little bottle in my pocket, turned back toward the coffin, and said my last goodbye before leaving.

Outside, I looked up at the stars. One seemed brighter than the rest for some reason. I like to think it was her spirit suspended in the heavens, free from pain and at peace.

"Thank you for making me feel special and safe," I whispered into the night sky. "And I promise — I'll never stop writing."

I kept my word.

— Marya Morin —

47

The Hockey Coach

Courage is fire, and bullying is smoke.
~Benjamin Disraeli

My second son, Derek, was in the first grade and was having difficulties in school. His teacher was hard on him because he was the funny one; he always had to be telling a joke and his humour tended to be on the physical side. He would jump up on chairs or try to do back flips in class in order to get attention. And he did get attention, just not the kind that he was hoping for. He was being bullied.

Each day he would come home upset. He was afraid to go to school; he would refuse to get up in the morning, his eating patterns changed and he became very thin and pale. His smile faded as the weeks of bullying turned into months. The school did everything they could to help us but the bullying continued.

It was late February when things changed for Derek. He was walking home from school and it was dreadfully cold. His hat had been stolen and his snow pants were soaking wet after he had been shoved into a puddle. Our neighbour Cody, who had only recently finished high school, spotted Derek walking home from the bus and noticed how cold he was. He ran out of his house straight away and wrapped Derek up in a warm, wool blanket. Cody walked the rest of the way up the street and knocked on the door to speak to me. I saw how sad Derek was and I fell to my knees to hug him and help warm him up.

I wasn't sure if he was bored, or he was just simply an amazing kid, but Cody offered to spend some time with Derek every day after school. Cody waited at the bus stop for Derek to get home from school and he took him out on excursions. At first I didn't know where they went, but Cody had him home promptly at six. Initially there was no change in Derek, but after three days he came to me and asked me if I would buy him a pair of hockey skates. I looked at him; his little six-year old expression was serious as he waited for my reply. I smiled and said, "Alright." For the first time in as long as I could remember, his face lit up with the biggest smile. My heart melted and I knew that something great was happening for my son.

After I bought those skates for Derek, he spent every day with Cody learning to skate and learning to manoeuvre a hockey stick across the ice. A few times Cody allowed me to come to the arena in order to witness the skill Derek had acquired in only a few short weeks. I could hear Derek's laugh as he joked with Cody on the ice. It was music to my ears.

At the end of March, Cody asked if Derek could play in a hockey game. Cody was an assistant coach for the house-league hockey association in town, and he had special permission to allow Derek to play in one of the final games of the season. We were hesitant because we knew that Derek had only just learned to skate, and we were afraid of him getting hurt. But Cody assured us that he would be right there the whole time.

The day of the game we were so nervous for our little boy. But Derek had gotten up early that day, had eaten his breakfast in front of the fireplace and was half dressed by the time we got up that morning. As a family we all piled into the van and drove to the arena. Anxiously we waited for the game to begin. Cody took care of everything. He had a hockey sweater waiting for Derek and all of the equipment he would need. All suited up and ready to go, Derek joined the rest of Cody's team in their box.

Derek sat on the bench for the entire first period. We weren't sure why and we could see Derek's smile fade slowly as the game wore on. My eldest son whispered in my husband's ear during the second period and afterward got up and walked around to the other side of the ice in order to speak to Cody. By this point Derek was nearly in tears as Cody urged him to go onto the ice.

Derek was timid as he skated around during that second period. When he was on the ice he stayed far away from all of the other players, and steered clear of the puck. By this point I wasn't sure I even understood why Cody had wanted him to play in the first place. My "mom" instincts were kicking in and I wanted to get my son off that ice.

The third period looked like it would be much of the same. Despite my yelling and encouragement from the stands, Derek remained far away from the action. Slowly two players from the other team had made their way over to where Derek was skating, and they tripped Derek, causing him to fall on the ice. As his head hit the ice, his mouth guard fell out and he bit his lip. Blood was flowing from his bottom lip and dripping down the front of him. The events unfolded in slow motion and I stood up screaming like a mad woman.

My eldest son pulled on my sleeve and tried to get my attention, but I was more concerned about what was happening with Derek. The referee placed the two players in the penalty box and then directed Derek to the opposing team's net. The referee dropped the puck in front of him and pointed toward the net. I glanced quickly at the scoreboard and realized that there was very little time left in the last period and the game was tied. (Scores didn't really make much difference in this age category, but it was our movie-magic moment so I mention it for that reason). I was still on my feet as I watched my son positioned directly in front of the net, and slowly my son took aim, lifted his stick in order to shoot that puck into the net. I had never seen Derek use that much concentration. The puck flew effortlessly past the goalie and right into the net, and the goal was awarded to Derek's team. After a few more minutes of play, the period was over and Derek had scored the winning goal. The sound of the cheers and applause from the stands made Derek smile and laugh as he skated off the ice.

After the game my eldest son finally got my attention, and it was then that he told me that the two boys who had tripped Derek were the two bullies who had been tormenting him all year in school. They were brothers who rode on the same bus as Derek. As I stood outside the change room waiting for Derek to come out, their father approached me in order to apologize for his sons' behaviour. We told him what had been happening all year and he promised that he would make it right.

Derek was not bullied again after that day. We witnessed our son's smile and sense of humour return, and we look back and realize that if it had not been for the selfless efforts of a young teenage boy and the game of hockey, our son might never have found his humour again. Cody continued to coach Derek long after that hockey game, and when Cody left for college that fall he left behind a young boy who could stick handle with the best of them, a boy with confidence and a killer punch line!

— Jennifer Litke —

A Scholar and a Gentleman

*The great thing about getting older is that you don't
lose all the other ages you've been.*
~Madeleine L'Engle

Vindication for the decision to become a writer doesn't always come from creative-writing teachers or even editors. One of my most powerful mentors came in the form of a scholar and a gentleman named Uncle Johnny. It happened the Christmas I was eight.

The big day would fall on Friday that year. I was relieved. That meant Uncle Johnny wouldn't be at our house for either Christmas Eve supper or dinner the following day. Wednesday was his day to visit.

I resented Uncle Johnny. His presence at our supper table every Wednesday evening never failed to spoil my enjoyment of the meal. My mother said Uncle Johnny was a graduate of one of Canada's leading universities and had been one of the most renowned literary scholars of his day, but I found that hard to believe.

Uncle Johnny was eighty-six. He had watery, red-rimmed eyes, sagging jowls, and trembling hands that slopped and spilled food and drink. Sometimes, drool seeped from the corners of his mouth. He smelled of mothballs. And he wasn't even my uncle. He was just my grandfather's second cousin, who'd ended up alone in old age. He always arrived wearing an old-fashioned, shiny-with-age, three-piece suit, a snow-white shirt, a threadbare tie bearing some sort of insignia, and down-at-the-heels black shoes glossed to a military shine. A polished fob crossing his vest terminated in the breast pocket that held his gold watch.

Uncle Johnny lived in a once-genteel, now-shabby boarding house beside the town's newspaper office. His proximity to this print shop facilitated the neatly bound typeset copies of his poems and essays that he never failed to bring to my mother.

He'd present one of these pale blue binders to her each Wednesday as we sat down to supper. "A gentleman never comes calling with his hands at his sides," he'd say as he handed her his gift.

My mother's meal would grow cold on her plate as she read. Uncle Johnny, with shaking hands, dribbled food down the napkin he'd tucked under his chin as he sent not-so-furtive glances in her direction, awaiting her reaction.

Repulsed, I tried to keep my eyes focused on the meal in front of me and ignore Uncle Johnny's effort to get food and drink to his mouth. My mother would finish reading, clutch the binder to her chest, and smile.

"Lovely, Uncle Johnny, absolutely lovely," she'd say. "I'll treasure it."

He'd cast her an adoring, watery smile as he patted his mouth with a corner of his napkin.

"Thank you, my dear," he'd reply softly, casting a gentle nod of appreciative acknowledgement in her direction. "You're too kind."

On Wednesday of Christmas week that year, aglow with hopes and plans for the Yuletide, I was willing to view even Uncle Johnny's weekly dinner visit in a kinder light. He wouldn't be around to spoil any of the Christmas feasts.

That morning, my mother shattered my anticipation.

"I've invited Uncle Johnny to come on Friday," I overheard her telling my father. "Last week when I asked about his plans for Christmas, I discovered he hadn't any. Oh, he tried to say Cousin George had mentioned something back in the summer, but I have a feeling he was fibbing. He didn't want us to invite him out of pity. I said that since there'd be just the three of us this year, he'd be doing us a favour by helping us to eat that big turkey you bought."

"No!" Startling my parents, I burst into the kitchen. "No! No! No! He'll spoil everything with his shaking and drooling and dribbling! And he smells!"

"Gail, how can you say such dreadful things?" my mother said in dismay. "Uncle Johnny is a dear, old gentleman. He's kind and clever and…"

"I hate him! I hate him!" I yelled. "If he's here for Christmas, I won't come to the table!"

I stormed up to my room and slammed the door.

A half-hour later (my usual allowed cooling-off time), my father entered. I knew from his expression I was in deep trouble.

"You've hurt your mother's feelings," he said, his face grim. "I want you to apologize to her." He turned to leave, then paused.

"And if you refuse to share Christmas dinner with Uncle Johnny, Santa definitely won't be pleased."

Consequently, Christmas Day saw me seated in my usual place across from Uncle Johnny. As my mother placed the steaming, golden brown turkey on the table, he drew a small, awkwardly wrapped package from inside his suit coat. With a shaking hand, he extended it toward me.

"Your mother tells me you enjoy reading and hope to be a writer some day," he said, his thin, old voice quavering. "I thought you might enjoy this."

I stared down at the crumpled wrappings. Some tatty old thing not even wrapped in new paper.

"Open it, Gail." My mother beamed down on both of us.

Gingerly, I untied the wrinkled ribbon and spread out the paper. Inside was a book, *Emily of New Moon*, by L. M. Montgomery.

"It's about a young lady about your age who, much like yourself, aspires to be a writer," Uncle Johnny explained, a tremulous smile on his moist lips.

"How thoughtful, Uncle Johnny." My mother put an arm around the shoulders of his worn jacket and hugged him. "Gail, wasn't that thoughtful of Uncle Johnny?"

"Yes." I was turning the book slowly over in my hands. Used. I liked fresh, new books. But Uncle Johnny had said it was about a girl who wanted to write. "Thank you, Uncle Johnny."

"You're most welcome, my dear. I hope it will inspire you."

Uncle Johnny passed away that spring, alone in his room at the boarding-house. Few people attended his funeral. In his poverty and isolation, he and his past scholarly achievements had been forgotten.

I stood by his grave, clutching my mother's hand and *Emily of New Moon*, the book I'd come to cherish and whose author would have a major influence on my literary life. I knew I would never forget the man who'd given it to me or the fact that he was a scholar and a gentleman.

— Gail MacMillan —

Chapter
5

We Are Family

49

Meeting the Gods with My Dad

*Generosity lies less in giving much than in giving
at the right moment.*
~Jean de la Bruyère

When I was a little boy, about nine, I was diagnosed with pes planus. Or for those of you who don't speak fluent Latin... flat feet. I would have to go to a specialist. My dad, William James Davidson, took it upon himself to take care of the situation. He had a doctor friend, a specialist, and we set up an appointment.

On a crisp winter morning we jumped into the car and headed into Montreal from our farm in Châteauguay. We headed up Atwater Street toward the children's hospital. I knew where it was because I'd been there to have my tonsils out, which for a little kid is really traumatic until after the operation when you are offered all the ice cream you can eat.

But I digress.

So there we were, heading to the hospital. Suddenly I realized my dad had driven right by it and was parking the car in front of the most important building in all the world. A building that represented everything that was good and true to a little kid in Quebec. Le Forum de Montréal, home of the greatest hockey team in my universe. Les Canadiens!

We walked in and Dad headed straight to the team's locker room. I couldn't believe he actually knew where to go. He opened a door and I walked into the office of the team's physiotherapist, Bill Head.

My dad actually knew the team's physiotherapist? They actually KNEW each other? I was dumbstruck!

Dr. Head had me take off my shoes and hop up on his examination table… the same table that the Montreal players sat on. My friends were going to be so jealous.

He began his examination. I had to concentrate on the instructions he was giving me, so I wasn't aware that two other people had joined us until Dad, who was perfectly bilingual, started rattling away in French. All very jovial and sprinkled with lots of interesting words that he would never say in English and that I wasn't even supposed to know.

Dad excused me from the doctor and said, "Son, say hello to a couple of my old friends." I turned to see who he was talking to and looked straight into the eyes of Jean Béliveau, who stuck out his hand and shook mine, like I was somebody important. Then he turned and said, "You probably know this guy, eh," and there he was, the player I wanted to be every time we played hockey — Bernie "Boom Boom" Geoffrion. The world's greatest right winger. The hardest slap shot in the league!

It was like being on Mount Olympus and meeting the gods. My dad just stood back and took it all in.

Boom Boom and Jean, my two new best friends, got into a discussion with Dr. Head and everybody was really interested in my feet and how to fix my condition.

Just about the time that I thought nothing was better than the moment I was living, there was another flurry of French and my dad said, "Maurice ceci est mon fils. Bruce say hello to Mr. Richard." I looked up and there he was, the god Zeus, the Greatest Hockey Player in the World, Maurice "The Rocket" Richard. My nine-year-old heart felt like it stopped beating!

After that I don't remember exactly what happened because my tiny nine-year-old brain seemed to explode. I do have an image burned in my mind of Gentleman Jean, Boom Boom and The Rocket all hunkered down on the floor in front of me talking flat feet with Dr. Head like it was the most important thing in the world. Fixing the problem was all about being able to pick up marbles with your toes, they said. They assured me that they all did it every day to keep from getting flat feet.

Then, to drive the message home, Boom Boom took off his shoes and socks, and proceeded to demonstrate the intricacies of Elite Athlete Marble Picking.

When the appointment ended, I left with a list of foot exercises that I had to do each day to strengthen my feet, along with a hockey stick that belonged to Boom Boom and was signed by everybody, and an official Canadiens puck.

I also left with a newfound respect for my dad. He wasn't just a salesman for Dominion Glass. He knew the Hockey Gods and more importantly... they knew him.

Even as I write this I can remember the drive home. Me babbling about all the exciting things that happened to me that day. How I was going to pick up marbles every day until I was as good as Boom Boom. And Dad nodding and smiling and smiling and smiling.

Years later my mother told me that Dad had said the day he introduced me to The Hockey Gods was one of the best memories in his life. It was one of mine too!

I still have flat feet.

— Bruce Davidsen —

50

The Christmas that Never Was

Christmas, children, is not a date. It is a state of mind.
~Mary Ellen Chase

I'll never forget the moment that celebrating Christmas ended for me, forever. The year was 1978. It was the strangest sensation when I stopped — heartbreaking and yet strangely liberating and exhilarating at the same time.

When I was a kid, my parents used to call me Little Miss Merry Christmas. My mother didn't like Christmas. She didn't know how to cook so she despaired every holiday when cookies or turkeys were needed. She hated decorating the house. Couldn't stand shopping for Christmas presents and she complained about nearly every present she received. They weren't thoughtful enough or too practical. And Lordy how she hated trimming Christmas trees!

The only real festive moment my mom enjoyed was making fudge — a recipe she and her friends had learned during World War II. They'd made batches and batches of the confection and sent them to soldiers fighting in that war. Fudge was the big Christmas tradition for Mom that she absolutely had to do. But if the fudge didn't turn out just right, she'd end up in a fit of tears.

Mom also loved being with her family even though she and her sisters usually fought whenever they were together. Christmas Eve was spent with her siblings and their kids.

I was the opposite of my mother. I loved everything about Christmas. When I was ten, I took over decorating the house and setting out the Christmas cards we received. By the age of twelve my father and I made the Christmas turkey. I found a farm in the country where we could cut down our own Christmas tree. My dad and I went every year and chopped down the biggest tree we could find. I'd spend the rest of the day decorating it while listening to Christmas carols and drinking homemade eggnog.

By the time I was eighteen I had pretty much taken over the preparations for Christmas, even baking cookies. All Mom had to do was make the fudge.

Then I went into nursing school and stayed in residence. My mother bought a fake tree. We argued about it. Fought. Battled as if it were World War III, but my mother was determined to have a fake tree so she could put it up December the first and not worry about needles falling.

No more garlands of holly, no more putting out the Christmas cards. It was too much for her to do without me. But there was still fudge.

I had been a nurse on a chemotherapy unit for two years when my mother pulled me aside one Christmas Eve and showed me a wound on her shoulder. I recognized it immediately. It was a secondary metastases from a tumour in her breast.

Some things just don't need to be said between mothers and daughters. We both knew in that moment that there would not be very many Christmases left for my mother.

I didn't sleep that night, just couldn't, and I watched the sun rise and kiss the sugary snow with its brilliant light. After a moment's hesitation I donned a sweat suit and my running shoes, went outside, and began to run. Within minutes I found myself running through a woodland nestled at the end of my street. I ran past a herd of deer, bunnies, squirrels. I felt as if my lungs would explode from the frigid morning air, but I still ran.

I ran along the river and mountains of piled ice on the frozen bank.

And then I ran past our neighbourhood church and stopped. Long icicles hung all along the side of the roof. They were prisms for the sun and rainbows danced on the wall.

"All right," I whispered. "If You are going to take her, all I ask is that it be swift and without pain."

As I walked home I began to think of my patients. Four of them were stranded at the hospital for Christmas because their families couldn't or wouldn't take them home for the day. None of them would live to see another Christmas.

"Dad," I called when I returned home. "How big is our turkey?"

"Why?"

"Do we have enough for four more people?"

"Sure."

"Good. We're having company."

After setting the table and making sure everything was prepared, my father and I signed my four patients out and brought them home. Two were in wheelchairs, one had oxygen. The fourth one, Mrs. M., my father and I had to carry inside.

We ate turkey, pumpkin pie, sang carols, and settled around the tree with hot cocoa and — my mother's fudge.

"I used to make this fudge for my husband when he was a soldier overseas," said Mrs. M. with a wistful smile on her face. "He hated it. He didn't tell me that until twenty years later, God bless him."

After several heartfelt thank yous were made, my mom made "care" packages for our four guests and we returned them to the hospital.

Three weeks later Mrs. M. died. The others were gone shortly after that.

That was the last year Mom made fudge. She didn't have the strength anymore. Dad and I tried to make it under her supervision but Mom was never satisfied with the texture.

The following year the Christmas tree went up in November and remained until February. Not only did Dad and I make the fudge, we tried our hand at Divinity, a confection my grandmother had made. We failed miserably at that as well.

I knew my mom was doing poorly; she didn't even get together with her family anymore. In August of 1978 my mother died. She was fifty-four.

Strangely enough I was okay. God did as I had asked of Him. She awoke one morning not knowing where she was. The cancer had spread to her brain. She was afraid to leave her home so I nursed her there.

She smiled at me two weeks later as I tucked her into her bed. "I'm tired," she whispered.

"I know. It's okay if you let go, now. I'm okay; so is Dad."

Mom died in her sleep that night.

I had realized on that Christmas day with our four guests that there were a lot of "forgotten" people around, especially senior citizens. After my mom died I found myself spending more and more time with my cancer patients, giving them simple pleasures like afternoon teas, picnics in the warm sun. Pumpkin carving. Homemade fudge. Holidays weren't really necessary anymore. I had learned to cherish each moment of each day.

My dad took my mom's death much harder than I had imagined he would. I tried to spend as much time as I could with him. In December I asked if he had set up the Christmas tree yet and he shook his head no. Three days before Christmas I tried to help him, but his heart wasn't in it.

"Dad, if you don't want to do this, it's fine by me," I said. "You and I can change the traditions, you know. We can do Chinese food and see a movie. Or go on a vacation."

"But what about your mother's tree?"

"I know what we can do," I said cheerfully. "Come on."

We packed up the tree and all of the decorations and drove to the hospital where we gave it a new home on one of the chronic care units that didn't have a tree. The patients and staff were thrilled.

My dad gave me a nervous glance. "You're really okay with this?"

And that was the moment I knew I'd never celebrate Christmas again. Didn't need to. I was celebrating life every day.

I smiled at him. "Yeah, Dad. I'm doing great."

— Pamela Goldstein —

51

Dad and the Grand Canyon

The desert tells a different story every time
one ventures on it.
~Robert Edison Fulton, Jr.

"**D**ad is there anything on your bucket list that you missed? Anything that you wish you could do before you leave us?" I asked sadly as I watched Dad struggle for his next breath.

Dad's eyes brimmed with tears. He whispered, "I've only been to the Grand Canyon six times. My favourite number is seven. It's my favourite spot on earth."

"Well, Dad, how about we ditch this place and enjoy our last road trip together?"

His eyes sparkled, his face took on a new life, even his breathing seem to improve.

"What about your work, Barb? Can you afford it? How am I going to get out of this dark, dingy, stinky hospital?" he asked apprehensively.

"I can't afford not to go Dad. I'd never forgive myself if I didn't at least try to grant your dying wish," I answered.

"Then why are you still standing here? Go find that doctor!" His voice got stronger and more excited by the minute.

I hunted down Dr. Pierce and told him about our plan. Shaking his head, he asked, "Are you prepared to bring your father home in a box?"

"Dad, do you mind coming home in a box?" I laughingly asked.

"Throw me down the canyon and I will be in heaven there," he answered, laughing back.

"I don't advise it," Dr. Pierce stated emphatically. "I will not discharge him. You will have to take him without my permission. Please think this through, I'm begging you. Your father is one sick man."

I packed Dad's few things and we escaped that drab hospital room, ambling out into the cold December air. Dad's colour came back into his cheeks. He said that the fresh air was healing him. I think it was just the cold air burning his face, but he insisted that he hadn't felt this good in a long time. I never saw his smile broader or his shoulders squarer. There was a spring in his shuffling steps. Dad was not the weak, tired, sick man we had brought in a week ago with an enlarged heart.

On December 2nd, bright and early at 6 a.m., I packed the car, said a prayer to St. Joseph for a safe and enjoyable trip, and we hit the road. The Grand Canyon was not just Dad's favourite place but mine too!

We drove for two hours and stopped in Kalamazoo, Michigan for breakfast. Dad ordered bacon and eggs. He'd had enough of that soggy toast and watered-down orange juice. "A healthy man eats meat and potatoes," Dad stated.

Besides inhaling his breakfast, Dad also interviewed people at the surrounding tables to see who would make a suitable husband for me. "She's all alone and way too much for an old man like me to handle," Dad said, chuckling.

"Smiling Archie" was Dad's nickname. Always a tease, he outdid himself that morning. His body might have been compromised, but his sense of humour was still as devious as ever.

Once back in the car, we both sang along with our favourite country songs. The day before, Dad had been fighting for his every breath. Today he belted out songs as if he were performing on stage.

Further on our drive, Dad insisted we stop at the Meramec

Caverns. Our eyes burned with tears of amazement and we held our breath as we witnessed God's majestic handiwork above and below the ground. The beauty of the multi-coloured stalactites and stalagmites was awe-inspiring.

Dad's water pills and my tiny bladder made it impossible to pass any rest stops. We both got restless and loved to stretch our legs. Dad couldn't wait to strike up a conversation with fellow travelers. "Where you all from? Can't believe the traffic, eh?" Smiling Archie made friends with everyone.

In Oklahoma, Dad insisted that we look for a Western shop. He wanted to buy a suit and a red shirt with tassels to be buried in. Dad loved the colour red. He got his wish.

Northern Texas presented us with large ranches, but New Mexico was our favourite with a multi-coloured, wondrous surprise at each twist and turn. But the roads were treacherous. We were lucky to be alive when we pulled into the Best Western in Albuquerque. The snow was so thick that it was impossible to drive and the roads ahead were impassable for three days. Dad became fidgety.

He mapped out a new route, and the next morning we headed south to Tucson. He loved the cactus in the desert and needed to say goodbye to them too, especially the saguaros, his favourite.

That night Dad was sore and decided to soak in the bathtub. I ordered in dinner. When dinner arrived I knocked at the bathroom door.

"Dad, the pizza is here," I announced.

"Help, help, potlicker!" Potlicker was his favourite word when he got stressed or annoyed. He sounded desperate.

"Dad, are you okay. Do you need help?" I was suddenly scared.

"I'm stuck, and I can't get out!" He sounded frightened.

I banged open the door and found Dad wedged in, his shoulders stuck under the lip of the tiny bathtub, his knees bent and his feet under the faucet. I tried soaping his shoulders. I tried pulling his arms. I rubbed him and the tub with baby oil to grease him out.

"Gosh darn it, Dad, wiggle yourself out or we'll have to call the firemen."

"If you do, I'll kill you," he snapped.

I panicked and ran to call the front desk. But he finally squirmed himself loose. "I'm out, now put down that blasted phone!"

Once I saw that he was all right, I laughed. I still can't control myself when I think back to Dad's bathtub imprisonment.

The next day, Dad's dream came true. If I could put a face on happiness, it would have been Dad's that day on the south rim of his beloved Grand Canyon. It was an emotional, spiritual experience for both of us. I took a dozen pictures of him glowing with joy and appreciation. Two minutes later, as I snapped pictures, Dad slouched down to the ground. His breathing was laboured, his face chalky and he was soaked with perspiration. His pulse was weak and he couldn't speak.

"Oh my God, Dad, can you hear me?" I screamed.

People came running. Someone called 911. We helped Dad to the car and crossed the road to the nearest hotel. Dad refused the ambulance. We stayed at that hotel for the next three days. Enough of his strength finally came back that we could drive home. He insisted on one last look at his heaven.

The drive home was quieter. No boisterous singing, no embarrassing me, not much conversation. But by the third day, Dad picked up again. His silliness returned, his voice was teasing and strong, his whole manner was light and bright. "We are stopping at Gene and Louise's home in Arkansas," he announced.

"We're doing what? Are you kidding me?" I asked.

"You heard me. I always stop there on my way back from the Canyon," Dad declared.

Gene and Louise were his first cousins. Dad and Gene hung around together as children and were great friends. Louise, a talented, beautiful, funny lady, was a joy to know and love. We spent two glorious days with them and their family listening to music, reminiscing and playing cards. Dad was back in all his glory.

On the way home, just before Cincinnati, Dad bellowed: "Pull over! You heard me. If I have to spend one more day in this car with you behind the wheel, I'm going to wish that I was dead!"

He drove the rest of the way home. He had a new lease on life.

We got to enjoy him for an additional nine months.

I still remember Dad's last words to my sister Cathy, my brother Gerry, and myself: "I love you! And you! And you!" He looked at each one of us with pride in his heart, love in his eyes, and contentment and peace in his soul.

With his bucket list complete, Dad went into God's welcoming arms in his new handsome Western suit and his red tasselled shirt.

Every five years, we children make a pilgrimage to the Grand Canyon to honour and visit our adventurous, loving Dad's spirit.

— Barbara Bondy-Pare —

52

Family Day

*Being a family means you are a part of something very
wonderful. It means you will love and be loved
for the rest of your life.*
~Lisa Weedn

I love Family Day. It's a Canadian holiday that occurs during
the same weekend as President's Day in the U.S. It was created
to give people a chance to spend more time with those they
cherish most, and that's exactly what we do. I plan something
every year to celebrate it. It's become one of my favourite days of the
year, a blissful time with my two boys and my amazing husband,
Mike.

It also always reminds me of the day I learned the true meaning
of family.

Right after finishing university, I got married and enrolled in a
college to get some more hands-on education. While going to school,
I also worked in a group home for adults with mental and physical
disabilities. It was there that I met Terry, a thirty-eight-year-old man
with Down syndrome. Terry had the mental capacity of a small child…
but one of the biggest hearts of anyone I've ever met.

Unlike many of the other residents, Terry hadn't grown up in
facility housing. He'd always lived with his mom and dad, until they
passed away. I could see that the drastic change in lifestyle was a difficult adjustment for him. Terry and I quickly formed a bond. I'd look
forward to seeing him every day. We'd often have coffee and donuts

together, or dance in the living room, two of Terry's favourite activities. He was funny, caring, and loved the *Three Stooges*. He was my friend.

Two years flew by. During the week of my college graduation, my first husband and I learned that we were expecting a baby. As the months passed and my delivery date grew closer, I felt both happy and sad. Though thrilled that I would soon be a mother, I knew that once I was on maternity leave, I wouldn't get to see Terry regularly anymore. Then it hit me. *I should just take Terry home to live with me.*

I know it sounds crazy, maybe just a result of all the pregnancy hormones. All I knew was it was the right decision. After countless conversations and a towering stack of paperwork, a forty-year-old, five-foot tall, stocky Ukrainian man with Down syndrome moved into my house. When Terry first moved in with me, his skills and vocabulary weren't the best. His parents had done pretty much everything for him, and even in the group home it had been largely the same.

I knew that with a baby on the way I had to start teaching Terry more life skills. It was a slow process, but he was gradually catching on to the basics, day by day. I never felt frustrated, because it just felt right to have his beautiful energy in the house. When Michael was born, Terry immediately fell in love with him, and affectionately nicknamed him Bugaboo — a funny name that stuck for years.

Michael's first year was wonderful, and Terry was right by his side for everything. To my surprise, Terry was absorbing everything I was teaching Michael. As the years passed, Michael and Terry became inseparable. They were the very best of friends. And as Michael's abilities increased, so did Terry's. They learned a lot from each other. We never really discussed who Terry was in our lives, and Michael never thought to ask. Terry had just always been there, eternal and beloved.

When strangers would ask Michael if he had any siblings, he would respond, "No, but I have a Terry!" It was cute.

Then one day, when we were out getting Michael's hair cut, something happened that forever changed the way I thought about family.

While the stylist cut his hair, she asked him questions like, "Are you in school?" "What grade are you in?" "Do you like your teacher?" He confidently answered all her questions with his adorable little voice. And then she asked him if he had any brothers and sisters. Michael responded, "Yes I do. I have a brother named Terry and he's forty-five years old!"

"Forty-five!" the hairstylist responded, confused. "Don't you mean four or five years old?"

"Nope, he's forty-five!"

I looked up from the magazine I was reading. I laughed, but as I thought about his answer, I realized the significance of what he'd just said. On the drive home I asked Michael why he told the hairstylist that Terry was his brother. In a very matter-of-fact way, he said, "Because he is and I love him." I was dumbfounded by his incredibly profound answer. I drove home speechless, tears rolling down my face.

Without being taught or told, my five-year-old had figured out that we were a family.

From that day forward I introduced Terry as Michael's brother. Some of the looks and questions I received over the years were hilarious. Terry lived with us for more than thirteen amazing years, until his health deteriorated and he needed to move into a nursing home. In that time I watched Michael quickly evolve into the role of big brother, even though Terry was forty years his senior. Michael read to him, protected him, cared for him, and watched him grow older. They were truly brothers.

We all miss Terry a lot, but what he brought to our family can never be replaced. He taught us that family doesn't just exist in the DNA. Family is a feeling. Family is love. Since Terry left us, we continued growing our family unconventionally. Many of Michael's friends have lived in our house at times, and all of them are considered close family members. Though they've left the nest and moved on, they're still in our lives and still in our hearts.

For Family Day this year, I arranged for my family to celebrate at a new restaurant that had just opened. To my great surprise, as the afternoon progressed, all the friends who have called our house a home stopped by, one by one, to celebrate this day with us. As I sat there listening to everyone joke and share stories, I thought about Terry and the gift he brought our family.

In reality, I only have a small family, but to me it's larger than life. And what a life it is.

— Heidi Allen —

53

The Last Time

*Only in the agony of parting do we look into
the depths of love.*
~George Eliot

The last time I looked into his eyes, I couldn't see him. He was dying. The nurse said he couldn't hear me. I knew he could.

"Oh my love, stay a little longer," I whispered.

The only sounds in the room were the machines keeping him alive and his son's weeping as he held his father's hand, willing him to live.

I had gotten the call at work. My daughter's frightened voice asked me to go to her father's side; he had suffered a major stroke that morning and was not expected to make it. She lives at the other end of the country and was scrambling to find a flight. Her brother was on his way to the hospital and she didn't want him to be alone.

All the way to the hospital, I gulped deep breaths of air, my stomach threatened to turn, and my hands shook. I couldn't believe he was dying. Dying? He was far too young. Trepidation seeped through my mixed emotions as I approached the hospital. The waiting room was filled to overflowing with family, and ex-wives.

We had been divorced for many years, and I wasn't sure what kind of reaction I would receive; anger, disbelief at my presence, indifference. I needn't have worried. From the moment I entered the waiting room, they opened their arms and hearts to me. His brothers and sisters held me. We cried together. And I knew I was where I should be.

"David's on his way and Marlene is taking the first flight out," I assured them.

"Do you want me to go in with you?" asked my ex-brother-in-law.

"No, I need time to be alone with him."

When I entered the room, I was overwhelmed with grief. He looked so small, surrounded by machines, a myriad of tubes threatening to engulf him. My first reaction was to touch his forehead with my lips as I had done so many times with my children, looking for a fever. I shook my head in disbelief. Imagine... looking for a fever?

As I took his hand in mine, our son, David, came in and together we began the vigil — the final journey. David reached out to me and as I held him, his thirty years melted away. He was a toddler once again, needing solace.

Too soon, the doctor told him, "Let him go. There is no hope; his system is closing down." Such a terrible decision for a son to make; my heart broke as I watched him nod his head.

"Yes," he whispered, "It's time."

One by one, his family came in to say goodbye. The machines were turned off, the tubing removed and soon all that remained was the soft whisper of his breathing. The silence frightened me. I had to accept that we were no longer fighting, but accepting the inevitable.

I was surprised at the intensity of my feelings. I thought that I had divorced my memories when I divorced him, but there they were, turning back the hands of time.

I remembered the young man I had danced with and married; the arms that had held me with such tenderness and love; the young father who wiped his children's tears and kissed them better. I had not been in love with him for many years, but I knew that I would always love this man. I often wished that things could have been different, that our first brush with love had bloomed into the "ever after" kind, but fate had a different road for me to travel.

I leaned over and whispered into his ear, "It's okay, go to your father — he's waiting."

We sat on either side of his bed, holding his hands, waiting. His breathing was barely audible. I lifted his hand up and said, "Okay, Da."

I am sure that his father took his hand and walked with him as they took the path home. He died holding the hands of love and for the last time, I whispered, "I love you."

—Shirley Neal—

54

Chicken Soup for the Soul

Worth More than Money

All that I am or ever hope to be,
I owe to my angel Mother.
~Abraham Lincoln

I slid my arms into my old gray coat and buttoned it as I looked at the wear around the sleeves. I hated that coat. Hated having hand-me-downs that neighbours had discarded as not good enough for themselves.

Biting my tongue, I forced a smile as Mom handed me my school lunch. "You could use a new coat," she said. "We'll have to see what we can do about that." She patted my shoulder as I hurried out the door, hoping she didn't see the tears in my eyes.

Seeing what she could do about it meant she'd find another old, used-up coat for me. I brushed the tears away and took a deep breath. The fall air was getting crisper. Soon winter would be upon us. I shivered, pulling my coat tightly around me. It did little good to wish that my parents had money like my friends' parents had. With six kids to feed, there was little cash left to spend on clothes and I couldn't remember when my mother had ever had a new coat. I told myself that I'd better get used to wearing castoffs. At least I had a coat, even if it wasn't fancy.

"Look what the neighbours sent over," Mom said, a few days later. She was beaming as she caressed a soft, short-sleeved sweater. She handed it to me. "This will look lovely on you. The collar is so soft."

I ran my fingers over the white angora collar. It was the softest thing I'd ever felt and added a beautiful touch to the bright red of the sweater.

"And look at these," she continued, as she lay two skirts side-by-side on the sofa.

My jaw dropped. One skirt was pink and the other was light blue. My older sister and I could each have one.

There were other things too, but these were my favourites. I lay awake a long time that night, suddenly grateful that our neighbours grew tired of their clothes.

The next morning I put on my old gray coat. I buttoned it, kissed Mom goodbye and turned toward the door. She was smiling. "Yes," she said, almost to herself, "you definitely need a new coat."

Mom had a twinkle in her eye and a hum on her lips for the next few days. She was up to something, but what?

The weather suddenly turned cold. I put an extra sweater under my old coat and tied a scarf around my neck, but the wind chilled me to the bone, long before I ever reached school. I was still shivering when I went to bed that night, and Mom looked worried.

I had a fitful sleep. My room was upstairs and therefore usually quiet, but that night I thought I heard a sewing machine whirring all night. I pulled the covers up to my neck and put the pillow over my head. Finally, I dozed off.

Wind whistled, blowing snow into drifts. I groaned the next morning as I looked out the window. I had to go to school and I shivered at the thought of another cold walk in my threadbare coat.

Mom looked tired as she made us breakfast. But there was a twinkle in her eye and she was back to humming.

As usual, I was the last one to leave for school. As I sullenly slid into my gray coat and began buttoning it, Mom said, "Why don't you leave that old thing at home?" Then, before I could answer she slipped into the living room, returning with a beautiful green coat that sported a real fur collar. "Try this on," she said proudly.

It fit perfectly. I marvelled at the softness of the green wool fabric, the heavy lining and the light-brown fur of the collar. "Where did you get it?" I was in awe.

She smiled. "It was in the box of clothes that we were given. I altered it to fit you."

"You mean, it was for a lady, and it would have fit you, Mom?"

"I suppose it might have," she nodded, reaching out to help me button the coat. "But you need a coat more than I do. And look how lovely it looks on you. Now hurry up, slowpoke, or you'll be late for school."

I wrapped my arms around my mother; my heart so filled will love for this woman who had always put her family's needs above her own. Who could ever ask for more than that? My friends' families might be better off financially than we were. But I had Mom, and she was worth far more than any amount of money.

— Chris Mikalson —

55

Boeuf Bourguignon

For some moments in life there are no words.
~David Seltzer, Willy Wonka
and the Chocolate Factory

Tuna casserole. Spaghetti and meatballs. Pork chops with sautéed mushrooms, and classic fried chicken. Towards the end of my first pregnancy, my mother began to fill my freezer with all of these and more. Several times a week she would drop off a portion of their dinner from the night before, a foil container neatly labeled with the contents, the date, and reheating instructions. I was to keep these containers in our rapidly filling deep freeze until after the baby came.

"Why on earth do I need so much food?" I was astounded by the sheer volume of frozen dinners waiting to be consumed. "I'm just having a baby, you know. It's not like I'm getting a limb amputated."

To this my mother shook her head, obviously in possession of some knowledge that I wasn't privy to, and simply brought over more food. Though I really thought that she was going overboard, I kept on rearranging my freezer, knowing that each of these containers had been filled with love — even those with the spaghetti, which after twenty-seven years I still wasn't able to convince my mother I hated.

Two weeks before Julie, our baby girl, was due, the unthinkable happened. Sitting in a hospital bed after delivering a stillborn infant, the words on everyone's lips were, inevitably, "You have to eat."

I didn't want to eat. What was the point? Not to mention that the very smell of the food that was delivered on a plastic tray to my bedside made me ill, saturating the air as it did with scents that were full of life.

"Eat something. Even if you don't want to, you have to eat something." These words came from my doctor as we prepared to leave the hospital, to go home and try to make sense of our lives.

"Yeah, right." The frustration that I felt at everyone's insistence that I eat — in effect, that I go on living when I didn't want to — threatened to boil over.

The doc wasn't the only one. We arrived home to find a pantry stocked by a well-meaning aunt. Deli meat, crusty rolls, pickles and fresh fruit. Cookies and crackers, fancy cheeses and paté.

When someone dies, people bring food. That's just what they do, and my aunt was no different. But though I knew that all of this food had been provided with love, I still couldn't bring myself to eat anything.

The food just kept coming. Friends, neighbours, more relatives — everyone brought something. And truthfully, I preferred a potato chip encrusted casserole to a bouquet of flowers that would wither and die before my eyes. But still I couldn't force anything down my gullet.

Three days after we'd arrived home from the hospital, someone — I can't remember who — announced that it was dinnertime.

I could have cared less. I went upstairs for a bath, and spent an hour crying salty tears that evaporated in the steam.

But when I went back downstairs, wrapped in my husband's housecoat, I saw that my father-in-law had opened one of my mother's foil containers. It lay empty on the counter, a wine red residue staining its innards, and the cardboard lid soggy and discarded in the sink.

In a pot on the stove was my mother's boeuf bourguignon. A dish made with stew meat, baby potatoes, onions and red wine, it was far from my favourite thing to eat. In fact, it would probably have languished in the freezer for months, being pulled out for consumption only when there was nothing else left but spaghetti.

But something about the sight of that container on the counter changed things. As I smelled the tang of the meat and the wine, my stomach rumbled, protesting its nearly week-long emptiness.

Still, I wasn't sure I could actually force anything in, or that if I did, it would stay down.

I filled a bowl mechanically anyway, and added one of the crusty buns that my aunt had purchased that lay in an open bag beside the stove.

Curling up next to my husband on the sofa, steaming bowl in hand, I took a bite. It was hot, and I could trace the path of the scalding liquid all the way down to my gut. But somehow, some way, that hot boeuf bourguignon began to thaw something inside of me. So I kept eating, lifting spoonful after spoonful to my mouth.

When I took the bowl back to the kitchen and saw that foil container, now empty, I began to cry again. This time, however, the tears were a little bit different, and at that moment I realized why my mother had been so diligent about filling those containers.

Though she hadn't anticipated the exact circumstances, she'd known that somewhere along the way I would need some help, some comfort and some love.

And though I'd initially been amused by her zealous efforts, had been annoyed by the food being heaped upon us by our nearest and dearest, I finally understood.

The food was her way of continuing to care for *her* baby. The food was love, and I wasn't alone.

—Lauren Murray—

56

The Cancer Christmas

Christmas is perhaps the only time in the year when
people can obey their natural impulses and express
their true sentiments without feeling self-conscious
and, perhaps, foolish.
~Francis C. Farley

The first Christmas after my father was diagnosed with brain cancer, I realized everything had changed. Up until his diagnosis, my father's life revolved around working. When I was growing up, I found that if he wasn't at the office, he was teaching me how to change the oil on our car, finishing my grandparents' basement, shushing us because he was listening to the stock reports, or forcing me to do fractions well before I understood them.

But he knew how to have fun, too. He was the one who picked us up and hurled us on the bed over and over again, while my brother and I bounced to our feet and begged for more. He showed us how to limbo under a broomstick. And, years later, when my first pregnancy ended in a stillborn baby girl, although he said little, he made her a blanket embroidered with her name and date of birth and death.

The summer of the following year, around his fifty-sixth birthday, my parents came to visit me and our new son, Max. Dad mentioned having trouble remembering people's names and having to work more slowly. Since I was an emergency room doctor, albeit on maternity leave, I asked if he wanted to come to the hospital to scan his head.

He said no, his family doctor had referred him to a memory clinic.

On November 2nd, the scan showed a tumour too deep to remove. When he first heard the news, his first reaction was, "I guess this means I can't work." His second was to point at my six-month-old son, Max, and say, "I just wish I could watch this one grow up." His third was to tell me and my brother, "I've done what I needed to do. Take care of your mother."

By Christmas, the first treatments had already taken their toll. The anti-epileptic drugs gave him a rash. The high-dose steroids made him dizzy and hungry and moon-faced. And who knew what side effects came from the radiation. But he still kept nearly all of his hair and he looked much the same. He was just very, very tired.

I didn't realize how tired until my family came to visit for Christmas. Dad posed for pictures in the kitchen. He put presents under the tree. He accepted his stocking. He even offered to take care of baby Max, since his number one goal in life was to be useful. But when I searched for them fifteen minutes later, I found Dad sitting on the toilet lid while Max ripped handfuls of paper off the toilet paper roll and threw them on the floor, cackling with delight.

The environmentalist inside my breast cried out, "No! Toilet paper comes from trees!" The clean freak in me yelled, "What a mess!" But I bit my tongue. I realized that my father was too exhausted to carry Max or push toy cars on the floor with him. The most he could offer his beloved grandson was one treat his mother never allowed: destroying toilet paper.

I wish I could say that I laughed with them, but I wasn't that enlightened. I cleaned up the paper and carted Max away so my father could rest.

The following Christmas, my father was hospitalized. He'd fallen several times at home. He needed two people's help to stand up, so he couldn't even go home on a day pass. And I have to say, despite the candy cane decorations and the tinsel on the ceiling, it saddened my heart that my father was spending Christmas on the cancer ward. But when I brought Max to see him, Dad opened his eyes and started to play.

I was amazed. How could this man, who couldn't even sit up on his own, play with his nineteen-month-old grandson?

Each patient had received a small Christmas stocking filled with candy. The oncology nurse pulled a small candy cane out of Dad's. Max had never tasted a candy cane before, but he sucked on a small piece and smiled.

My father took a piece of candy cane into his own mouth. Then, using his lips, he pushed it back out toward Max.

Max giggled and reached for it.

Dad pulled the candy cane back into his mouth. Then, after Max gave up, Dad pushed it out again: peekaboo!

Max laughed and laughed.

I stood silently by the hospital bed. My father had lost nearly everything: his ability to work, his sharp intelligence and memory, and even his ability to walk to the bathroom by himself. But this holiday season, he had not forgotten how to love or how to make his grandson laugh.

And maybe I had learned something, too, because when Dad said he didn't want any presents this year, I understood. I asked my family to write letters to him instead. We gathered around his bedside and took turns reading stories about our time together and how much we appreciated him. Dad snuggled in bed and closed his eyes in order to concentrate on our words. And so, before he died in May, we were able to tell him exactly how much we loved him.

I can't say this was my best Christmas, because it was mired in sadness. But it did teach me the spirit of Christmas: love.

— Melissa Yuan-Innes —

57

Home

There is nothing more important than a good,
safe, secure home.
~Rosalynn Carter

Has it really been fourteen years since I was placed into the invisible hands of the government? Fourteen years since social services first gained control of my life?

After all this time, I remember it so clearly, as if it were only yesterday. I was eight years old and sitting in a group home waiting patiently for my mom. Unfortunately, she did not return. Three months later, I found myself in a foster home. From that day on, my life became a case file; just a large manila folder held snugly under the arm of a complete stranger.

I learned to accept a foster home as I saw it; a place that I stayed. It was not a home to me but merely a house with four walls and a roof, just a building that social services deemed fit for my living requirements. It was a place that I slept and ate in, but it held nothing for me — no love, no family and no values.

I spent the first five years of foster care envying my friends, secretly wishing for everything that they had. I wanted to know what it felt like to be so loved. I yearned to have a real home. I wanted so much to belong, to know what it was like to not feel like an intruder in somebody else's home. I ached deeply to not spend each day believing that I owed those people something for accepting me into their house.

At thirteen, right after I spent three months in the hospital for anorexia nervosa, I learned that I would be leaving the foster home that I had been in for the past five years, and I was going to be placed in a new foster home. I really didn't believe things could get much worse. It felt as though my world was crashing down upon me once more. I cried at the cold realization that my foster family was not going to show me the meaning of "home."

The tears fell for days as I slowly began to understand. A home in my world was like a fairy tale, a far off place of magical beings and magical events where everything would end in love and happiness. I envisioned a world that could make me feel wonder and fascination, but deep in my heart, I felt like such a place could not truly exist. I had never known "home," and I suspected that this would always remain the same for me.

I was sent to what they call a relief home after I got out of the hospital. It felt comfortable, and the family was very loving. I felt at ease the moment I stepped within the warm, cozy walls. But I knew I could not get too comfortable, because shortly, I would be sent to my new foster home. Then, when my two weeks in the relief home were nearly up and my anticipation and terror of being sent to a new home were in full force, the world I had come to know changed.

My relief family sat me down at the kitchen table one evening just before bed, and they all looked at me. The mom spoke in gentle, soothing words.

"We know that you have gone through a lot after finding out that you were not returning to your first foster home." She went on with a quiet breath, "And we don't want to scare you off, or force you into any decision that you don't want to make, but we really want you to stay here with us and be a part of our family."

I stared at her in shock. I couldn't believe what I was hearing. The others smiled.

"We want you to think about it. Take as much time as you need." I nodded and quietly rose from the table and went to the room where I had been staying while I was living there. I put my pyjamas on, lay down in bed and silently cried. They weren't just tears of sadness, but also tears of happiness and tears of relief. A part of my life was ending and now a greater part of my life was about to begin. If I would let it.

Later that night, as my tears finally began to dry, the youngest daughter popped her head into my room. "Are you asleep?" she asked. I shook my head in reply. "Have you made a decision yet?" This time I nodded, and she waited for my answer. Without thinking any more about it, I replied with a quiet "yes."

"She's going to stay!" she yelled as she ran out of the room.

I slowly got out of bed and prepared to be welcomed by my new family. I smiled as I walked out the door. For the first time in my life, I felt I belonged. For the first time in my life, I felt comfortable and cared for. For the first time in my life, I was a daughter and a sister. I was finally a normal girl.

For the first time in my life, I truly knew home.

— Cynthia Lynn Blatchford —

58

Writing on the Wall

Let love and faithfulness never leave you;
bind them around your neck, write them
on the tablet of your heart.
~Proverbs 3:3

Colourful chalk designs on summer sidewalks had always brought a smile to my face, whether I was the artist or the admirer. But I never expected that finding chalk markings on the interior walls of my house as an adult would have the same result, or that I would be the artist!

Between picking up socks and sweeping away dust bunnies from under my sons' beds, I came across a discarded piece of white chalk. The idea came to me in the instant I touched it, and I pursued it before my mom-mind caught up with me. I took to the walls with that chalk and wrote each of my sons a note, listing some of the many things I love about them.

Satisfied with my work, I headed to my own room to pick up socks and clear out the dust bunnies from under my bed. Upon coming up from under the frame, I came face-to-face with the empty space of blue wall above the bed that my husband and I have been blessed to share for thirteen-some years. The words I had written on my sons' walls rolled through my mind, and a question formed in my heart: What words would I have for my spouse? I sat on the edge of the bed for a moment and allowed this thought to linger.

Words have always held great value to me. The very words of

the promises and love that God has for me have built up my faith and relationship with Him. I began to think of all these promises and gifts of words that have been written on my walls — the walls of my heart. These words were given at times when I needed to recall that I was loved and cared for unconditionally. As a mother, it took little persuasion to give similar words to my little men, but what about my husband? Did I have words to offer to him? Was I willing to give the gift of words to build and form our relationship? Could I write on his wall?

Ignoring the freshly folded sheets and well-placed pillows, I retrieved the chalk, stood on the bed, and began to write words for my spouse. Even after thirteen years of not-always-wedded-bliss, but of real-life love, I offered the very same gift that is constantly bestowed unto me — words of affirmation and love. As I stepped off the bed, and re-adjusted the sheets and pillows, I smiled.

When my husband came home that day, the boys excitedly showed him their messages. As he entered our room to change after his long day of work, I could almost feel the smile on his face as he took in the message written for him on the wall above our bed. Words don't come easily from me in my marriage, but they are worth all the effort. As God continues daily to write His messages of love and affirmation on the walls of my heart, I can continue to pass on messages of love and affirmation on the walls of my spouse's heart in the hope that our relationship will not only represent the one we can have with our Heavenly Father, but so that it can be built upon the foundation of it.

— Angela Wolthuis —

59

"What If..."

We must love men ere they will seem to us
unworthy of our love.
~William Shakespeare

I was working in the high tech sector of Ottawa when I was sent to a one-week database course downtown.

Each day that week, I enjoyed a nice casual walk downtown during my lunch hour to unwind from the complexity of the program. Two days before the end of my course, while on my walk, I noticed a terrible unavoidable stench of urine coming from a homeless man who had just walked by me. My first reaction was of repugnance as I walked away farther from him. Then, for some inexplicable reason, I decided to sit nearby and observe this man. Downtown Ottawa had plenty of homeless people, but something told me to keep my eyes on this particular one.

What I saw next truly shocked me. He stood near a storefront and simply let the urine run down his pants. First I was appalled, then a compassionate thought came to me with the reality that he most likely had been kicked out of every establishment and was not welcomed anywhere in such condition.

How sad, I thought, to see a grown man get to the point where he no longer cared for his own presence, who probably had nobody caring for him. How low and rejected he must have felt. Still, with perceptible pessimism, he had enough strength to go on one more day.

I went from feeling disgusted and numb, to feeling overwhelmed by sadness.

Realizing that this man was probably hungry and cold, I rushed to the nearest fast food restaurant, where I purchased a warm bowl of chicken soup, a sandwich, and a warm cup of coffee. With hesitation, I approached him, wondering how he would react. As I offered him the meal, my fear dissipated when he gently reached to take the free lunch. His eyes hardly rose to meet mine. Then, he gave me a humble "thank you" and a grateful smile.

I looked at my watch and realized that my afternoon class was about to start. I ran to the building where my course was taking place, just a couple of blocks away.

That afternoon, all the sophisticated database tools and lectures seemed quite irrelevant. I found myself drifting and thinking about the man and the mystery of his life. This was not the first time I had offered food to a homeless person, but something about this man truly captured me in a deep and puzzling way.

That night I had a very vivid dream. I saw my own dad as the one being rejected by his family and society. In my dream, my dad was the one now living in the streets and looking and smelling just like the man I had seen the day before. The dream felt truly real, and so was my frustration and feeling of helplessness to get him back on his feet, back to his family and feeling of self-worth.

Waking up from this terrible nightmare gave me great relief. It had all just been a dream! However, as the day unfolded, I kept wondering,

What if that had really happened to my dad, or someone else I loved dearly. What if the man I saw the day before had lost someone who he loved and missed dearly?

I felt the urge to do something. Something that would help him believe that he could have a fresh new start, something that would give him a sense of self-worth.

In a flash I had a very clear vision of what I was going to do next.

During my lunch hour, on the last day of my course, I bought this man a "Caring Kit" containing a new comb, mirror, shaver, soap, nail clippers, aftershave, a towel, underwear, socks, pants, shirt, some food and snacks, and a specially chosen card. Feeling an unbelievable boost, I carefully packed them all together in a zippered bag and included the card I picked for him. It had a quote from the Bible with a reassuring message that God is never too far and His love is eternal.

I eagerly anticipated the end of my course. I kept checking the time and wondering if I was going to find this man again. During rush hour? Who was I kidding? What were the odds? He could be anywhere!

Regardless, I knew I had to try. If I could not find him, I would just find someone else who could still make use of all this stuff.

An inexplicable sense of being guided took over me. Without resistance, I started to walk in a totally opposite direction from the area where I had seen the man the previous day. I went down a few blocks and walked briskly, filled with purpose, while mentally questioning if indeed I was heading in the right direction. Regardless, I continued to walk farther and farther away. I was now quite a few blocks from where I had started and at this point I told myself that when I reached the next corner, if I did not see him there, I would simply turn around and take the bus home.

When I reached that corner, I felt shivers down my spine.

The man I was looking for was standing at that intersection.

I found myself quickly searching for the right words to say. I paused for a moment. Then I walked toward him and asked, "Excuse me, what is your name?"

He looked up and with a faint voice he said, "My name is Danny."

I took a pen from my bag and wrote his name on the envelope holding the card I had carefully chosen for him. As I handed the card and the bag with the gifts I said, "Danny, your guardian angel has sent me to you. This is for you."

His eyes lit up, and the smile on his face said it all. "Thank you, thank you, thank you," he said as he anxiously looked inside the bag like a kid opening a present on his birthday. Then he briskly walked away.

I felt blessed and filled with incredible joy.

I never saw Danny in the streets of downtown Ottawa again. I often wonder how he is. I pray for him and wish him a better life with dignity, self-respect, and love for God.

And I wonder, "What if..."

— Miriam Mas —

Chapter 6

Doggone Kind

60

Choosing Ophelia

Acquiring a dog may be the only time a person
gets to choose a relative.
~Author Unknown

O phelia is the dog we almost didn't want. My son's living arrangement wasn't working out and, unable to find a place that allowed pets, he debated whether he could keep his new German Shepherd puppy. Adding to his stress were complications with his job and the ending of a long-term relationship.

I will never forget Barrett sitting on our kitchen floor with three-month-old Ophelia in his arms as we discussed the possibility of returning her to the breeder. "She's such a wonderful dog," he kept saying, while she looked up at him trustingly. There was an edge of grief in his voice.

After several discussions, my husband and I suggested Barrett move back home until he found a place to live. "But you don't want a dog," Barrett said.

He was right, we didn't. "We'll make it work," I promised.

Ophelia arrived with her crate, toys, dishes, and puppy food. A timid little soul, she soaked up hugs and praise, and couldn't seem to get enough of us. I braced myself for dog hair drifting across the floor, "toilet training" gone awry, chewed furniture, and a house that smelled doggy.

Accidents did happen; in fact, one morning I almost stepped in a large, fragrant one in the kitchen. She chewed through the phone cord and tore off a chunk of wallpaper with a ripping sound that brought me running. The vacuum cleaner remained permanently plugged in. Sometimes the house smelled like a dog.

But something else happened, too. A miraculous creature with a passion for stealing socks and an astounding capacity to give and receive love bounded into my heart. In my mind's eye life is now divided into Before Ophelia and After Ophelia.

Before Ophelia, I was annoyed by a cupboard door left ajar. Before Ophelia, a speck on the couch was vacuumed immediately. And no one could wear shoes in the house Before Ophelia. After Ophelia, not even a dog hair floating in my coffee, or muddy paw prints on the sliding door fazed me.

Now a year old, Ophelia follows us from room to room, reluctant to be separated for even a few minutes. Her greeting when we come home is equally joyous, whether we've been gone half an hour or all day.

Her beautiful tail almost reaches the floor. Her huge ears stand up perfectly and her coat is glossy and soft except for a bit of unruly business on her back that swirls crazily like a cowlick and makes me laugh.

One day Ophelia and I were interviewed by Vicky, Recreation Manager and Volunteer Coordinator of Chateau Gardens, a long-term care residence. Ophelia's enthusiastic interest in people and sweet spirit made her a good candidate for pet therapy.

"Where's your leash?" I asked.

She looked at me, head cocked, expectation shining in her dark eyes.

"Get your leash, Ophelia," I said. "Let's go."

She smiled (German Shepherds can mimic an owner's smile), bounced out of the room and came back, carrying her leash in her mouth, tail wagging excitedly; at fifty-nine centimetres that tail has sent cups on the coffee table crashing to the floor.

She took up the entire back seat of my Echo, ears brushing the roof, and watched as I fastened my seatbelt and turned the key.

Vicky met us outside and we sat on a bench where Ophelia promptly decided to leap on me. Vicky laughed, which seemed to egg on Ophelia. She rolled on her back, legs in the air and began chewing on her leash.

"Ophelia!" I said sternly. This wasn't going the way I envisioned.

As we chatted, Ophelia jumped on Vicky, tried to chase a bird, and ripped open her bag of treats. By now my reassurances that she was well behaved sounded feeble and contrived.

But Vicky was encouraging and gave Ophelia a pat on the head before sending us on our way with paperwork to fill out. We were scheduled for our first visit in a few weeks; Torin, a resident with multiple sclerosis, couldn't wait to see us.

To my surprise, Torin appeared to be in his forties and beamed at us despite a debilitating battle with his disease. Before coming to live at Chateau Gardens, he owned a German Shepherd named Whitney. Giving her up broke his heart; and when he heard she'd been put down, the wound was ripped open again.

Ophelia eagerly entered Torin's room, ears up and tail wagging. She snuffled his hand, into which I'd placed a doggy treat, put her paws on his pillow to get closer and then, to everyone's astonishment, made a gigantic leap into his hospital bed and lay down beside him.

I stood there, wondering in a sort of panic if such a thing was allowed and what the staff would do, but they crowded into the room and began clapping. Although Torin's body had betrayed and trapped him, it couldn't quite contain his laughter. He grinned and shook with almost soundless delight and tried to pet Ophelia with a pale, uncooperative hand. Ophelia put her head on her paws and snuggled closer.

I wouldn't have expected Ophelia to be such a natural for pet therapy. She is, after all, just a year old and brimming with energy, yet she's endlessly curious and gentle with the residents. She hops on their beds, pokes her head into purses, licks frail, trembling hands, does tricks for treats (her high-five is everyone's favourite), and gladly accepts petting and fondling. When I brought in cupcakes to celebrate Ophelia's first birthday, an elderly woman in a wheelchair couldn't stop giggling as Ophelia carefully licked all the icing off her fingers and then drank the water out of a Styrofoam cup she was holding.

Next month Ophelia and I are scheduled to begin orientation

with the St. John Ambulance Therapy Dog Program. The program has grown to become a recognized leader in animal-assisted therapy and is a wonderful opportunity for the two of us to work even more closely together, providing comfort and companionship.

To me, Ophelia is much more than a dog. She's a reminder each day that challenges are meant to be met as a family; the overwhelming and impossible become the strong, true lines and spacious rooms of a sanctuary we build together. Some of its finest features are designed by the most difficult circumstances.

Barrett's career as a pilot could take him almost anywhere, but I've told him that Ophelia stays. And I think he's okay with that. She is part of our family and she is loved. Her life has become entwined with the lonely and vulnerable, and the joy of it fills us both every time we enter Chateau Gardens. It's there when she looks up at me and nudges my hand with her nose as we walk down the hall, and in the way she expectantly enters a resident's room.

One of the nurses said it well, "You don't choose an animal; it chooses you."

— Rachel Wallace-Oberle —

Dirty Harry

Courage is almost a contradiction in terms. It means a
strong desire to live taking the form of readiness to die.
~G.K. Chesterton

He was a downright plain, homely dog. A big old mutt with matted, orangey-brown hair hanging over his eyes and tangles all over his skeletal body. His breath reeked of rotted meat, onions and other garbage he'd been scavenging from the community dump where, my husband and I guessed, the aging animal had been abandoned when his callous owners moved away from the small northern community where we were living.

Remembering back, I didn't want to keep the mangy stray who limped into our back yard and sprang into my kids' hearts faster than I could say "no." But what's a mother to do when her three children are bawling their heads off to save a pitiful animal from certain death? After all, the pathetic dog had already been wounded by a gunshot to its hind leg — an indication that someone was trying to put the nuisance beast out of its misery.

So there came to our family a dog the kids named Dirty Harry. After a costly trip — more money than we could afford — to the vet in town to get the bullet removed as well as shots, pills and papers, Dirty Harry was on the mend.

I laid down the law. Dirty Harry could live in the garage and that was that! I don't know how it happened, but within days he was snoozing on the porch. Next thing I knew he had graduated to the laundry room. From there he took over the whole house. Sleeping, for that's mostly all he did, anywhere he wanted. Of course, by then, he had weaseled his way into our lives and there was no turning back.

At first I didn't think Dirty Harry liked me very much, for let's face it, it was I who had to do all the scolding when he chewed up the vacuum hose, ate carpeting or gnawed the runners off my rocking chair!

One late spring day when my husband was at work and the kids were in school, I decided to take Harry along with me up the hydro line that ran for miles through the woods behind our house. I had to do a photo shoot of some wildflowers and figured the walk would do him good.

I usually went alone on my picture-taking outings, but since the vet warned us that Harry was getting fat and needed more exercise, I coaxed him along.

That's how he happened to be with me on the trail that fateful day. And that's how he came to save my life. I was about a mile from home, kneeling on the ground trying to get a good close-up of a rare Pink Lady's Slipper. Dirty Harry had gulped his fill from a muddy puddle and, exhausted, had laid down in the shade to snooze.

In the quietness of the forest, I sensed something behind me and slowly rose and turned around. To my horror, not more than a few feet away stood a huge mother bear on her hind legs with two cubs romping playfully at her side.

The bear let out a roar, looking like she was ready to charge. I froze, too frightened to breathe. Usually Harry could sleep through anything, but the ferocious roar woke him up and, out of character, he sprang to his feet. In an amazing burst of speed, Dirty Harry dove at the bear.

The bear swept her huge paw at Harry and sent him flying and yelping through the air. He landed with a loud thud but, miraculously, was back on his feet and snarling at the bear with a protective viciousness I never knew he had.

After tossing the old dog a few more times in the air, the mother bear decided she'd had enough. The cubs had already disappeared into the gully and, after a final loud warning roar, she turned and took off.

I managed to catch my breath and ran to Harry. There was a huge gash in his shoulder and his stomach was torn and bleeding. He was whimpering but licked my hand when I laid it on him.

Until that moment, I had never shown the homely old dog much affection. For after all, I never really wanted a dog! But there I was, praying with all my heart to keep him.

I laid my face on his shoulder. He licked my cheek. Then he was gone. Dirty Harry taught me one of life's most valuable lessons: Only in love do we see true beauty.

— Linda Gabris —

The Natural

Fun fact: Therapy dogs at hospices provide comfort not only to dying patients, but also to their families.

After responding to an advertisement for volunteers at the hospice, I sat chatting with the volunteer coordinator. The hospice had been open for about a year, a very welcome addition in our community, and now was looking for special personnel to visit and comfort residents in their waning days. I reached down and unfastened Roxy's leash as she kept her big brown eyes on the coordinator, as if she was taking it all in. "She's not exactly what I was looking for," the coordinator stated. "I was hoping for a lap-sized dog, but she certainly is gentle and talks to you with her eyes."

"No, she's not a lap dog; she's a Lab — a small one as she was the runt of the litter — but she thinks she should be a lap dog, too," I stated. "She also understands grief. She curled up beside her mother when she was dying, and she grieved for several months. So when someone is feeling down or not well, she senses it and tries to offer her empathy and comfort. She works hard at trying to please."

We walked down the hall with the coordinator. Roxy started to enter one of the rooms, but I told her, "No," and she continued to follow. The coordinator took her into the next room where she was fondly greeted. Immediately, Roxy cuddled up to the patient, who was sitting in his wheelchair. "Well, she's winning me over. Let's try her and see how she works out," suggested the coordinator.

Doggone Kind | 221

As I was a full-time caregiver to my daughter, we arranged for us to drop off Roxy and pick her up again at the end of her shift. Another volunteer would oversee her. And thus Roxy became the first dog volunteer at the new Foothills Country Hospice.

The first few visits, she arrived with her leash on, but after a couple of weeks it was no longer required. Upon entering the facility, she would stop at the door while her feet were wiped and, when given the okay, she would first say "hi" to the volunteer at the front desk and anyone else close by, and then be escorted to a resident's room. Soon, she was also strolling unleashed alongside wheelchairs as residents enjoyed the fresh air and beauty of the pathways and gardens outside. Being on duty, she never took off chasing gophers like she did at home on the farm.

Baths before visits became a regular chore, and Roxy obediently stepped in to the shower even though this was not one of her favourite activities. Rolling in stinky things was more to her liking, but she quickly associated baths with volunteer days.

For weeks, one volunteer helped hoist Roxy up on the bed to lie beside a resident who was extremely weak. Roxy lay quietly beside the resident, soaking up and giving as much attention as she could. Eventually, the volunteer discovered that Roxy didn't need help, just a small invite and she would climb, ever so gently, onto the bed by herself. Before long, she was up on the couch or bed whenever she felt someone wanted her love. She found her way into the fireside room and the chapel area when functions were going on and greeted everyone. One day, she lay unsupervised beside the tea cart during a memorial tea. She did not even try to take a morsel of the tempting goodies for herself. She never barked in the facility and always seemed to be looking for approval that she was doing the right thing. If she wasn't needed, she snoozed by the front desk.

Roxy always arrived for duty with a smile, and as her popularity grew, one shift a week became two. The residents, staff and volunteers looked forward to her company and sought her out. She did, however, seem to have a built-in clock and would often be watching the doorway if we were a little late in picking her up. People would go in and out, but she never tried to escape. She just waited for her family.

We were told stories about how much comfort Roxy was providing. One young woman was losing her husband. When the volunteer came to check on Roxy in that room, the resident was asleep, but Roxy and the young wife were curled up together on the floor as the woman poured her grief into Roxy's fur. One family had the hospice call us when their loved one passed away. They needed Roxy's companionship, so she made her rounds to console the various family members in the fireside room as they grieved and made funeral plans. Another family made special mention of Roxy's care in the loved one's obituary.

People had their pictures taken with Roxy, and one woman had hers enlarged and hung over her bed. Visiting children loved playing with Roxy. Older ones took her for walks. Regardless of how rough some little ones were with her, sometimes pulling her tail or poking her eyes, she never showed any signs of aggression and gave them all the kisses they could want. It gave their parents time to spend with their failing loved ones.

People who saw us downtown began recognizing us as Roxy's family. Knowing that sometimes residents did not have many visitation days left, we were happy to provide this service for them. We felt bad when we had to be away, causing Roxy to miss her visits.

Other dogs have since joined the program to visit different days accompanied by their owners. Having watched how Roxy worked, we decided that even if we were available to accompany her, she worked better without us. She was totally trustworthy and sensed what people needed. As things were, when a volunteer escorted Roxy to a room and left her with the family, they were free to seek her comfort privately, and she would respond unconditionally.

For six years now, we have continued to bathe, groom and transport Roxy to and from the hospice twice weekly as well as to other occasional special events. Roxy, now ten years old, remains top dog—a hospice favourite—and she relishes her time there. Last year, she also began volunteering with the Literacy for Life Foundation, which uses dogs to help reluctant or struggling readers in elementary schools. The kids read to the dogs and feel more enthusiastic and less self-conscious that way. She gives cuddles and kisses there, too.

Roxy is a busy girl, and she keeps us hopping with her volunteer schedule. We are happy to help Roxy, the little yellow Labrador Retriever, make a difference. She gives her heart to everyone who needs it.

—Irene R. Bastian—

Breaking the Silence

Dogs have a way of finding the people who need them,
and filling an emptiness we didn't ever know we had.
~Thom Jones

We visited the special care facility on the first Wednesday night of every month. My six-year-old retired racing Greyhound, Itssy, had passed a behaviour test that allowed her to visit the residents as a therapy dog. We usually visited with a group of two or three other dogs and their owners. We would travel through the building, making stops at the common areas throughout the facility, where residents would gather if they wanted to visit with the dogs. Most were wheelchair bound and eagerly anticipated the dogs.

There were some residents who did not enjoy being around other people or activity. The care workers would try to convince some residents who they believed would benefit from contact with the dogs to join us. On this particular night, they had convinced a ninety-year-old lady to join us. They mentioned that she had not spoken for a long time and they were surprised she agreed to leave her room. They pushed her wheelchair into the common area where we had gathered. The residents' chairs were in a semicircle and the dogs and owners moved from chair to chair visiting.

"Say hello!" I said to encourage Itssy to move closer to the ladies and gentlemen in the room. She moved her long snout into laps and allowed shaky hands to stroke her head and move down her sleek brindle-coloured back. When she reached the quiet lady, Itssy did not require any encouragement to move closer. Even though she had been on her feet for close to an hour, she seemed to immediately perk up with excitement. She moved her head close to the lady and placed her head in her lap. The woman's eyes seemed to become more aware and Itssy looked into her tired face. Her watery blue eyes looked into Itssy's brown ones and they seemed to say something to each. The lady's hand trembled as it moved along Itssy's head, playing with the points of her ears lying flat against the sides of her head. And then the lady spoke.

"What a good dog," she murmured softly.

The care worker standing by the woman's chair looked at me, then back to the woman and Itssy in astonishment.

"Do you know," she said, "that she has not spoken a word in at least a year?"

It was difficult to take my eyes off the pair and their special moment. The woman continued to pet Itssy's head gently and speak softly to her, telling her what a good dog she was and how pretty she was. She spoke of her own dog from long ago.

"She was my dearest friend," she said as she looked off into space, a smile on her face.

The woman seemed to be taken away to a special place. All of the care workers gathered around her chair. They were so happy she had agreed to come out of her room, and wondered how this dog had inspired such an engaged reaction from a resident who had been withdrawn for so long. I smiled as I watched Itssy and her new friend, and listened to the amazed people around me. I was pleased that Itssy had made such an impact, but I was not surprised she had. I knew my dog and how special she was. She had a way of bringing joy to everyone she crossed paths with. It was all in a night's work for one amazing dog.

— Kimberley Campbell —

One Season

Dogs are always good and full of selfless love.
They are undiluted vessels of joy who never,
ever deserve anything bad that happens to them.
~Steven Rowley

It was the first day of spring many years ago when my husband, Don, looked up over the newspaper he was reading and grinned at me. "Let's get a dog!" he said.

"We already have two cats," I pointed out, gesturing to the windowsill of our basement apartment where they were wriggling their butts excitedly, watching the antics of a squirrel outside.

"So?" he shrugged. "Cats are boring. You can do stuff with a dog."

"Yeah, like mop up after them, clean up their poop, and listen to them bark at nothing," I quipped, but I was already caving. I loved animals, so within minutes we were in the car on our way to the local shelter.

We heard the loud, yapping cacophony before we even parked. It became deafening as we entered and began our search for the perfect pet.

Though I wished I could adopt every single dog maniacally throwing itself against its cage, none stood out until I made a second tour.

In a far corner sat a small, nondescript Collie/Shepherd mix. There was nothing remarkable about him except for his pose. He sat ramrod straight in alert sphinx position staring at me.

Don called him over, but the dog didn't budge. When I crouched down, however, grasping the grating of his enclosure for balance,

Doggone Kind | 227

he came over immediately, placing his paw on the back of my hand through the small hole.

"He's scheduled for tomorrow," we heard a voice say behind us. I turned to see a female attendant standing there.

"Scheduled?" I echoed.

"Yes, he'll be euthanized. He's been here too long. He's a good dog, but too plain. No one wants him."

"I do!" I exclaimed.

I heard my husband sigh. Clearly, this was not the muscular, tough-looking, manly dog he had visualized accompanying him on his daily jogs, but he smiled and nodded at the woman.

"At least she didn't fall in love with a Chihuahua," he joked as the dog regally pranced out of his cage to plop himself at my feet in the position that would earn him his name.

Sphinx fit into our life beautifully, quickly adapting to basic commands, leash etiquette, and outdoor potty training. He did none of the chewing damage one would expect of a dog acclimatizing to new surroundings. He never barked either. Neighbours attested that he made no sound while home alone.

Rigid as his posture always was, he was loving, friendly, playful, and happy. He showed so much joy when he was chasing balls or greeting us after work. He'd go and get his leash for us in order to go on his walk sooner.

He bonded with both of us, but he seemed more partial and protective toward me, rarely leaving my side, yet careful not to get in my way while I went about my housework.

Even the cats tolerated him the way cats disdainfully endure anything they find beneath them. They would swipe at his muzzle occasionally to remind him who was boss, but his only reaction was a friendly swish of his tail and a slight adjustment in his ever-vigilant position.

Sphinx had been with us three months when he demanded a second walk. I had already given him a quick walk when I came home from work, but now I needed to go to the bank. To my surprise, Sphinx stood up and went to get his leash again.

"Not now, sweetie," I told him. "I'll be back in a bit, and I'll take you for a longer walk, okay?"

I jumped when he barked. I'd never heard him do it. I tried to pass, but he barred my way with his body, barking again — more insistently this time.

"You must need to go pretty badly," I commented, puzzled. He paced in agitation. "Okay, come on, but I'll have to tie you up outside the bank, and you have to be a good boy," I added sternly as we left the house.

Oddly, he didn't need to relieve himself. He trotted beside me, not even stopping to smell every new blade of grass, tree, or hydrant, as was his habit. Nothing interested him — not even the chipmunk that crossed our path.

My banking took longer than expected, so I decided to take an alley shortcut to get back home. Sphinx wasn't happy with that decision either. He barked again, startling me. I tugged at his leash, but he balked and kept pulling away. By then, I was tired and had enough of his odd behaviour.

"Come!" I commanded, my voice sterner than he'd ever heard. Immediately, he stopped struggling and became his usual obedient self.

Halfway down the alley, a man stepped out from a recessed stairwell and approached us. His smile made me a little nervous, but I continued to walk.

"Hey, babe," he leered. I could feel goose bumps pop on my skin. He came closer, blocking my path. I heard a soft growl from Sphinx, then saw the fading sun glint against something in his hand — a knife!

"Stay quiet, and let go of the mutt. You and me are gonna have some fun," he murmured, grabbing my arm.

Frozen, I couldn't even scream. I didn't have to. In a nanosecond, Sphinx pushed forward between us. His jaws clamped around the man's wrist, and he screamed in agony, dropping to his knees. My dog continued to bite into the soft flesh, never releasing his hold.

I ran! As soon as I was far enough away, I yelled for Sphinx, who instantly let go and tore after me.

Needless to say, Sphinx got more than his fair share of treats that

Doggone Kind | 229

night. As we fawned over him, he clung protectively to my side.

Three days later, Sphinx became extremely sick. Within two hours, the seizures started. Terrified, we rushed him to the vet. By the time we got there, he was unable to walk, and we carried him in. The prognosis — advanced distemper — made me sag in disbelief. Even though he was current on all his vaccinations, somehow he was unable to fight the disease. It was recommended that he be euthanized immediately.

"No!" I bellowed at the vet. "This just started today. Fix it!"

The vet shook his head sadly. I continued arguing and screaming until something touched my fingertips. I looked down to see Sphinx nestle his paw into my hand. Our eyes locked, and his message was clear. He knew, and wanted me to know it was time to say goodbye. Within minutes, my beloved dog was gone, peacefully and painlessly.

I sobbed all the way home. When we got there, it occurred to me that it was the first day of summer. Sphinx had been with us for only one season, but thanks to his courage and loyalty, I had my whole life ahead of me.

— Marya Morin —

The Dog that Couldn't Bark

Love is, above all, the gift of oneself.
~Jean Anouilh

Many years ago, in what appears to be a different lifetime now, I had a friend named Jonathan who lived only a few houses down the street. He was a cool kid and a real pal, and in retrospect I can see that he had all the usual qualities and hang-ups of a typical boy. He was fun to be with because of his innocent enthusiasm, and he knew all the best places to hang out in the neighbourhood, but he also had severe acne that made him self-conscious, and his round face often looked like a ripe honeydew melon that sprouted bright red raisins.

The best part about Jonathan, though, was his dog. This is not to say that my friend was any less memorable than his pet, but that dog had a very peculiar quality about him. A friendly Bulldog that never met anyone he didn't like, or immediately want to lick, Bowzer was born without any vocal chords. It was a freak of nature, and a congenital condition that had no plausible explanation, but here was a dog that simply couldn't bark. He would yap his mouth all day long like any canine, but no sound ever came out. Jonathan's parents affectionately used to refer to their pet as "the mute brute."

Even though he couldn't make any sounds, Bowzer sure made his presence known anyway. We couldn't play a pickup baseball game in the neighbourhood park without an extra infielder, outfielder, base runner, or ballboy running around on four paws like his life depended on bumping into every single player on the field, regardless of which team that player played on. For all of us, it became an accepted part of our playtime that Bowzer would somehow be involved in whatever activity we decided on.

Except for the local public swimming pool, of course. Jonathan never had a need to tie Bowzer to a leash and to wrap the leash around a tree or a post, because we all knew there was no way that Bowzer would run away. Oh no. If that dog had fingers and feet, I could swear that he would have climbed that chain-link fence to come frolic with us in the water.

Then, one day, something terrible happened to Jonathan, and we all had to grow up much too quickly. His parents were called away to the hospital because his grandmother was ill, and so Jonathan was left at home by himself. It was early in the evening and no one really thought anything bad could happen to him. But, as it turned out, two men had chosen that house for an unannounced visit.

Soon after his parents locked all the doors and left in their car, with Jonathan securely ensconced inside their home, the men broke into the house from the back door, with theft on their mind. Jonathan's family wasn't super rich, but even as a kid I could tell they had nice things in their house. I suppose the robbers thought so, too.

Jonathan was in his bedroom and heard the noise from the break-in, and maybe because he panicked, he didn't yell or scream for help. Bowzer was in the bedroom also, and heard the noise as well, but because of his birth defect, he couldn't make a sound. I bet, though, that his face was yapping like mad. Had the robbers heard a dog barking, maybe things would have turned out differently.

As Jonathan tells the story, the robbers made their way through the entire house and probably figured that no one was home. Maybe, just maybe, they would leave before they came to Jonathan's bedroom. But no such luck.

One of the robbers opened the door to Jonathan's bedroom, and was startled to find a boy huddled amongst the pillows of his bed.

The robber was even more startled though to discover a fifty-pound Bulldog charging at him. Maybe Bowzer couldn't bark, but that didn't mean he didn't have teeth. And, as Jonathan recalls, it certainly didn't mean that Bowzer was not intent on taking as big a bite out of that robber as he could.

With an angry dog chewing on his arm, the robber began yelling in pain. The second robber suddenly appeared, and that's when Jonathan saw the gun. The last thing he remembers is hearing one gunshot. And then it all went black.

Jonathan survived that horrific episode, luckily, without any physical scars, but he was never the same afterwards. He lost his youthful enthusiasm and innocence. He lost the desire to play and was seldom seen in our usual hang-out spots. He eventually lost his acne as well, and his awkwardness. But, even now as an adult in mid-life, he still mourns the greatest loss of all.

That gunshot had a target, and the target wasn't Jonathan. After that night of the break-in, the dog that couldn't bark never even yapped his face anymore. He didn't run around a baseball diamond like a demon. He didn't pretend he could bore a hole through a chain-link fence to play with us in the water of a swimming pool. The only thing Bowzer got for defending his territory and protecting his master was a nine-millimeter bullet through the heart.

The robbers were arrested and jailed a few days after the break-in. Jonathan's parents never left him alone in the house again, and they never got another dog, either. How could you replace a dog like Bowzer?

Whenever Jonathan and I cross paths now, we reminisce about the many good times, and the one bad time. And it never fails to move us to tears to talk about Bowzer and his courage. The lesson has stayed with us always: some things are irreplaceable. It doesn't matter that we're both grown men now and that some people believe men aren't supposed to cry. The memory of Bowzer is worth every single tear of laughter and sadness.

By the way, if you're wondering what profession Jonathan chose, it should not come as a surprise. He's a veterinary doctor. Me? I became a lawyer, and I sit on the board of an animal shelter. Every once in a while a Bulldog comes through the shelter. I call Jonathan to see if he wants to volunteer that day. There's no need to tell him why, and he never asks. He just shows up, in memory of Bowzer.

—Joseph Civitella—

Volunteering
from the Heart

The purpose of life is a life of purpose.
~Robert Byrne

Are we all guided by a sense of purpose and do we live to fulfill that purpose? I am often reminded of the value of living with purpose and passion by our precious dog Toby, a seven-year-old Chesapeake Bay Retriever, who volunteers from the heart. I firmly believe that people (and animals) come into our lives for a reason and I now know the reason Toby chose us: he reminds us daily of the importance of passion, unconditional love and living with purpose.

We adopted Toby from a rescue agency two years ago. He came to us with some baggage; his original owners loved him and struggled when the time came to surrender him for adoption due to tragic circumstances within the family. Toby was about twenty-five pounds overweight when he entered foster care but when we adopted him several months later he was at a healthy weight for his size.

Several months after welcoming Toby to our family, little quirks, odd habits and strange behaviours began to surface. It was almost as if when he knew he was home to stay, he could relax enough to be himself. He began to exhibit extreme separation anxiety. When we would leave for work he would empty the front hall closet contents into the middle of the entranceway, knock things over and try and lock himself in rooms. He would also close himself in the bathroom and when unable to escape, he would crash the toilet tank lid to the floor (we have gone through four tank lids to date).

Toby is an excessive barker. Not only would he bark at neighbours, other animals and noises, but he seemed to bark just to hear his own voice. Every Monday, which is garbage day, Toby empties the hall closet contents into the middle of the floor and sometimes removes all the coats from their hangers. When it is meal time, Toby either goes outside to bark, or goes into the bathroom and bangs the shower doors with his nose or knocks the shampoo bottle into the bathtub. While frustrating at first, these behaviours and odd habits have now become somewhat amusing for our family. They are our daily reminders of Toby's individuality and personality.

Then there was what we refer to as "the incident of all incidents." My husband Christopher arrived home from work first, and by phone he described our house as a "murder zone." He explained that Toby was fine but there was blood and mess everywhere. Apparently Toby knocked a number of items off the counter including the kettle, teapot, knife block and in doing so, must have cut his foot. Then knocking over plants and the water cooler, he trekked dirt and ran through the house spreading blood and muck everywhere. It even appeared he might have tried to call for help as the phone was all bloodied.

After this incident, we took Toby to the vet as well as an animal behaviourist and trainer for help. Maggie, from Capable Canines, provided us with a range of suggestions and helpful strategies. The most profound was her conclusion that Toby was uncertain of his role — Toby needed a purpose.

Wow! What an incredible "ah ha" moment. Just like people need a purpose, so do animals. Toby and I explored the potential to become part of a volunteer team so that he could work as a therapy dog. We were introduced to the Chimo Project, a well-respected pet assisted therapy program in Edmonton, Alberta. With tremendous excitement and curiosity, Toby passed his obedience and temperament tests with flying colours. We were then accepted as volunteers with Chimo and were soon placed with Alberta Hospital Edmonton.

On the way to the volunteer coordinator's office, Toby seemed to somehow know he was "working." He walked up the steps to the building in a confident manner, stopping with me at the reception desk. Of course everyone was very interested in Toby, and he had to greet everyone by stopping in each office as we walked down the hall. Toby was curious, happy and very social with the volunteer coordinator, and slobbered all over her, just like he does with us. It was like he was saying, "I have arrived!"

Wednesday afternoons are clearly the highlight of Toby's world. The moment I bring out the Volunteer Bag (a knapsack used solely for his volunteering and containing toys, treats and his uniform), the non-stop barks of excitement begin. This makes putting on his special harness and volunteer vest an interesting challenge. The drive from our home to the hospital typically consists of Toby smiling, barking and panting with excitement. Once at the hospital we put on his special red bandana and his Volunteer Photo Badge.

When the door opens to the hospital and particularly to the unit we volunteer on, Toby's sense of purpose is evident. He greets everyone he sees with curiosity, acceptance and joy. The fascinating part is that he clearly seems to understand his purpose and proves that by interacting with each individual in the appropriate manner needed at the time. With some individuals Toby is playful; with others he is quiet and gentle. Some are blessed with his affection while others are treated with a respectful distance — Toby is intuitive enough to recognize that around some people, he must be quiet, and respectful of their need for space and distance.

His activities change each week. Sometimes patients take him for a walk or to play fetch outside. On other visits he performs tricks and shows off. Patients also help him with his obedience class homework.

Toby finds simple pleasure in things that many of us would not even notice, like a dust bunny, a leaf tumbling across the grass, a rabbit or squirrel hiding behind a tree or a dog barking in the background on the TV. When playing fetch, his sole purpose and focus is on the toy and the individual playing with him (nothing else matters to him at that moment except his purpose). And when it comes to people,

Toby connects through the heart. He unconditionally accepts each and every person he visits.

As I watch my dog each week, I see the growth and change in him becoming more pronounced. Each week he lives his purpose! This program has also been therapy for the therapy dog. Since volunteering, we have noticed that Toby's barking is less of a problem as he is confident in himself and in new situations. He is more comfortable being away from my husband and me. In addition, his weekly interactions with the patients have clearly helped him grow, change and live life fully.

His story has inspired me to pursue a number of purposeful activities including developing my own Life Purpose Statement, consciously living more purposefully, and writing more about strategies for people to live a purposeful and intentional life, all based on lessons I have learned from our precious Toby.

— Charmaine Hammond —

The Magic of Colleen

Dogs are not our whole life, but they
make our lives whole.
~Roger Caras

I n 1981, I went to work in a nursing home as a Nurse's Aide. My duties included waking the residents in the morning, bathing and dressing them, and getting them to the dining room in time for breakfast.

My first day on the job, I met Anna. She was a petite, beautiful woman with a sweet disposition and silver-gray hair. As I brushed her hair, she would sit with eyes closed, enjoying the attention I gave her.

There was only one thing that bothered me about Anna. No matter how much I coaxed her, she wouldn't say a word. Upon inquiring about her lack of speech, I was told that Anna hadn't spoken since she'd come to the nursing home. No one seemed to know why—Anna had always been a very social person with lots of friends.

The only time that Anna left her room was for meals. As soon as she had finished eating, one of the staff would push her wheelchair back to her room. She sat all day, gazing out the window, which faced a farm and pasture.

One day I walked into Anna's room. The sight that met my eyes stopped me dead! Anna was standing, clutching the windowsill. A chortle of laughter escaped her lips. I craned my neck to see what she was looking at. She was watching a Border Collie round up the cows and head them back toward the barn. Silently, I backed out of

Doggone Kind | 239

the room and went directly to the administrator's office. Ruth was a wonderful woman with an open-door policy. She wanted the best for the residents.

After I explained to Ruth what I'd seen and heard she told me that Anna had spent her entire life on a farm. Ruth explained that she had been thinking for weeks about starting an animal therapy program here at the nursing home. The theory that animals could help people heal was fairly new at this time but she felt that there might be a lot to be gained by allowing animals to visit the residents. Of course it would take some time to implement such a program; the animals would all have to be carefully screened.

It took six months before the program was initiated. The animals were to visit three times a week for two hours. Their owners would accompany them and the residents who wished to be a part of the program would gather in the Recreation Room.

The first day, only three animals visited — a Husky, a Poodle and a Persian cat. Ruth wanted to introduce the animals slowly so the residents could get used to their visits.

From the first day, the staff knew the program would be a success. The residents loved the pets. There were only two exceptions — Mr. Mannen, who was a crotchety old soul, and Anna. Neither of them paid any attention to the creatures that moved freely around the room.

Within a few weeks, the residents looked forward to Pet Day with much enthusiasm — all except Anna and Mr. Mannen. Hours before the pets were to arrive, the Recreation Room would be filled to capacity. I continued to ensure that there was always a place for Anna and Mr. Mannen.

At this time, Ruth decided to allow three more animals to visit. A total of sixty residents were taking part in the program and three animals were not sufficient to meet the demand. The newcomers were all canines; a Husky, a blond Labrador Retriever and a Border Collie named Colleen.

Colleen was a gentle, loving animal and a hit with all the residents. The first time she visited, Anna was in bed with the flu. However, Colleen proceeded to work her magic on crotchety Mr. Mannen. She continued to return to his chair time after time, laying her head on his knee. Instead of brushing her away, as I expected, he sat and stared at her.

As Colleen was saying farewell to all of the residents, she ventured to Mr. Mannen one last time and laid her head on his knee. To my astonishment, he patted her head and spoke to her in a soft, gentle voice. This was a step forward, as Mr. Mannen never had spoken a kind word to anyone.

The following week, Anna was feeling much better and her doctor gave his permission for her to take part in the program. A half-hour before the pets were to arrive, I pushed Anna to the Recreation Room. She sat, staring into space, ignoring everyone around her. That is until Colleen walked into the room. As soon as Anna spied this lovely black and white creature, she laughed with delight and clapped her hands. Colleen immediately trotted to Anna's side, wagged her tail excitedly and danced on her hind legs. As Anna bent to touch her, Colleen began to lick her, her pink tongue lapping in and out rapidly. Anna hugged her close, tears coursing down her cheeks. As fast as they fell, Colleen lapped them up.

"Oh my dear Laddy, I've missed you so much," Anna cried. By this time there wasn't a dry eye in the room. Even old Mr. Mannen's eyes sparkled mysteriously. Everyone was surprised to hear Anna speak so plainly after two years of silence.

The next time Anna's sister, Mildred, came to visit, we told her that Anna was talking. She could hardly believe it. Ruth explained what had happened. Mildred told Ruth that when Anna had come to the home she had left behind a Border Collie named Laddy. The farm had been sold and a neighbour had adopted Laddy. He had been a direct descendent of a Border Collie that had been given to Anna by her father when she was a child. In fact, until she had come to the nursing home, Anna had never been without at least one, and more often two, Border Collies in her life.

Over the next few months, Anna and Colleen bonded in a special way. Anna began to talk to the other residents and walk with a cane. Every staff member of the nursing home knew that if Colleen hadn't come into Anna's life, the healing process would never have taken place.

Two years later, at the age of eighty-seven, Anna passed away peacefully in her sleep. As I stood at the cemetery and listened to the eulogy, I looked across the lawn. What I saw brought tears to my eyes and a smile to my face. There on the outskirts of the mourners lay Colleen, her nose on her paws, sad eyes gazing at the coffin. I was sure that Anna knew Colleen was there and I whispered a prayer of thanks for the magic that the wonderful Border Collie had brought into Anna's final years — the magic of Colleen.

Colleen taught me much about the human response to animal companions. I have never looked at a dog in the same light since Colleen brought the miracle of love to Anna.

— Mary M. Alward —

The Tail of Little Guy

*Our perfect companions never have fewer
than four feet.*
~Colette

"There's a hurt kitty in the field," my husband said solemnly. "I think it's going to die."

It was Canada Day, July 1st and I was in the midst of preparing a barbecue for friends. I really didn't need this right now. Not that I hate animals. In fact, I'm queen of the strays. Aside from one, the German Shepherd, Kali, all our animals have come from desperate situations. But I just did not need one more vet bill. Sensing I might be swaying, Kali whined and looked up at me.

"What's wrong with her?" I asked.

"Well Kali found it. She thinks it's our responsibility to care for it now. Finders, keepers I suppose."

"And how are we supposed to pay for another stray?" I sighed, not looking up from cutting vegetables for the salad.

Kali barked and made the "let's go find the kitty" motion towards the door. But I was adamant. I had too many strays already. We were a two-cat one-dog two-rabbit family. Several chickens and one bad-tempered cockatiel rounded off the mixture. That was enough, even for the country.

My husband hung the leash on the hook and went inside the living room. I made tea while pondering what to do next. Obviously we had to do something.

"How bad?" I asked as I brought in the tea.

"The back legs look broken. Or maybe the spine. It's also really weak, probably been without water."

We looked at each other and I sighed. "Well, we'll take it some water and see how it is."

Together we strolled down, dish in hand. But the place the cat had been was empty except for a mark in the tall grass where he had lain. "Well, he must have gone somewhere," I said as we looked around.

"But he couldn't walk!" my husband contended. "He can't have gone far."

We searched and searched through the tall grass and by the creek that runs through our property. An hour later we found him. He had crawled 150 feet over a bridge and up to our shed. He had crawled after a dog and a strange man, not away from them, and had settled inside the shade of the entrance. He managed a whispered meow of thanks as we put down the water and he struggled to stand up. This cat was a fighter and I knew we had to save him.

Putting the food for the celebration back in the fridge, we made some hurried phone calls and left a note for the friends who we hadn't reached. They would understand, for anyone who knows us knows how crazy we are for our animals. The barbecue could wait for another day.

Canada Day is a national holiday—so finding a vet willing to come in even for the call-in price wasn't easy. And what if the cat belonged to someone else? The only option was to take him to the SPCA and drop him in as a walk-in case. Surely they would take care of him. We finally found a place willing to accept him forty-five minutes away.

I sat in the back with the cat on the way up. His breathing was tortured and every now and then he seemed to fade. His emaciated body was a mass of matted fur, burrs and dried mud. There were maggots on his open wounds. "Hang on," I whispered. "Hang on, little guy."

At the center they examined him. He was too far gone to be considered adoptable, but as it is law, they kept him alive and fed for three days and waited for someone to claim him. I phoned in often, checking on his progress. Surely someone would call and claim him.

He was such a sweet, determined little cat.

But no one called. The vet care to save him was going to cost hundreds of dollars. The SPCA only allotted a maximum of $150 for each animal. I didn't blame them. It was all they could afford and this cat had already used up his funds. A few hours before he was to be put down humanely, I made the decision. Somehow we would have to find the money. I couldn't give up on him and I couldn't see him being put down after he struggled so hard to survive.

Our wonderful vet in Sooke took on the responsibility of helping us care for him.

Even with rehydration and food the cat was still in rough shape. He weighed just over six pounds and his fur came off in your hands, a sign of malnutrition. Maggots had eaten away at his back end. His spine was broken near his tail. His tail hung lifeless and limp. "This," the vet said, "will have to go." Luckily his legs were intact and the determined sparkle was coming back in his face. He defiantly swiped a paw at the vet when he got too close to his wounds. "How do we proceed?" I gulped. "We'll have to see after the surgery," the vet said, "but he sure is a fighter, isn't he?"

The tail came off in an operation; also something else came off, which cured him of being a future father and wanderer. We went in the next day to pick him up. "Stick him in a box, keep him quiet. His spine may knit," the vet said. We took him home and set him up in an upstairs bedroom with glass doors. The other cats and dog kept interested vigils over the next month as the little guy recuperated, ate tuna, had antibiotics forced on him with a syringe, and got stronger. Kali especially took great interest in her charge.

In three days he was up and walking. In four days he had managed to break out of his cage and was atop the furniture when we went in to feed him. At three weeks he managed to fire himself at breakneck speed out the room and down the stairs to meet the other members of his new family face to face.

That was three years ago. Nowadays we call Canada Day "founding day" and usually have a party with our animal-loving friends. Both Little Guy and Kali get a special treat to share with their family friends and Kali gets a hero cheer for finding Little Guy. Yes, it is my country's birthday but this experience gave us something more important to celebrate — a tailless cat who taught us to never give up fighting, and a German Shepherd who wouldn't let us shirk our responsibilities.

— Nancy Bennett —

Chapter
7

Purrfect Compassion

The Assignment

What greater gift than the love of a cat?
~Charles Dickens

W e all know someone who loves angels. You know, the kind of person who has every nook and cranny of her home filled to capacity with those endearing porcelain, china or dollar store knickknacks?

I have always pictured an angel as a soft, feminine form with cascading luminescent tendrils of hair, porcelain skin and eyes the colour of the Caribbean Sea. That was until… I actually met one.

Not the feminine form I'd imagined, but feline. Not cascading tendrils or porcelain skin, but soft, silky, taupe fur. Beautiful turquoise, soulful eyes, albeit somewhat crossed. Yes, my angel was a Siamese cat!

My daughter Jessica was nine years old at the time. She had fallen off the monkey bars in the playground. A compression fracture wrapped in a cast was her souvenir after spending eight hours in the emergency room. Nice gift to get the week before summer vacation! At our one-week check-up with the orthopedic surgeon, X-rays were taken, an exam made, and we received disappointing news.

Although things looked okay on the outside, the bones weren't in perfect alignment. The surgeon recommended a return visit to the operating room the next day to remove the cast and re-set the bone. My daughter was terrified, especially when she learned that her dad and I weren't allowed to be with her during the procedure.

The ride home was very quiet. You could see the worry in her watery eyes and in her body language. There was no consoling her. After encouraging her to have some lunch I suggested she go outside to get some fresh air.

At her age, most kids were pining for the latest video game or electronic gadget, but she was pleading for a cat. Being an only child was lonely and I had always felt guilty about not providing her with any siblings. I was trying to come up with an activity to distract her, when all of a sudden I said, "Look!"

A beautiful Siamese cat was walking atop the fence in our yard. Strutting her form like an Olympic gymnast, she was showing off her beautiful lines and languid curves.

Where did this exquisite cat come from? We'd lived in this neighbourhood for fifteen years and had never seen this cat before. I couldn't believe it. The one thing that would truly make my daughter happy had just appeared out of thin air! The cat dismounted with gymnastic perfection and crossed the yard to softly rest at my daughter's feet.

She let out a meow as if to say, "All is well; I'm here for you." That Siamese angel was hugged, rubbed, petted and loved all afternoon. She followed my daughter everywhere and was a faithful companion and confidante. I kept peeking outside in utter disbelief.

Dinnertime rolled around and I regretfully called my daughter inside. Her trusty companion kept vigil outside the patio door for a few minutes, making sure she was in good hands. Then as quickly and quietly as she had come into our little world, she vanished, her assignment here on earth completed.

We never saw that cat again, but we have a photo that we truly treasure. I was so moved by the encounter that I wrote this story and originally titled it "Angels Among Us." I was thrilled to be able to submit it to this book with the same title.

— Catherine Rossi —

70

Oliver's Ministry

But ask the animals, and they will teach you.
~Job 12:7

Oliver was next on the list at the local shelter to be euthanized. An irresistible tabby with markings that looked like thick black mascara outlining his friendly green eyes, he was doing his feline best to attract the attention of my sister and her pastor husband. They fell for his charms and took him home to their church rectory where he was free to explore the large rooms, spacious yard, and cemetery next door.

One hot summer day, the church door was left open as a funeral got underway. Oliver took the organ music as his cue to check things out. He went up the wide stone steps on little cat feet and sat in the doorway listening to the service. As the pastor read the part of the eulogy that described the deceased as an avid animal lover, Oliver padded down the aisle, all the way to the front row of the church, where he approached the grieving granddaughter. He sat at the end of the pew and stared up at the little girl. She stared back at him for a moment and then invited him to hop up and sit with her. Oliver accepted the invitation, curled up on the child's lap and stayed there until the closing prayer, as if in tribute to the dearly departed. His mere presence offered a comforting distraction to those in mourning. When the service ended, Oliver left the way he had come.

Parishioners often talk about visiting the cemetery and the graves of their loved ones and finding Oliver there at just the right moment, purring, looking for a scratch behind the ears, ready to offer a gentle rub up against a mourner's leg. Oliver can sometimes be seen perched serenely on a monument, as a reminder that we are watched over and not alone.

But something was different this time. The hearse had already pulled away from the graveside and the casket, draped with flowers, was resting on racks waiting to be lowered into the ground. There sat Oliver as usual, present in the moments that can be the saddest for family and friends. He seemed once more to provide a pleasant, even hopeful, distraction from overwhelming grief.

Suddenly, Oliver flicked his tail and dove into the hole under the coffin just as the lowering device was switched on. My sister gasped, "Oh! Get the cat!" The pastor sprang into action, his clerical robes billowing white around him. He reached out in the nick of time to grab Oliver by his hind legs and haul him to safety.

As people chatted and milled about, chuckling over Oliver's narrow escape, he wound his way through the legs of the crowd and settled at the feet of the widow. She bent down to pick him up. As she stroked and Oliver purred, she looked him in the eye and whispered, "You stay with him now and I'll be back soon to visit you both."

—Jo Yuill Darlington—

71

Therapy Appointment

Fun fact: Only female calico cats are fertile; males are few and they are usually sterile.

"Y ou want out again, Marmalade? You were just out. What, not the back door, you want out the front?" I was very surprised that our beautiful, longhaired, ten-year-old calico cat wanted out again.

Several days later, I realized that almost every day she had been asking to be let out at 1:00 p.m. and always wanted the front door instead of the back door she normally used to go to the yard. As a busy housewife and mother, I hadn't been paying much attention, but I realized this had been going on for a while, and I had no idea why. Therefore, the next time it happened, I watched out the front room window to see what Marmalade was doing at one o'clock every day.

"Marm" meandered down the front stairs and out to the city sidewalk — then just sat there. About three minutes later, she flopped down and rolled over so her belly was showing.

"This is weird," I thought. "She never does that unless she wants to be petted — but there is no one there." I looked up the street — no one; I looked down the street — no one. Wait — on the sidewalk just crossing a block down from our house was a group of about fifteen young adults from the nearby group home for young adults with Down syndrome. They were out for a walk with their chaperone.

As they approached, I could hear, "There's the kitty; there's the kitty," coming from multiple mouths. When they were close enough to touch Marm, she lay quietly while each person took a turn petting her. This took quite a while, and obviously these teens were very comfortable petting her and talking to her. When everyone, including the chaperone, had given Marm a petting and a belly rub, she turned over, stood up and gave herself a shake, then meandered back up the sidewalk to the front door where I heard her scratching to be let in. As I opened the door, I watched the group continue on their walk down the street.

It had been a breathtaking experience to see.

The next day, at the same time, I watched it happen again.

After a few more days of this, I needed to find out how long this had been going on, so I went out just as the last few were giving Marm the required petting, and asked the chaperone.

What I was told was both interesting and humbling. Our wonderful cat had been doing this every weekday for months, and these young adults thought it was the highlight of the walk to be able to have a chance to pet her.

How she had come to understand that these young people would enjoy petting her and could trust them, only God knows.

Marmalade had the most loving and caring personality I have ever seen in a cat. She would cuddle any of the family when they felt sad, and she would lick away the tears and purr in their ears until she had made them feel better. To see that she extended that love to others was incredible.

— Shirley K. Stevenson —

72

Summer of Skooter

The power of love to change bodies is legendary,
built into folklore, common sense, and everyday
experience…. Throughout history, "tender loving care"
has uniformly been recognized as a
valuable element in healing.
~Larry Dossey

I fell in love the instant I saw him. He scooted across the room and hopped into my lap. With one little eye open, he fit in the palm of my hand. He was the cutest, tiniest, most mischievous-looking, pink-and-black nosed tuxedo cat that I had ever met. The kitten was the last remaining of a litter that had lost their mother, and my friend, who wasn't much of a cat lover, was looking for a home for him. That summer I worked full-time, and, because my home life was so miserable, I took on as many extra shifts as I could, often working six or seven days a week.

My live-in boyfriend, John, stayed home every day in our secluded, three-bedroom house. His only hobbies were playing video games and consuming drugs in an attempt to drown out the desolation and emptiness of his life. The more he was alone, the more depressed he became, and in turn, this only made him seek isolation even more. It was a vicious cycle. It was lonely in our big house, and the kids were away, hiding from the angry, empty atmosphere my partner and I had created. I thought of all this as I climbed into my van with my little passenger curled up in my lap for the drive home.

He was so tiny, and with no mama cat to feed him, he was voraciously hungry. I was the only mother he had, and he did what any hungry baby would do — he looked for something to suck on. He found my thumb, and my heart melted. I was floating with happiness when I introduced the kitten to John. With a scowl, he told me that I couldn't keep him. I convinced him to at least let me wait until after work the next day before taking him back. I was nearly heartbroken, but glad to be allowed to keep him for one night.

The kitten seemed to think that he was a furry little person. He followed me everywhere, and copied me while I watched TV, sitting on his rear end, front paws at his sides as if they were his arms. That night he stayed in our bedroom with us. The night was long since the kitten woke me up every couple of hours, trying to nurse, sucking my hand, telling me it was feeding time. John grumbled every time I got up to get the kitten's milk, and complained that it wouldn't be soon enough when I took the kitten back to my friend.

However, something changed in the morning as I was leaving for work. When I popped my head into our bedroom after my breakfast, I announced, "Okay, I'm going now." As soon as the words left my mouth, the kitty scooted to the end of the bed with a frightened and sad look, and emitted the tiniest and saddest little meow, as if he understood. It was irresistible. John's face softened for a moment and then he smiled.

"Awww, that's so cute, he's crying for you, Betty," said John.

It was the first genuine smile I had seen from John in months. Right then I knew my little tuxedo cat was staying. When I arrived home that evening, it was to an excited John telling me all about his day with the kitten. Happily demonstrating all the games that they played and how the kitten would hunt John, thinking that if he stood very, very still he was invisible and John wouldn't see him. John announced that we should come up with a name. I thought for a few minutes, watching the kitten race around the house chasing him.

"Skooter. He's a Skooter-cat," I said.

That summer was long, lonely and difficult until Skooter came along. He helped us both smile at least once a day, whether it was because I couldn't break him of his sucking habit — he salivated at the sight of any exposed human flesh, and he mauled me when he had the urge to suck — or his fascination with watching the water in the toilet swirl around. He loved it so much that he figured out how to flush the toilet himself just so he didn't have to wait for a human to do it. John spoiled Skooter, feeding him only the best cat food we could find, and caring for him as if he really were an actual human child. And Skooter saved John. I knew John's drug use, chronic depression and self-imposed isolation were driving him crazy. On more than one occasion, John has told me that he had been suicidal before I brought Skooter home. Then, in this tiny kitten, he could see the beauty and wonder in life again.

John and I have since parted ways, healthier and happier. John went off to a rehabilitation program and cleaned up, and I'm enjoying a peaceful life with my two kids, who no longer need to escape their home to find love. When Skooter came into our lives, he fit in the palm of my hand, not even weighing one pound. Today, he is three years old and weighs a whopping twenty-five pounds. He isn't fat — he's just a big healthy guy who still thinks he's a baby. Yup, he still tries to suck on my thumb.

— Louise Nyce —

73

Emily

There's a bit of magic in everything,
and some loss to even things out.
~Lou Reed, Magic and Loss

A few months after our dog passed away, my son Jason begged me to go have a look at our local SPCA. Suffice it to say, the idea did not thrill me. I was still in mourning. I felt like a traitor just thinking about getting another dog.

"Come on Mom, we don't have to get anything. I just want to look. Please!" he begged.

"Oh alright!" I snapped. "We will go just to look." I could already feel my resistance starting to wane. When it comes to saying no to adopting an animal, I have the backbone of a slug and my son knew it. As we headed off towards the SPCA, I kept reminding him that we were just going there to look.

"Don't worry," he replied. "I know that we are not going to bring home another dog. I just want to visit some animals because I miss Sam so much."

Goodbye strong matriarch, hello slug woman. Once inside our local chapter, I was surprised to see my fair-haired son ignore the dogs and zero in on the cats. I started to feel a little bit at ease. He would never pick a cat. He has allergies. It was simply out of the question.

"Hey Mom, come look at these kittens, they are so cute! I know we can't have one but if we could, which one would you choose?" he asked.

I looked down into his sparkling blue eyes and knew that I was a goner.

"Jason," I said softly, "I would love to get you a kitten, but you know that you are allergic to cats."

"But that was a long time ago. We have been here for almost an hour and if I was going to have a reaction, it would have happened by now," he reasoned.

That was true. His allergies would usually kick in within minutes of being exposed. I was weakening. "You know it wouldn't be fair to the kitten if you suddenly became allergic to it," I said. It would be a disaster for all of us I thought.

"Mom, really I am fine. Please just give us a chance," he pleaded.

"Us? What us?" I asked.

He pointed to the lower cage. A little black paw had snaked its way through the bars and was clinging to the hem of Jason's T-shirt. I looked through the bars to see a very small and scrawny black-and-white kitten with a little pink nose. She had a Herculean grip on Jason's shirt. Every time I would get one paw free, another would take its place.

"It's no use Mom. She thinks she is coming home with us and I don't think that she can be told otherwise," he said.

Fifty dollars later, we were on our way home with Emily.

The little cat that I didn't want became a very special little friend and companion for the next twenty-one years. She was there through happy times and sad. She watched Jason grow into a man, and I think she was just as sad as I was when he left home.

A few years ago I had an operable form of cancer and had to be hospitalized for a few days. God was ever gracious, and they managed to get it all. I was told that I would be laid up for about two months. For the next little while I was not allowed to use stairs or drive my car.

Once I was home, that sweet little cat never left my side. She fretted over me when I groaned, and snuggled close when I cried. About three weeks into my recovery, I started to notice that Emily was not herself. Her arthritis was really causing her pain and her appetite was off. Now it was my turn to fret. I called my veterinarian and explained Emily's condition. He reminded me that she was an ancient cat and advised me to just make her as comfortable as possible. As long as she was still eating and drinking, that was as good as it was going to get.

I selfishly looked at her and pleaded, "Please Em, just wait until I'm on my feet and I promise I won't let you suffer."

Two weeks later on an early September morning, I kept my promise. I held her until she was no more. I gently kissed her goodbye and thanked God for this precious little gift called Emily. That funny little cat kissed my heart the day we met, and in my heart she will remain.

— Avril McIntyre —

74

Lost Friend

You cannot look at a sleeping cat and feel tense.
~Jane Pauley

T he day we lost Colonel was a cold and miserable day in January. The year was only a few days old and somehow the magic left over from Christmas and all the promises of the new year ahead vanished as I gently lifted my small gray cat into the carrier.

His body was limp and his normally white beard was covered with yellow slime from the countless times he had vomited. The vet knew my husband, James, would be bringing him in, and as I closed the door to the carrier, I stroked the slate-gray fur of his forehead. He looked at me, pain filling his eyes, and I knew that we were saying our last goodbyes. I looked at my beautiful cat one last time, and tried to fight the tears sliding down my cheeks.

I busied myself with our two young boys of two and five. I spent the time trying to calm their worries about Colonel but as each minute slowly slid into the next, those worries only grew.

Despite all my reassurances, I knew that Colonel wasn't coming home. I prayed that I was wrong, prayed that Colonel wasn't as sick as I thought. I didn't want to believe that our young cat, not even two years old, was going to leave us. I had always thought that he would live to fill out his name and become the grouchy Old Colonel, much like our nine-year-old cat, Lobo, was the grouchy Old Prince. It wasn't fair that this cat, the same one who slept with my older son and allowed my younger son to use him for a pillow, was sick. It wasn't fair that I was going to have to tell them that he wasn't coming back.

Lobo was a wonderful cat, but he didn't have the same patience with kids. Colonel was Gabriel's cat more than he was anyone's, and I found myself worrying about what would happen to my five-year-old son's heart when his cat died.

When James walked through the door, tears shining in his eyes, the handle of an empty carrier clenched in his fist, I knew that my prayers had gone unanswered; Colonel was gone.

In a voice filled with grief, James told me that Colonel had had liver failure; there was nothing the vet could do but help him along. Tears stung my eyes and I felt a lump form in my throat as I thought about all the chin scratches he would never have. I thought of Gabriel and the nights he would spend alone without his living teddy bear, and the lump grew larger.

We told the kids and Gabriel was devastated. Tears choked his words as he asked us why, and tears choked our hearts as we explained that God had called the Colonel home.

The evening passed slowly and each moment found my thoughts returning to Colonel. Returning to the happy moments we had shared and all the moments we would miss. I thought about how empty our home would be without him and I worried about the nights ahead of us when no Colonel was there to snuggle against Gabriel.

When it was finally time for the boys to go to bed, sobs wracked Gabriel's thin body, and no matter how hard I hugged him, he couldn't stop. Instead, he shared with me all the grief that his small body held.

While James and I tried to calm Gabriel, Lobo entered the room and sat in the doorway staring at us. His yellow gaze scanned the room, and his tail flicked slowly as though in deliberation, before he slowly crossed the room towards us. Jumping onto the bed, Lobo did something that he had never done before; he lay down beside Gabriel and started purring. We stopped and the sobbing ceased. I said quietly, "Lobo is here to sleep with you."

Gabriel laughed, a tear-filled sound, then buried his face in the brown and gray tiger-striped fur. Lobo lay there, his purr deepening, the sound filling the room with assurance that all would be well. I scratched his ears and said a silent thank you to the grouchy cat who had sacrificed his space to bring a little comfort to the boy he shared a home with. Although Lobo had spent the last five years with Gabriel, he had never warmed up to this child who filled his life with noises and smells. He would avoid the kids, preferring to come to James or me for the occasional scratch. The fact that he was lying there, with a child grasping him tightly, proved that he was a remarkable creature.

I knew that Lobo wasn't Colonel for Gabriel, but on that cold night, Gabriel was able to sleep with Lobo by his side. The days continued and the heartache lessened. We didn't forget Colonel or how much we loved him, but we forgot the pain of losing him. Each night became a little easier and Gabriel cried a little less. Each night, Lobo would sit in the doorway, watching the little boy in his bed before finally climbing up with him. Each night, Gabriel would smile a tear-filled smile, curl up with one arm wrapped around Lobo and fall asleep.

Six months have passed and Gabriel can finally fall asleep more easily, but every night Lobo still curls up on his bed. Gabriel doesn't hold him like he used to, but Lobo's strong purr still fills the room as he fulfills the Colonel's legacy.

— Sirena Van Schaik —

75

Duet for Fiddle and Viola

When a cat chooses to be friendly,
it's a big deal, because a cat is picky.
~Mike Deupree

When you live on a farm, you choose your cats for mousing ability rather than for their cuddlesome qualities.

It's the reason I chose Fiddle, a skinny, green-eyed tortie with long paws and a fearsomely quick pounce.

Of course, I didn't know she was a good hunter when I got her. But her mother was a good mouser, according to my friend Nancy, whose grain storage was mouse-free, so it was worth the risk.

She was cuddly when she was a kitten, round, with soft fur. As she matured, her baby fat melted from her bones and she became a skinny, spooky, predatory cat. She reverted to her cuddly kitten self only when she was pregnant. When the kittens were weaned, she returned to her career as Lurker-in-the-Shadows. My grain storage was mouse-free.

When Fiddle was five years old, I had a run of spontaneous abortion in my ewes. The distressing part was that the ewes miscarried late in the pregnancy. In the middle of the thrill and hustle of lambing, all that new life, my favourite part of the year, came the shock of lamb after lamb emerging from the womb, tiny, perfect and dead. Over half my lambs never drew breath, or had any possibility of it.

Belladonna was one of the last to lamb and, like most of the others, she delivered early. She'd shown no signs of imminent delivery; no triangular hollow in front of the hip to indicate the lamb had dropped into position, no swollen udder, no nesting behaviour. She just pushed out a tiny black lamb, covered with the slime of birth, onto the manure of the barn floor and stood looking at it.

Without hope, I wiped the remains of the sac away from the muzzle and was astonished to hear a little gasp. The tiny thing shook its ears and produced a barely audible bleat. Belladonna strolled away. I tucked the baby, slime and all, into my jacket and headed for the house through the late-March snow.

I kept colostrum in the freezer for just this kind of emergency. While I was feeding the newly dried lamb her first meal, Fiddle, who must have sneaked into the house on my heels, came creeping across the room and put a tentative paw onto my knee. Before she could pounce, I brushed her off.

"Not a mouse," I said to her, although I could hardly blame her for thinking of the lamb as prey. I could cup it in my hands with the legs dangling through my fingers. On my kitchen scale, it weighed a bare two pounds.

A newborn lamb has to be fed every two hours. A barn full of lambing ewes has to be checked every three or four hours. I was already strained from the lack of uninterrupted sleep. Keeping Fiddle out of the house was impossible; she was not Lurker-in-the-Shadows for nothing. Time and again I found her at my knee as I fed the lamb.

I kept the lamb in a box with a towel and hot-water bottle, in the spare room with the door closed. When I got up at night, I would check first to see if it was worth warming the bottle. I fully expected the lamb to die between one feeding and the next, but she hung on.

Finally the inevitable happened, and I failed to close the door properly when I went to get the bottle. Padding back upstairs in my nightgown, I was shocked to see a wide line of light falling across the hall floor from the guest room.

When I got into the room, I could see that my worst fears were confirmed. Fiddle was in the box with the lamb. From the sharp motion of her head, she was biting. It was probably already too late. I didn't want to look. But I would have to put her out with her prey — I didn't want blood and guts on my guest room floor.

As I looked down into the box, Fiddle looked up. Her green eyes were slitted and she was purring. Her paws were wrapped around the lamb, who shook her wet, cat-licked ears at me and bleated. At the bleat, Fiddle turned and took the lamb gently by the neck, as I had seen her do with her kittens when they wouldn't hold still for washing. Then she went back to work on the lamb's face and ears.

I waited until she was done, marvelling, grateful and sleepily amused. When the lamb was washed to Fiddle's satisfaction, I gave her the bottle and tucked her back in. Fiddle curled around her, purring.

"Two points off your predator license, Fiddle," I whispered, stroking her head. I went back to bed for another snatch of sleep, leaving the guest room door open.

I named the lamb Viola.

— Elizabeth Creith —

76

The Guardian

Fun fact: The blue-eyed Siamese cat is one of the oldest breeds, treasured members of the Thai royal family, seen in ancient manuscripts as far back as 1350.

Long ago I lived in Vancouver with a Doberman named Sasha and a Siamese cat named Paxton. Now, Paxton was a great cat, tolerant of people in general and kids in particular, but he hated dogs. All dogs, any dogs, he made no distinction. The day we moved into our new home I remember a black Lab wandering across our front yard and hearing, later, some high pitched, dog-type yips. Shortly after a very irate dog owner showed up claiming my cat had chased his dog down the street and swiped its snout, which now sported some (relatively) minor gashes. Pax loved sitting at the end of our driveway hissing at the dogs walking by on leash. He didn't discriminate: large or small, pure bred or mutt, if you were canine he hated you.

The only dog he tolerated was our Doberman Sasha, probably because she had been there first. He completely ignored her attempts at friendship, but they coexisted more or less peacefully. At least Sasha never turned up with her nose in shreds.

As Sasha aged she started to have trouble walking and controlling her bladder. I took her to a specialist. We learned she had a tumour wrapped around her spine. There was no treatment that would work so we just brought her home to let nature take its course.

Sasha deteriorated gradually, to the point that she became unsteady and sometimes had to be helped to stand. But it was summertime in Vancouver, which allowed for Sasha to be outside most of the day, slowly making the rounds of the back yard or basking in the shade. It was a good summer.

Toward the end of July I had left Sasha in the back yard and gone with the kids for the weekly grocery shop. I noticed, coming back to the driveway, that there seemed to be an inordinate number of ravens sitting on top of the fence that surrounded the yard, hopping on and off and calling incessantly. I knew instantly they were after Sasha.

My heart pounding, I ran to the back yard, but something beige whizzed past and beat me to it. There was Sasha, unable to get up, surrounded by a mob of ravens edging ever closer. The ravens, sensing an easy target, had gathered to defeat her by numbers. But the real action was happening a few feet away. Paxton literally had one raven by the leg, another by a wing, and was going for a third. They were attacking him but he wasn't giving up.

Paxton drove the ravens off and they retreated to the top of the fence. The cat remained crouched, every hair on end, spitting and yowling in a way that would have made a wolf think twice. I'd never heard anything like it. After a couple of minutes the ravens dispersed.

Amazingly, neither Sasha nor Pax was really injured. Given the number of black feathers littering the yard I'm not sure the same could be said for the ravens.

Summer passed into a long, uncharacteristically warm and dry fall. I never again let Sasha into the yard unless I was home. But she loved lying in the grass, watching the bees and smelling the earth, so I did let her enjoy long periods of time outside. And ever after that day, she had a guardian. No matter where he was, within a few minutes of Sasha going outside, Pax would appear, sitting on the fence above wherever she lay, sharing the last warm rays of the season. Sometimes they would sleep together, dog on the grass, cat on the fence above, but the cat was always there. The dog was never alone again.

As the fall grew colder, Sasha reached the point where life was more pain than joy, and I let her go.

Some may say Pax was being territorial, defending what he saw as his own. Some may say he just figured Sasha was the best bird bait the cat goddess ever made. But after I put Sasha down, that cat sat on her bed for three days and, other than to relieve himself, did not move. So judge as you will.

Paxton lived to tolerate another dog in our family, a German Shepherd named Kia. As with Sasha, Pax seemed to barely stand her and spent a lot of time glaring at her down his very long Siamese nose. But he didn't fool me, not for one second!

— Trish Featherstone —

77

Good Vibrations

I simply can't resist a cat, particularly a purring one.
They are the cleanest, cunningest, and most intelligent
things I know, outside of the girl you love, of course.
~Mark Twain

Sometimes it feels like there are two major groups of people in this world: those who adore cats and those who hate them. My husband, Harry, however, exists somewhere in the middle. He enjoys snippets of their existence, such as playing with kittens or petting them when he wants. But when it comes to the constant shedding, sharpening claws on furniture or yowling to make their wishes known, well... he has had to learn tolerance. After all, when he fell in love with me it was clear that animals would always be a major part of my life.

One summer morning, I'd gone out to the barn to feed my horses. A low, guttural, eerie wail stood my neck hairs at attention. I found a large, orange and white tomcat lying on the dirt floor. A quick examination revealed two large abscesses that had swelled one back leg to twice its size. He also had a fever and was quite weak.

As I picked him up, the cat purred and head-butted his appreciation.

I set him up in our bathroom, cleaned and opened the abscesses to allow drainage and put a poultice on his leg. He purred quietly throughout the procedure and again each time I treated him, three times daily. In two weeks, he was healthy and ready to be introduced to our animal family.

For several months I tried to find him a good home, but everyone seemed to want him as a barn cat and he was far too interested in home life for that.

So, Orion became the newest member of our family.

Harry and I were closing in on thirty-eight years of being together when he was diagnosed, over Christmas, with Stage II colorectal cancer. Two weeks later, he was in surgery.

After ten days in the hospital, I brought him home and helped him get slowly out of the car and up the stairs. He sank into his recliner, lifting his feet and legs with the handle. Grimacing, he tried to find a comfortable position.

Orion was not allowed on that chair; Harry didn't appreciate the hairs he left behind. But once Harry was settled, Orion scrutinized him carefully, considering the situation. Then he made his move. Gingerly, he jumped onto the footrest. With careful consideration, one toe at a time, he inched up further, still surveying. And then, with a ballerina's grace, he slid onto Harry's lap, edging as close to the incision as he could without actually touching that painful area.

Finally, he'd found the exact spot he wanted and lay down. Within seconds, the whole room filled with a purr symphony — without a doubt, the loudest purr I'd ever heard. He didn't move or stop purring for a full hour. When he eventually left, he did so in the same careful manner.

Some scientists suggest that a cat's purr vibrates at a healing frequency. Orion certainly seemed to use it therapeutically for himself and then stepped up to help Harry. And although Orion and Harry eventually returned to their normal relationship, tolerating each other's presence in the house, for that one hour, the synchronicity and symbiosis between these two roommates defined pure harmony.

— Diane C. Nicholson —

Chapter
8

The Joy of Giving

78

Thriving While Grieving

Help your brother's boat across,
and your own will reach the shore.
~Hindu Proverb

part of me felt guilty, but I knew that I needed to honour my brother by moving forward with my life's purpose. I never expected to be launching a new business and a personal development seminar one year after my younger brother suddenly passed away.

On the day Taranveer passed, my world came crashing down. Just four days prior, I had told a friend how completely happy I was for the first time ever. My parents were also strong emotionally and ready to conquer the world. Taranveer had gotten his dream job, one he had been seeking for a year.

I had moved back in with my parents three months earlier, so I had spent every day with my brother before he left for his job. He left two days after my birthday, and I was mad at him for not wishing me a happy birthday or saying Happy Father's Day to our dad.

When we said goodbye, I hugged him and told him I loved him and wished him the best. He called me a few minutes later from the car to remind me to find his speakers. That was our relationship — we were really close friends who forgave each other and went back to our dynamic relationship as siblings.

The morning we learned he had died, I was standing with my parents and it felt like his spirit was standing beside me, telling me that we have a greater purpose and not to grieve for him too much. We decided as a family that we would celebrate him, laugh and tell his funny stories. We kept that atmosphere in our home instead of the pain and sorrow in traditional Sikh grieving households. Not following the norm, we laughed at the funeral and his pictures. Some elders of the community commented that we seemed unaffected by the death, but they didn't know we cried ourselves to sleep every night.

The year after his passing became a year of travel and self-discovery for me. I finally did the international consulting work I had always wanted to do. I was healthy and I made new friendships. I was a changed person.

Now that I had lost my identity as a sister, I had to rediscover who I was. And I had become the sole caregiver for my parents. I had to take that into consideration for all my decisions — where I wanted to live, where they would live, how I could support them as they aged and what emotional support they needed. I knew I wanted to be there to support them while they rebuilt their life.

In the Sikh culture, there were some who told my parents they had nothing left because now they didn't have a son. My parents fought back, telling everyone that their daughter was everything and more.

I had a powerful conversation with my dad, who said, "We are meant to be of greater service and contribute to our community and that is why we are facing such hardships. We need to step outside ourselves and be of service as that is how we can honour him."

As soon as my brother had passed, I had decided to have a ball hockey tournament in one year as a fun way to get everyone together, celebrate him and contribute to kids in sports. I cried each day of the tournament, but in the end knew it was the right thing to do. We contributed happiness and memories to those who attended the tournament and those who benefited from it.

I also had decided that a year after his passing, I would step up my contribution in a big way. So I launched my personal coaching company, focusing on ethnic women aligning to their passion/message by building the career and life they love.

I came forward and hosted a weekend seminar two days after what would have been Taranveer's birthday. He was always the proudest of me when I helped change people's lives. He was always telling his friends about me and all the cool things I did. I hope that he's talking about me wherever he is, saying, "That is my sister, the one who realized that living her life with purpose is more important than crying for my loss."

— Manpreet Dhillon —

Learning to Ask

*The strong individual is the one who asks for help
when he needs it.*
~Rona Barrett

I arrived early, dressed in black slacks and a white top as requested, and tried to calm my nerves as I approached the man and woman standing at the kettle. The greeting was not what I'd hoped for. "You were supposed to be here yesterday, not today," the man told me after I introduced myself. "We wondered what happened to you."

I could not have felt worse. For weeks, I had geared up for this. I put the instruction sheet on my refrigerator and re-read it many times.

I was volunteering for a few shifts of bell ringing for the Salvation Army. That probably doesn't seem like a big deal. Every Christmas, people in shopping malls, grocery stores and on street corners collect donations for the Salvation Army's programs for those in need.

But in addition to helping raise money for an organization I believe in, I decided to volunteer for a personal reason. I find it difficult — in fact, ridiculously hard — to ask people for anything, even though I quite enjoy helping others when they need a hand.

My friends will tell you that I'm outgoing, independent, even adventurous. Yet, when I'm sick I'd rather stagger out the door half-dead to buy some chicken soup than ask a friend or neighbour for help. When I sign up for a run to raise money for cancer, I donate the cash myself rather than asking others. The thought of asking a friend for a ride to the airport is way too stressful, even though my rational mind knows the answer would be yes.

So, I decided one Christmas I would take a baby step in learning to ask. I'd do a few shifts as a "bell-ringer" to see how it felt to ask perfect strangers to give.

By the time I returned for my shift the next day, I had learned that the mix-up wasn't my fault. There had been a computer scheduling error for which the supervisor of volunteers apologized profusely.

The man I'd met briefly the previous day was there again. He was a driver who made the rounds collecting money from each kettle every couple of hours to deliver to the local headquarters.

He gave me a few friendly pointers, since he had been a kettle volunteer for a decade or so before being hired as a seasonal driver. He also revealed that he had gotten help from the Salvation Army years ago, which had changed his life.

That gave me something to think about. This cheerful guy, with the responsibility of handling thousands of dollars in cash, was one of many who had been helped by the donations dropped into the Christmas kettles.

As I slipped on the Salvation Army vest and took my spot beside the kettle, I consciously tried to follow the "tips" provided to volunteers. Stand (don't sit), smile, make eye contact, and don't ring the bell too loud or too often. (That can get annoying to those in nearby stores.)

It felt awkward at first. My location on the second floor of a shopping mall wasn't a busy spot, so I tried to smile and catch the eyes of every passer-by. Most quickly glanced away. I worried I was making them feel guilty. I didn't like that at all.

I was starting to wonder whether this bell-ringing thing was for me when a man emerged from a store some distance down the corridor and marched purposefully toward me. "Well, this won't do," he said as he slipped a twenty-dollar bill into the slot of the clear plastic globe that topped the collection kettle. "We can't have this sitting empty."

I thanked him for his donation and for "seeding the pot." The smiles we exchanged were more than polite. It was like we were on the same team.

Even then, it took me a while to relax. When people walked by with nothing but a quick glance and then turned away, I felt like I wasn't doing this right. Should I smile more? Say "Merry Christmas?" Try more eye contact?

But little by little, I began to see that people who had passed me once, or even two or three times, were coming back later to drop money into the kettle. It was a revelation to me that many of the people whom I thought were dodging me weren't doing that at all. Whether they needed time for the idea to percolate, or felt pressured to get their shopping started first, I cannot say.

For a while, I tried to guess who would return to donate later. But I gave up. There was no "typical" donor, at least, to my unpractised eye. They came in all ages and apparent income levels, and for their own reasons.

By the time I had my last two shifts, in the week before Christmas, I had relaxed and enjoyed watching people bustling by. I still stood tall, looked people in the eyes, smiled and occasionally rang my bell. But inside me something had changed.

I no longer felt I was "targeting" people, or that my success or failure depended on whether they gave a donation. I felt much more like I was part of the cheerful, busy crowd. Once people noticed my presence, their own circumstances and feelings would determine the rest.

It was surprising how many people came to talk to me. One woman shared how her brother had been helped with addiction; others told how they look forward to helping the Christmas kettle campaign each year. Quite a few parents took their small children aside for a talk about the kettle, and then gave them coins to drop in.

A few dropped money into the kettle without a word. That was the case with my biggest single donation. A middle-aged, casually dressed man stopped a short distance from me and began pulling bills from his wallet. He walked over, dropped eighty dollars in the kettle and quickly walked away.

The weirdest donation came from someone in a group of twenty-somethings, dressed in elf costumes, who were racing around the mall early one morning. I thought they were Santa's helpers, doing a few errands before the Santa House opened.

But it turned out they were on a scavenger hunt. Once they spotted my bell — a musical instrument was on their list — they beseeched me to ring it and sing "Jingle Bells."

"I just donated!" one of them shouted cheerfully, as if to urge me on. I would have done it regardless, of course. We sang with gusto, if not with perfect pitch, as one of them recorded it on his cell phone.

There was a lesson for me in this little venture into uncomfortable territory. It has given me a great appreciation for the good feeling that comes with giving, not just for me but for everyone. So it follows that asking for help is not such a bad thing. It is just another side of living in a caring community.

I'll try to remember that next time I'm down with a cold and in need of a little chicken soup.

— Kristin Goff —

I Would Have
Starved Without the
Food Bank

Not what we say about our blessings, but how we use
them, is the true measure of our thanksgiving.
~W.T. Purkiser

I stood there shocked. It was the day after my roommates and
I had thrown a huge party. I had just opened the cupboards
and realized that we had no food left.

When I first moved out on my own there was a tremendous amount of adjustment time. I was young, foolish and kept bad
company. To make matters worse, I didn't know how to budget, I
had bills to pay, I had to finish my schooling, and I couldn't find a
job better than a counter attendant/bakery assistant at a donut shop.
I worked graveyard shifts for over a year at the wage of $6.10/hour
and I did this while attending high school. How I did it, I really don't
know. Those were not the best times in my life.

I remember moving from cupboard to cupboard and feeling completely overwhelmed by their emptiness. To make matters worse, we
had no money. Nothing. Not a penny until our pay cheques, which
were over a week and a half away. I knew I could eat one free meal at
the donut shop every day but I had no idea what I was going to do
for my other meals.

That was when I realized: We needed to go to the food bank.

I remember trying to think of an alternative. I believed that food banks were for homeless people, that I would be taking from someone needier than myself. However, I soon realized that if I didn't go, there would be repercussions. I needed food to keep my mind and body healthy.

I swallowed my pride and went.

I remember being so fearful, wondering if they would turn me away. My stomach was in knots, partially from the hunger and partially from the anxiety of knowing that my life had come to this.

The staff at the food bank was kind, understanding and gave us more than enough food to get us through two weeks.

Due to ongoing financial challenges, I ended up using the food bank for almost a year.

This is something I haven't told anyone in my life... until now. I was afraid of being judged. I was concerned that others would think I was weak because I had to rely on a social service for help. I was frightened that it would change the way my friends and family view me.

However, the reality is, we all have times of need. We all have moments when we need to reach out for help. At that time in my life, I was thankful for the food bank and the services they provided. Their services helped feed my mind and body so that I could continue with my education.

A couple of decades later, I find myself regularly donating food and volunteering at the food bank. I've even written a post on how to help your local food bank. The help that they extended to me in my time of need will never be forgotten.

—Jennifer Bly—

81

Someone Who Cares

Unselfish and noble actions are the most radiant pages
in the biography of souls.
~David Thomas

I t was somewhere between spring and summer; just enough
sunshine to be warm, but not so much that it was blistering
hot.

My mom and I drove through the countryside — windows
open, long hair whipping around in the breeze.

We were a long way from home, but it didn't matter. It was nice
to just enjoy each other's company on the long drive. I was only eight
or nine at the time, but this journey from Grandma's house by the
lake back to our own house in the suburban city wasn't foreign to me.

A pot of flowers sat in the back seat, long ago forgotten by me,
even though their heavenly scent filled the car as best as it could
amidst the air blowing in through the windows. They didn't matter
to me — they were just something someone had given to my mom.

Suddenly, in the middle of nowhere, my mom pulled over.

"What are you doing?" I asked, fearing that the car had broken
down and we'd be stuck there, so far from home.

But that wasn't the case.

My mom hopped out of the car, grabbing the flowers from the
back seat.

"I'll just be a minute," she called back through the open windows.

As she walked away, I noticed the humble little building hidden by a hedge just beyond the ditch. My eyes quickly scanned the edge of the road before settling on a little sign, proclaiming that it was a nursing home.

I looked back to the building, utterly confused, as my mom reappeared — empty-handed. She climbed back into the car and we drove away, without a word.

After a mile or two, I spoke.

"Do you know someone there, Mom?"

She absentmindedly shook her head no, checking her rear-view mirrors.

"Then what'd you do with the flowers?"

She smiled slightly. "I gave them to the receptionist."

"Oh," I thought for a moment. "You gave the receptionist flowers?"

She laughed at my confusion. "No, I gave them to the receptionist to give to someone she thought really needed them, who hasn't gotten any in a while."

I sat in silence for a moment, thinking about this, before I spoke again.

"Did you leave your name?"

She answered instantly, "No. The receptionist asked, but I just told her 'someone who cares.'"

This time, I spoke quickly. "But why?" It had never occurred to me that people could purposefully give gifts without putting their name on them. "How will they thank you?"

My mother smiled again, speaking as though it was the most obvious answer in the world. "Because leaving flowers there for someone who will appreciate them more than we will makes me feel good. Knowing that those flowers will make someone smile is enough of a thank you for me."

My mom was oblivious to my amazement, as I stared at her in awe for quite a while longer.

For her, it was a simple act that she had done without even thinking.

But for me, it was a memory and lesson that would last for the rest of my life; the greatest gifts not only come from the heart, but are given without any expectations.

—Janelle In't Veldt—

82

The Gift of a Caring Companion

Fun fact: Studies have shown that the unconditional love of a dog can help people feel less depressed.

Back in high school, I had a hard time fitting in and felt really lonely. It was getting harder and harder to hold back my tears every day when I came home from school. I didn't know if the tears were of relief that the day was done, or of sadness that I had to get up and go back to a place full of bullies and people who didn't like me.

One day, I came home in tears and ran upstairs to my bedroom. I couldn't stop crying. I sat on my floor and started ripping pages from my diary. I can't believe I liked him, I thought. I had liked this boy for a long time and had actually been feeling pretty happy lately, but that day he had said he could never like someone like me. I was crushed.

I finished ripping the pages out of my diary and continued sobbing when I felt something brush against my leg. I looked up and saw Myla staring at me with a tilted head and a wagging tail. I scrunched up my face and began crying hysterically. Myla's tail stopped. She backed away a little bit and tilted her head to the other side. Her eyes grew wide. Then she started whimpering.

I curled my legs up to my stomach and hugged them with my arms. Myla nudged her head between my legs, put her paws up on my chest and sniffed my face. She had never done this before! She was a pretty placid dog who usually sat on the couch and unenthusiastically watched the cars go by. I knew she cared about me but I was shocked when she put her paws on me, sniffed my face, and licked my tears away. It was as if she was replacing a caring parent at that moment.

I patted her head, and her tail started wagging again. I laughed at her funny little tail trying to wag as fast as it could. She then started chasing it, and as I watched her, I forgot what I was so sad about. I took a moment to catch my breath and lifted myself up off the floor. Myla followed me to the bathroom where I washed my tear-stained face. I flicked some water at her, and she sneezed. Her tail never stopped wagging.

Myla followed me around the house until late into the evening. Every time I would sniff or make a sound, she would cock her head and look at me like a worried mother, as if to confirm that I was okay.

That night, as I crawled into bed, exhausted from the day's events, I realized how thankful I was for Myla. I had gotten her for Christmas the year before just as I had entered high school. I went through many emotional ups and downs throughout high school — as most people do — and came home to my favourite little pooch who would follow me up to my room and insist on comforting me the only way she knew how: with doggy kisses and tail wags.

Myla comforted me with her puppy compassion until someone else needed her. Two years after I started university, my mom told me her friend was lonely after being widowed. It broke my heart. I knew that Myla would be a perfect addition to her household, with her easygoing nature and huggable coat of fur.

It was really hard to give Myla away, but I will never forget the look on that lady's face when I gave her a new companion. Her big smile and happy tears made me feel like I did the right thing.

After caring for me for so long, it was time for Myla to care for a widow who just needed someone to talk to and feed. I think I gave the best gift one could ever give. From an emotional high-school life to a widow's bedside, Myla served her purpose as a caring and friendly presence in times of need. My darling Myla proved to me that dogs make not only the best pets, but also some of the best friends, teachers, and caregivers we'll ever know.

— Sarah Wun —

83

Santa in the 'Hood

Christmas, my child, is love in action. Every time we
love, every time we give, it's Christmas.
~Dale Evans

I was pregnant and my husband had just started a new job driving a transport truck. We weren't sure our finances were going to get us through the holidays. Things were tight and we already needed to make a nice Christmas for our first child and my husband's daughter. I felt as though I was failing as a parent in some way. We didn't have enough money for food and our marriage was going through a bumpy patch at the time. Being pregnant and alone a lot only served to deepen my depression, and I even mentioned to a friend how low I was feeling.

One day, I was babysitting for another friend. I was doing everything possible to earn a little extra money. I was in the bathroom when I heard a knock on the door; the kids must need me, I thought. I called to them to let them know I would be right out. I was shocked to hear a male voice answer me saying, "Hurry up! Get dressed. We are going for a car ride."

When I came out of the bathroom, I was surprised to see my friend Wayne standing in my living room smiling broadly at me. "I can't just go for a ride, I am babysitting and we don't have any car seats or anything," I replied. The truth was I wasn't feeling up to company and didn't feel like going anywhere.

Wayne was a persuasive man and always seemed to have answers to such problems. "Oh, that's no problem... I can just use my grand-daughter's seat." He smiled at me, almost bouncing out of the house. "I'll be right back. Be ready, okay?"

Realizing that my friend was not going to take no for an answer, I quickly brushed my hair, grabbed my coat, and got the kids dressed for the weather, just in the nick of time. In mere minutes, Wayne was knocking on the door. As I walked to the car I realized that it was my neighbour Stu's car, and he was there, smiling in the front seat.

"Where are we going?" I asked my friends.

Wayne quickly replied, "Oh, Stu needs to go into town to pick up a few things, and we just thought it might be good for you to get out of the house."

When we got into town, Wayne pulled into the grocery store parking lot, parked, and proceeded to get the kids out of the car.

I told them I would just wait in the car, but they wouldn't hear of it. I got out of the car, took the kids by the hand, and followed them into the store.

As we walked through the doors of the store, Stu and Wayne each grabbed a shopping cart and turned to me. I stood there waiting for them to start their shopping. "I'm ready," I said, trying not to hold up their shopping. They looked at each other mischievously, then back at me. "What?" I asked.

Stu smiled. "Okay, since you're ready, let's do your shopping." I was dumbfounded. I just stood there staring, as tears began to run from my eyes.

"Wh-wh-what?" I stammered.

"Let's do your grocery shopping, and no looking at price tags. Just buy what you want. I'm paying," Stu replied with a boyish grin.

"You can't do this," I said quietly.

"I can and I am," he replied, still smiling.

In a quiet whisper, smiling through tears, I told Stu, "I'll get you back for this." Slowly, I started to follow them.

As the two men ushered me through the store buying all manner of food, drink, candy, chocolate, and anything they deemed we needed, I couldn't wrap my head around it. Why were they doing this?

At the checkout counter, it suddenly dawned on me what was actually happening. I started to cry again, and the cashier asked timidly, "Are you alright?"

Yes," I replied. "These two have just done my Christmas shopping for me."

"I'm paying," Stu stated proudly. The cashier smiled and said, "Well, it's nice to meet you, Santa!"

Once we were packed in the car (believe me, there wasn't much room) and on our way back home, I asked Stu why he did what he did. He told me that since he didn't have children of his own, and his wife had passed, this was his way of celebrating Christmas.

It took me three days to find room to put all the food away.

In January of the following year, Stu was diagnosed with esophageal cancer. I had to let him know how much everyone in the community loved and appreciated him. Stu was a bit of a philanthropist in our small town. What could I do? How could we show him? We had to do something before it was too late.

Eventually, I came up with the idea that we could make him a quilt and have each of our families' names embroidered on a square so that he could be "blanketed in the warmth, love, and kindness" of us all. We called Wayne, who then got in touch with many of the people around town who knew, loved, and respected Stu. He planned a bit of a party and had the quilt embroidered. I told Wayne that I didn't want anyone to know it was my idea. We just all needed to let Stu know we loved him.

A year later, it was a snowy December evening near Christmas. My mom and I got the kids ready and walked to the community center to join in the festivities. When we arrived, we noticed Stu sitting at the front of the hall.

Then, Wayne took the microphone. "Tonight would not be happening without the thought and care of one person...."

Oh no, I thought. Here it comes. I stood there staring at Wayne, shaking my head slowly at first and then more violently. "Connie, can you please come up here?" I'm going to die, I thought, everyone is looking at me.

"Go on, Con," my mom whispered.

When I got to where Stu was sitting, tears were streaming down his face. I leaned down and hugged him. "I told you I would get you back," I whispered to him.

"That you have, darling, that you have. Merry Christmas!"

A month later Stu passed away from the cancer. Twelve Christmases have passed since he died and every year I think about him and say a silent prayer of thanks to him for being Santa to me all those years ago.

— Connie I. Davidson —

84

A Humbling Experience

*Judge tenderly, if you must. There is usually a side you
have not heard, a story you know nothing about, and a
battle waged that you are not having to fight.*
~Traci Lea LaRussa

It was my very first impression of Salt Lake City, Utah. My
best friend had dropped me off in front of The Cathedral of
the Madeleine, near Temple Square, before heading to the
university. Thinking I'd start my tour with this building, I
climbed the stone steps and pulled open the outer wooden door. I
found myself inside a small entrance, facing a second, locked door.
As I turned to leave, I noticed a man, a vagabond, asleep in a corner,
his head resting on a small backpack. Suddenly feeling like I was
intruding, I exited the cathedral as discreetly as possible.

Outside, I paused on the sidewalk and inhaled the cold winter
air. My encounter with the vagabond brought to mind an article I had
read on the plane. It was an interview with a pastor who had spent
a day walking around downtown Toronto, handing out change to
everyone who asked. At the end of the day, he counted how much
money he had shared with the needy, and it was less than ten dollars.
The lesson he wanted to impart with his story was that we shouldn't
show so much restraint about giving to those in need, because none
of us will go broke if we part with a couple of dollars now and then.

I could see the wisdom and truth of his words, but I still mistakenly believed that most homeless people were either drug addicts or drunks, and that giving them money would only serve to fuel their vice. When confronted with a similar question, the pastor pointed out that the Bible tells us we must strive to offer charity in whatever manner we can to whomever is in need. It is up to God, not us, to see that our gifts are righteously used. That last message was now causing me to re-examine my beliefs regarding homeless people.

"Miss?"

I turned to see the vagabond walking toward me. "Yes?"

"You wouldn't happen to have a bit of money to spare, would you? Enough to buy breakfast?" he asked.

"No, sorry," I answered. "All I have is Canadian money. I don't think that would be of much use to you."

"No, it wouldn't. Thanks."

I hesitated a few seconds before offering, "I have a McDonald's gift card. I could buy you something for breakfast."

"Thank you," he replied.

I followed him down the street to the nearest McDonald's. He looked to be about fifty years old and was dressed in layers of what I figured must be every garment he possessed.

After ordering breakfast and a coffee for himself, he asked me what I was having. I told him I'd already eaten and that I was anxious to start my visit of Temple Square.

"You have time for a coffee, Miss," he said. "The buildings don't open for another hour."

I couldn't figure out if he wanted company for breakfast or if he felt awkward after realizing that I had detoured by the McDonald's solely for his sake. His comment caught me off guard, and I was unable to come up with a polite reason to excuse myself, so I ordered a tea and resolved to sit with him for a while.

When we left, he thanked me again for the breakfast and asked if I was heading directly to Temple Square. I told him I was.

"I know this town well. I'll show you around," he offered. "To thank you for your generosity."

"It's not necessary."

"I insist."

What to do? I must admit that it was kind of him to offer to be my tour guide in exchange for breakfast. I didn't want to spend the entire day with him, but I didn't want to be impolite either. So, I reluctantly accepted his offer.

We started by the Temple gardens, followed by the Joseph Smith Memorial Building, the South Visitors' Center, the North Visitors' Center, and finally the Conference Center and the Tabernacle. We spent six hours together!

Initially, his presence bothered me. It troubled me to be accompanied by a vagabond. I worried about what others would think and how I would be seen.

At first, I tried every excuse I could think of to part ways with him: I need to rest a bit; I'd like to take some pictures; I need to call my friend; I need to use the bathroom... Nothing worked! He always waited for me patiently.

Eventually, I gave up and accepted my fate. That's when I began to see things differently. I realized he was a fantastic tour guide. He knew absolutely everything about everything: the details of the Temple's construction, the names of the plants in the Temple gardens, the history of Hotel Utah and of the renovations that transformed it into the Joseph Smith Memorial Building... everything!

Little by little, I got to know him and started appreciating the way he would tell me about his life while we walked. Over the course of our time together, the vagabond disappeared, and James appeared. James was an educated man and had once been a tradesman in Tennessee. He had resorted to sleeping on church steps following an injury and a series of unfortunate events that had left him without a job, house and money. He wasn't an alcoholic or a drug addict.

We parted ways in front of the Conference Center.

"I have to go meet my friend," I said. "Thanks for the guided tour. I had a nice time." I was sincere.

"Happy I could be of some use."

I pulled the McDonald's gift card from my pocket.

"Here. It's not much, but it should buy you dinner," I said, handing him the card.

"I can't accept… You've done so much already."

"I insist. I don't need it."

"Thank you."

"Goodbye and good luck," I said, holding out my hand. Instead of shaking it, he removed a necklace from around his neck and placed it in my palm. It was a large metal cross studded with plastic "diamonds."

"Keep it close to your heart. It'll protect you," he said.

It's not the type of necklace I would typically wear. I thought of protesting, but the sincerity with which he gave it made me think it would be futile to do so. He shook my hand, thanked me once again for my generosity and left me with a "God Bless."

Almost ten years have passed since that day. His necklace has become a permanent addition to my purse, constantly reminding me to never judge a book by its cover… or a man by his appearance.

— Kim Tendland-Frenette —

85

Kindness Gives Back

Carry out a random act of kindness, with no
expectation of reward, safe in the knowledge
that one day someone might do the same for you.
~Princess Diana

I had a quick thirty-minute layover in Detroit before heading home to Toronto. After rushing up the jet way I embarked on a brisk walk, knowing that my gate was on the opposite end of the airport. I got there with five minutes to spare and stood waiting for "Group 3" to be called.

I was tired and had a coaching call scheduled for an hour after I was set to get home. I guess you could say that time was of the essence. But then I heard the announcement: "It seems we have overbooked the flight. Would anyone care to volunteer to stay for the later departure?" There were 100-plus people and not a single person volunteered.

The next flight was in four hours, at 7:30 p.m. I looked around and saw businessmen needing to get home for work, moms needing to get home to see their kids, kids needing to get home to see their friends, and more importantly, I saw people that needed to be helped. Even though I wanted to be home just as much as anyone, something inside me said that I should volunteer. I should extend some kindness to this group of strangers. The gate attendant had said that the flight couldn't board until someone volunteered.

I picked up my bag and approached the desk. I said, "I volunteer as tribute!" The gate attendant smiled and understood the reference to *The Hunger Games*.

As she was processing my ticket, I looked around at all the passengers who could now board their flight and I was happy that I had been able to help. The attendant handed me my boarding pass for the later flight and then said, "This is for your kindness." She handed me another piece of paper and I saw that it was a seven-hundred-dollar voucher to fly anywhere in the world during the next year!

I got to my new gate and took a seat next to a power outlet so that my laptop would make it through the extra four hours. I rescheduled my coaching call. And then I got a lot of work done, which was a wonderful silver lining.

When my flight started boarding, I was surprised to discover that my new boarding pass was for a seat in first class. I boarded the plane, and I thought about how grateful I was for everything that had happened, and how it was all because of the ripple effect of kindness. I gave with the intention to serve others, with no thought of reward, and that kindness was returned to me with an upgrade to first class and a big voucher for future travel.

—Juan Bendana—

86

Conscious Kindness Day Lasts All Year

Your heart is a powerful force. Use it consciously.
~Amy Leigh Mercree

A few years ago, when United Way Winnipeg began their Conscious Kindness Day, a day to encourage everyone to do and say kind things, my family embraced it with enthusiasm! We pledged to complete many acts of kindness that day and had a great time.

Among other things, we wrote sidewalk chalk messages and baked treats for the kids' school staff. My daughter, Ainslee, also decided she wanted to give away homemade cookies and lemonade. Many people paid her anyway, so we took the money to the store and bought some flowers. We immediately gave one of the bouquets to a lady we met outside the store. It was fun to watch her face light up with surprise and delight when she realized she was the recipient of this random act of kindness from my little girl!

Another act of kindness my daughter performed that day was to call her grandparents and great-grandma to tell them she loved them. I posted a picture of that call on social media and United Way even used it in the newspaper! Such a simple act — reaching out and letting people know you love them — yet so important and transformative.

As a teacher, I have also supervised Kindness Clubs at my schools.

I've enjoyed being a part of this amazing movement, and the ripple effect of spreading kindness is very noticeable. These small acts, and an emphasis on celebrating kindness, create a positive atmosphere, build empathy, and create lasting change in our attitudes.

I have witnessed the desire to spread love and kindness grow in my own children, as well as those I teach. Ainslee now plans her own acts of kindness for Conscious Kindness Day. Most recently she made bookmarks for each of her classmates, as well as wrote them personalized compliment notes celebrating their individual strengths. Before Conscious Kindness Day, she spoke to her teacher about her plans and the class decided to write notes to all the school staff and write positive messages outside with sidewalk chalk that day. It warms my heart to see this kindness spreading.

Meanwhile, my students gave up many recesses to prepare for the day. They made bracelets, prepared notes for staff and neighbours, and also made plans for spreading kindness at home. These students met before school on Conscious Kindness Day to run around and deliver notes, write sidewalk messages and, generally, spread kindness. The excitement in the school was noticeable!

At lunch, the students met again to deliver the bracelets to other students and deliver the "nice neighbour notes" to all the houses that face our schoolyard. They each had three bracelets to share and they were challenged to give one to someone they had never spoken to before. This was a powerful addition to our plan. Making connections with people we don't know increases empathy and compassion. Many of the classrooms heard what our club was doing and they also found ways to spread kindness; some wrote notes for other classes, some gave treats away, and some made posters that are now displayed around our school celebrating the power of kindness!

The ripple effect of spreading kindness is tremendously notice-able! Each year my family, and now my extended family too, embraces Conscious Kindness Day with an open heart, excited to spread kindness, love, and empathy to those around us, whether we know them or not!

Of course, spreading love and kindness isn't limited to one day, but celebrating Conscious Kindness Day is a real boost to morale for both the giver and the recipient, and the impact lasts much longer than a day.

— Niki Card —

87

Charity Begins...

It is the thrifty people who are generous.
~Lord Rosebery

With three weeks before the end of the year, it's time to do the majority of my charity donations. I get my spreadsheet of charities where I track donations and income tax receipts, pull out the stack of pledge cards I've been saving throughout the year, and open my check book.

I pick up my pen, but instead of writing the checks, I hesitate. It's easy to give money to charity when you know you have money coming in. It's not so easy when most of the money is going out.

Over the last few weeks, I've been informed that two of the websites I write for have decided to "proceed cautiously because of the recession." An editor at a newspaper I've written for told me they're no longer using freelancers. And just yesterday I got an e-mail from a health magazine that I frequently contribute to. In response to my query, they told me they're not looking for any new ideas for the next six months.

In other words, I can't expect any more assignments from these places for at least that long, maybe longer.

Although I've been looking for other writing venues, so far I haven't done well. The marketing group that I belong to is mostly listing positions for bloggers and freelance writers that pay less than five cents a word, some as low as a penny. No one can survive on that.

While I actually had the best writing year of my career, it's becoming clear that next year is not going to come close to matching it. And I should add that "best" is relative. I read somewhere that the average writer makes less than $15,000 a year, and that's with factoring in the megastars who make hundreds of thousands of dollars. I'm still below average.

Although my substitute teaching helps pay the bills, I haven't been getting as many calls lately. To save money, the school board is closing schools, meaning fewer teachers are needed.

So, can I really afford to give to charity? Doesn't charity begin at home? My home. I'm tempted to close my check book, but I don't.

I look around my house. Yes, it's worth less now than it was before the housing market tanked, but I still have a small, nice house in a good area of town. Since I'm not looking to sell, I can wait out the market slump.

My fridge and cupboards aren't bursting with food, but that's because I haven't gone shopping this week. These days I don't buy a lot of meat or expensive prepared foods, but neither do I have to choose between food and paying for utilities. Unlike an increasing number of people, I've been able to donate food to food banks rather than having to use them.

A lot of the clothes I wear are second-hand, but that's partly because I'm inherently frugal and partly because I don't care about fashion. If I look carefully, I can usually find good quality clothes that have been "gently" used.

Then I think about some of my friends who aren't as lucky as I am. One lost six teeth over a couple of years because she couldn't afford regular dental care. I just had a filling replaced last week. Yes, the bill hurt almost as much as the procedure, but the pain wore off for both.

Another friend, with massive health and mobility problems, lives on a meagre disability pension while her husband works two jobs to keep them afloat. My knees may creak more than they used to, and my kidneys aren't in the best shape, but I can still get around.

A third friend lost seven years of her life when a stroke wiped out large chunks of her memory. Unable to work, she lives on government assistance, which, for her, means stale crackers and tuna fish—which she hates. Yet one month, when she had managed to save five dollars for a treat at McDonald's, she ended up giving that money away to someone she thought was needier. Me? I treat myself to breakfast out every Sunday and every couple of weeks my mother sends me twenty dollars to go out for dinner.

Suddenly, I feel very lucky and very rich. I grab my pen again and begin to write checks. I don't know what next year will bring, but for now I can share my good fortune with others.

Charity may begin at home but it doesn't have to stay there.

—Harriet Cooper—

88

The Children's Christmas

Christmas, in its final essence, is for grown-ups
who have forgotten what children know. Christmas
is for whoever is old enough to have denied the
unquenchable spirit of man.
~Margaret Cousins

I'd been up since the crack of dawn preparing a Christmas feast that would feed twenty-one friends and family members plus the three of us. It was almost noon, and the delectable aroma of turkey and stuffing permeated the house. I'd already prepared two gigantic pots of peeled potatoes and diced fresh vegetables. The glazed ham, roast beef and meat pies sat waiting to be popped into the oven.

I put the finishing touches on the appetizers, carefully storing them in the fridge beside cranberry sauce, salad, condiments, and other side dishes I planned to serve. As holiday music played softly in the background, I measured spices for my gravies and set the table.

Though the plates and cutlery didn't all match because I was feeding so many, everything gleamed and looked picture-perfect. Poinsettia centerpieces with matching crimson candles lay nestled among breadbaskets I'd fill at the last minute. I was admiring my work when the call came. It was my younger brother's girlfriend.

"We can't come," she groaned into the phone. "We have the

stomach flu."

"Oh dear," I gushed soothingly. "Get back into bed and try to rest. If you like, I can send some food over later." The gagging sound she made before quickly hanging up suggested it was the wrong offer to make.

The phone rang again. This time it was a friend. She'd just had a heated argument with her sister, another of our invited guests, and her husband. "Jake and I refuse to sit at the same table with those two and their annoying brats," she hollered, hanging up with a loud slam.

A second later a call from her sister came, saying basically the same thing. Before I could tell her it was safe to come, the dial tone hummed in my ear. I was down four adults and three kids.

I was just about to ask my fifteen-year-old son, David, to clear and dismantle one of the folding tables when the phone shrilled a fourth time. I picked it up warily.

"Mary, it's Janice. I'm so sorry, but we can't make it today. Glen's mom had a heart attack. We have to get to the hospital. I'm dropping all three kids off at my cousin's on the way."

I clucked sympathetically. As I was telling her I would send good thoughts, my call waiting beeped. With a quick "stay strong" to Janice, I switched over to hear my older brother announcing there was a blizzard in Ontario, and that they had no choice but to stay home. In the span of three minutes, my guest list had dwindled by nine more people. I could feel a headache rapidly approaching.

Seconds later, I heard my husband Don stamping snow off his boots in the foyer.

"Honey, I have bad news," he hollered.

"Who bailed this time?" I bellowed back, dragging my feet into the living room.

"Ursula called on my cell while I was walking the dog. She, Frank, and the four kids are all down with bad colds. They don't want to come and make us all sick," he said. "What's wrong?" he added when he saw tears starting to slip down my cheeks.

"Everyone cancelled!" I wailed. "It's only the three of us left! What am I going to do with all this food? I was expecting two dozen people."

He caught me in his arms right as I started to sag and sob at the same time.

"Shhh," he soothed. "We can always freeze the leftover food. It's not the end of the world."

He was right, of course. Except for two couples, everyone had a perfectly good reason for backing out. I was instantly ashamed of myself for feeling "inconvenienced" when people I loved were so sick. As for my brother in Ontario, if anything had happened to him while traveling through the snow, I'd never have forgiven myself.

My son got up from the couch and handed me a tissue. I smiled at him through watery eyes.

"It's Christmas," I hiccupped. "Let's make the best of it. I'm sorry I reacted like a baby."

"Mom," David began, "can I invite some of my friends for dinner instead? A lot of them have no plans. Some of them are pretty poor and have nothing special for dinner either — and we have all this food...."

Don and I stared at each other, both nodding at the same time.

"Of course. Go ahead and call them," I told our son.

"How many can come?" he asked.

"I have food for twenty more people... maybe thirty. Some may have to eat off paper plates," I warned, "but everyone is welcome."

The doorbell began buzzing at 2:00 p.m. By three, twenty-one teenagers and two of their little sisters filled my home. The kids proudly handed me a bouquet of flowers they'd all chipped in to buy, thanking me politely for inviting them. I pushed back tears at the sweet gesture, and shooed them all downstairs to wait for dinner.

The volume on David's stereo went up several decibels as heavy metal music drowned out carols, but Don and I didn't care. The house was alive with laughter and the spirit of the holiday. Many youngsters dribbled in and out of the kitchen offering to help, and as I delegated small chores, we chatted.

That Christmas dinner was one of the best we ever had. Our table was packed with hungry kids who demolished the twenty-pound turkey and the roasts, digging into the vegetables as if they were eating ambrosia. No one muttered about diets, indigestion or allergies. They simply enjoyed and appreciated every morsel of food that went into their mouths. As I watched them eat, any thoughts of leftovers being transformed into potpies, hot sandwiches or midnight snacks rapidly disappeared, but it didn't matter.

After dinner, those kids banished our family to the living room while they pitched in and cleaned up my kitchen until it was spotless. Someone had brought a newly released movie and before I knew it, my living room floor was covered with fifteen- and sixteen-year-olds, generously allowing the "old people" to sit on the couch and watch the movie. The two little girls curled up on either side of me, cuddling close. After passing out bags of microwave popcorn and canned soft drinks, we turned off the lights to enjoy the film.

By 10:00 p.m., everyone began to leave, but not without warm hugs and sincere thanks that made my eyes well up yet again. That night, I turned to my husband in bed. "Why is it we never thought to invite David's friends for Christmas dinner before?"

"I don't know," he replied sleepily. "You always hear that Christmas is for kids, but we seem to make the meal itself more of an adult occasion, picking and choosing who we want at the table."

"Not anymore," I vowed, remembering the grateful young faces that saved our day from being a quiet, lonely disaster.

—Marya Morin—

89

Devon's Story

To learn to read is to light a fire; every syllable that is
spelled out is a spark.
~Victor Hugo

I t was a cold, snowy day in January when I first met Devon at a local branch of the public library. Married with three children, he was a large man, dressed in a scruffy duffle coat that was open at the neck, exposing the ragged collar of his green flannel shirt. He thrust his hand out to shake mine and smiled.

"Nice to meet you, Miss June," he said. "I'm fifty years old and I never learned to read when I was a boy. But now I want to know everything."

Devon's eagerness was infectious. We quickly got to work using the library's literacy program materials. He could write his name and knew some capital letters but wasn't able to recognize simple words, such as "the" and "at."

We met for two hours each week, reviewing the alphabet with flash cards and stringing letters together to form simple words. He laughed at the passages about a bumbling man named Sam and his no-nonsense wife Pat. He would take the stories home and study them diligently.

When he got to the point where he could read these stories and other more challenging texts, he confessed to me something he'd wanted to do for a while.

"Do you think I could read to my three-year-old daughter now?"

We scoured the library for children's stories he could manage, such as *Good Night Moon* by Margaret Wise Brown and *The Very Hungry Caterpillar* by Eric Carle. He later told me that his daughter was so happy to spend time sitting on his lap and reading books before bed every night.

As well as literacy, we worked on numeracy — addition, subtraction, multiplication and division. He also wanted to learn how to tell time on a clock face.

"Miss June, what are the little dots between the numbers for?"

When I explained they represented minutes, his eyes lit up.

"Nobody never told me that before," he said, grinning.

Because Devon was the one responsible for the food shopping, he brought in grocery store flyers to figure out which items were on sale and which ones were bargains.

Devon noticed a single bottle of water cost seventy-five cents. "That is a good price," he said.

I pointed to a sale item. "What about this package of eight, same-size bottles of water for $4.00?"

"That's too much money."

"Is it? How much for each one?"

He did the calculation and figured out that the bottles cost fifty cents apiece. He looked up at me and said: "Them is tricky, eh?"

In the spring, the city was holding an election. On TV, Devon had been watching the candidates' debates and he told me he had a good feeling about one of the contenders.

"Devon, have you ever voted?"

"No, Miss June."

Together, we called to find out how he could register, where his polling station was located and what help was available. It turned out that an official could read out the candidates' names and instruct him where to mark his ballot. When his candidate won, he was thrilled.

As well as reading books, Devon loved reading lyrics to his favourite songs. That's when I learned that he was a musician and he wanted me to help him write down the lyrics to his reggae compositions. Secretly he had always wanted to submit his music for copyright, which meant he had to write a letter and address the envelope. We walked to the mailbox and he dropped the envelope in.

"That feel good, Miss June. I never do that before!"

Devon grew bolder. He asked me to help him learn how to use an ATM. When he saw a printout of his account transactions, he was annoyed to see how his wife and teenage son spent money on frivolous charges, such as extra ATM fees and Internet games. A few weeks later, he told me he had taken them to task.

"I talked to my wife. She no like that I know. But now she know I no put up with that no more."

In December, almost one year to the day that we began our time together, Devon texted me: "Morning miss June. Have the flue so I cannot make it to day."

I wrote back to say I was sorry he wasn't feeling well. But I was far from sorry to see those beautiful words typed out on the screen.

—June Rogers Flahie—

90

The Invulnerable Child

If you truly believe in the value of life,
you care about all of the weakest and
most vulnerable members of society.
~Joni Eareckson Tada

The call came in at 2:00 a.m. "Young female runaway needs help."

Police often called from the hospital when they suspected a mental health problem. As a Community Mental Health Nurse, I had spent many nights with students who had overdosed, women who had been abused, and teenagers who'd lived in far too many foster homes. The voice at the other end of the telephone sounded urgent.

Because of the hour, my husband insisted on keeping me company. He was used to driving me on late night visits. It gave us a chance to catch up on our busy lives.

In the hospital, I was rushed into a private room while my husband settled in the hallway with his book. A tiny girl of seventeen sat on a cot with her back to me. All I could see was her long, matted, vibrant red hair. Red "not her real name" turned to face me and my heart melted. I had never seen such a lonely looking child. She reminded me of a doll our girls owned when they were little — Miss No Name.

"But why?" I asked the policeman standing guard.

"We found her huddled in the stairwell of an apartment building, with a weapon. Refuses to pass it over."

"A weapon?"

"A jackknife, curled up in her hand."

Red opened her fist and showed me the little knife. Our eyes met as I passed her a cup of hot chocolate.

Conversation wasn't easy. I had to be patient. We sat for what seemed like hours while my husband kept sending in treats. My role was listening. Red's pain welled up with silence and then guilt. Between hugs, words seeped out, as if crying for release. Eventually, I learned her family had disowned her because of her erratic behaviour.

"I get wound up and run the roads," she said. "I can't help myself. I don't know why I do these things. I run and run and don't eat or sleep."

"And now," I asked. "How do you feel now?"

"Exhausted."

"But why the knife?"

"I don't know. I just want the pain to end."

While the policeman hovered close by and Red accepted the doctor's medication for sleep, I thought of my own family and wondered why some children suffered so much. After telephoning several numbers she'd given me, I reached an aunt who offered to help. As I explained the situation, the aunt said she would take Red into her home until she recovered.

"Life hasn't been easy for her or her family," she explained. "My niece was a terrific child when she was young. Kind-hearted and loving. Always helping others. But my sister is a single mom now and doesn't know where to turn during the frightening mood swings. There are so many arguments."

I asked the hospital staff to keep Red until the psychiatrist visited in the morning. While the attending doctor and patient advocate scrambled to find a bed for her, I gathered my thoughts and wrote my nursing diagnosis: bipolar disorder, a roller coaster ride with wild highs and devastating lows. Red's symptoms hadn't included hallucinations or delusions, but I still worried. With her persistent feelings of helplessness and hopelessness, I feared she was heading for a major depression, with suicide a serious risk.

I knew what I had to do. I had to protect Red from herself, with education, and most important, with loving care. I promised I would do all I could to help this little girl tackle her illness and the stigma involved. I reminded myself of a quote from the book, *The Invulnerable Child*: "Against all odds, they cope. And they survive." Although there's no cure for bipolar disorder, there is recovery.

By self-managing her medications, the cornerstone of treatment, and with support from family, friends, and self-help groups, Red could one day lead a healthy and productive life. She had already proven she was a survivor. Our journey into wellness had begun.

Several years after our daily, then weekly, then monthly appointments, Red visited me again. She wanted me to meet her husband. And her beautiful red-haired daughter. "And," she said excitedly, "I've been accepted into nursing school and plan on specializing in Mental Health."

As for Red's jackknife. I still have it.

A reminder that against all odds, they cope and survive.

— Phyllis M. Jardine —

Chapter
9

Holiday Helpers

91

Operation Christmas Thank You

There are no strangers on Christmas Eve.
~Adele Comandini and Edward Sutherland,
Beyond Tomorrow

I t was October and we were attending the fire hall's open house with our five-year-old son Isaiah and three-year-old daughter Angeleaha. Isaiah stood in awe of the massive yellow trucks, with all of their shiny chrome and interesting gadgets. The firefighters were more than happy to answer his many questions about each piece of equipment. He fidgeted with his plastic firefighter's hat as he studied the collection of scale models in the large glass display case in the office. "When do you get to play with those?" he asked the accompanying firefighter.

The firefighter hid his amusement as he answered very solemnly. "We don't get to play with them. The chief keeps them locked away in that cabinet."

Isaiah was lost in thought as we walked home that evening.

Halloween came and went, as did Remembrance Day. With colder weather setting in, our thoughts turned to Christmas. It was important to us to keep the true spirit of Christmas at the forefront of our holiday activities. The last thing we wanted was our children seeing Christmas as a commercial event.

We sat the two children down and explained that there were many children that didn't have the same things they did. Some children didn't have a mommy or daddy, enough food to eat, or new toys to play with at Christmas. We explained that Santa Claus sometimes needed a bit of help from Christmas Ambassadors to provide gifts or food for those in need.

Both children listened very intently. Isaiah's eyes shone! "Can we take presents to the firefighters? Santa doesn't visit the fire station and they aren't allowed to play with all those fire trucks! We can take them toys to play with on Christmas!"

At first we didn't know how to respond. We had long since forgotten about the model fire trucks in the display case at the fire hall! Apparently Isaiah had not. His dad cleared his throat. "Well, that is a good idea, but they don't really have time to play with toys because they are too busy keeping us safe from fires at Christmas."

Isaiah became very serious; he knew his dad was right. Being a firefighter was a very important job. Angeleaha had been sitting quietly playing with some blocks. "Candy... they want candy," she said quietly.

I looked at my husband. "Not quite what we had in mind," I said.

"It's not a bad idea though," he replied.

That first year we set out on Christmas Eve, led on foot by our two children to the fire hall, police station and paramedic stations to deliver boxes of chocolates. The kids were given a warm welcome at each stop and a tour of the units and their trucks.

As the children grew, the operation matured. We added coffee, lunch, dessert trays, and candies. We began deliveries to the Ontario Provincial Police and the hospital emergency room, too — six emergency response locations in total. We began taking photographs and posting to a Facebook page in hopes that others would start the campaign in their own cities.

We have five children now, and the fourth was born with a serious medical problem. For the first time we fully understood and appreciated the role of emergency services in a very personal way. During one medical emergency, which occurred during a blizzard, we had to call an ambulance to take Nathaniel to the hospital as he screamed in pain. The roads were too dangerous to navigate, but the paramedics still came, and they got us to the hospital safely.

Then on December 18th, 2014, while crossing the street, a car hit my husband and me. The car had slammed into me first, sending me scraping across the pavement several feet before coming to a stop. My husband had been picked up and thrown onto the hood by impact. A fire truck was first on scene, and I was helped onto the truck step, shaking and crying. Firefighters kept me talking, making sure I was coherent until paramedics arrived on scene.

I was helped onto a stretcher and rolled into the ambulance, where one soft-spoken paramedic assessed my vitals and provided me with ice packs for my bruises. The other paramedic climbed in the driver's seat and called back, "These are the parents of the kids who bring us goodies on Christmas Eve!"

I was shocked. I'm not sure why, but I didn't think we were recognizable, and I really didn't view what our children were doing as anything out of the ordinary. We were saying thank you, showing our appreciation.

Our first little Christmas elves, Isaiah and Angeleaha, are now teenagers. They raise money each year to pay for the treats that they and their siblings deliver to all our first responders.

This year will be our twelfth Operation Christmas Thank You. It's the highlight of our family's Christmas.

— Danielle Kuhn —

92

My First Away Christmas

*The greatest thing you'll ever learn is just to love
and be loved in return.*
~Eden Ahbez

In the winter of 2015, I spent my first Christmas away from home. When I say away from home, I mean everything that goes along with home too. I was away from my mom and dad, my sister and nephews, my pets, my Christmas tree — everything.

I was worried about spending such an important holiday away from the people I love so dearly. I was afraid I'd be a nervous wreck. I was scared I wouldn't be able to appreciate the holidays as much. And to top it all off, my family (for the first time ever) was going to spend the holidays somewhere warm. They were visiting Florida to spend Christmas on the beach. And I was choosing not to go.

All for the new love of my life: Devin.

I am from Ontario, and Devin is from Nova Scotia. Our two hometowns are roughly 2,000 kilometers apart from each other (1242 miles for you American readers). Although Devin and I were both going to school in Ontario, we knew that the distance between our families was something that was going to be a challenge for the rest of our relationship. But we knew we *had* to spend this Christmas together.

Devin and I had both had a rough semester at school. And we

were both really good at supporting and comforting each other — we just couldn't imagine being away from each other during our first Christmas together as a couple. My family said they understood, but from their not-so-subtle hints, I knew they were trying to get me to reconsider going to cold Nova Scotia instead of warm Florida right up until our flight left Pearson Airport. But I was resolute: Devin and I were meant to spend this Christmas together and, though it would be a bit of a sacrifice on my part, I wanted to see it through.

We landed in Nova Scotia to hugs, kisses, and squeals of joy from Devin's mom and dad. I was so happy that they were pleased to see me. From the first moment I stepped off the plane, I felt immediately welcomed into Devin's family. They plied us with appetizers and finger-foods when we got to Devin's childhood house, and his mom treated us to her famous "silver bells" — a holiday drink made up of milk, Kahlua, and some other tasty spirits. The house was decorated to the nines. Even the bathroom had Christmas decorations! My family was usually not so enthusiastic in their decorating.

But even though Devin's family was supportive, loving, and excited — more than I could ever hope for in prospective in-laws — I kept finding myself drawn to the bedroom or to the television. I felt myself get upset with Devin more quickly than was normal. I got a little quiet and sullen. I felt depressed. My family kept sending me beautiful pictures of their Christmas vacation in Florida. And I kept sending them pictures of Nova Scotia snow banks (which are beautiful in their own way, I suppose).

Devin's family did things a little differently than mine. In my family, we have one big dinner with our extended family and that's it. The rest of the holidays are time for our immediate family. My mom and I would play board games, my dad and I would go to the movies, and my sister's family and I would play in the snow. My sister's husband has an amazing tradition of creating a "snow track" around their back yard, where he uses his tractor to pull as many people as can fit on a sled around the track. We usually go until we all fall off.

In Devin's family, there are several family dinners. There are maybe two or three big dinners with extended family and several smaller dinners or get-togethers in smaller groups. Now, I know I might be sounding completely ungrateful — but it got pretty stressful! I am used to holidays where we try to relax and recharge, but instead I felt like a piece of cargo getting shipped from one Christmas event to the next. And trying to remember all of the names and faces — impossible!

Christmas morning arrived and I was surrounded by Devin's family: his mom, dad, sister, brother-in-law, and his little nephew. We watched his nephew open all of his amazing presents, and he loved every one of them. Then came our presents: and I was completely and utterly overwhelmed. Devin's family piled gifts on me: clothes, jewellery, fancy soaps, chocolates — it was amazing. All I could do was say, "thank you so much" over and over, but I felt like it didn't fully express the gratitude I felt to them for including me so whole-heartedly in their Christmas. And I tried to tell them over and over that they didn't need to get me all those gifts. I already felt so loved and accepted by them; that was gift enough. They reminded me that although I was "away," I had a new home with them.

But there is one gift from Devin's family that will remain in my heart's memory for a long, long time. During one of the big family get-togethers, Devin's grandma approached me with a gift.

Now, Devin's grandma, Dodie, is the sweetest, loveliest lady I think I've ever met. I loved her from the first time I met her; I felt that we instantly connected — just like she was my own grandma. She is full of stories and knowledge; she's caring and compassionate and her family is her greatest source of pride and joy.

She approached me at the party with a gift and I instantly felt guilty: I didn't have a gift for her. But she insisted I accept and open the gift she brought me.

The party was loud, children were playing, grownups were drinking wine and beer and "silver bells" and catching up on the latest family news. New babies were being cooed over, folks were sitting on chairs and couches nibbling on food. The room was buzzing with noise, and even though it was chaotic, it was clearly filled with love.

And in a quiet, unacknowledged corner of the room, I opened the gift from Devin's grandma. Inside a lovely box was a piece of delicately twisted, knotted coloured glass. It looked like a small piece of art. With the glass, there was a card that read:

This knot represents a never-ending connection. This gift unifies the giver and recipient; it links our fate and binds us together.

She looked into my eyes, beaming and smiling.

"As soon as I saw this I thought of you," she said. "We love you so much. Welcome to our family."

— Emily Bednarz —

93

A Gift from the Heart

While we try to teach our children all about life,
our children teach us what life is all about.
~Angela Schwindt

I t had been a tradition for my husband to give me a box of Nutchos chocolates at Christmas. They don't make them anymore, but at the time, they were delicious: a swirly mound of milk chocolate filled with ground nuts.

In one of my "woe is me" moments, facing the first Christmas after my husband and I had separated, I moaned and asked who was going to buy me my Nutchos that year.

Days later, I took the kids to the local department store and handed them money so they could do their own Christmas shopping. They had been instructed to stay together, and we had a set time and place to meet before we headed home.

A short time later I saw the kids lugging their purchases. It made me smile to see their excitement with their first foray into holiday shopping. But as we walked home, I saw one of my son's purchases hanging out of his bag.

It seemed that instead of using the money for gifts, he had spent the money on a huge bag of Doritos or some sort of junk food for himself. I was annoyed, thinking that was not the giving holiday spirit I was trying to teach him.

"Why did you buy chips?" I asked. "That money was for gifts for the family, not for you to buy yourself a snack."

He looked at me, his sad eyes looking hurt, holding back tears. "They're not for me," he said. "They're for you. You wanted to know who was going to buy you your nachos, and I wanted to make sure you got some."

Nutchos... made from chocolate and nuts. Nachos... a chip made by Doritos. I guess they could sound very much the same to an eight-year-old boy.

I gave that thoughtful little boy a big hug right there on the sidewalk.

— Deborah Lean —

94

Being Santa

Everyone has been made for some particular
work, and the desire for that work has
been put in every heart.
~Rumi

"There you are. I found you!" exclaimed a young woman as she rushed toward my husband as we were browsing in a toy store. "Flowing white hair, a kindly smile," she continued. "You even have a twinkle in your eye. I'm the president of a local costume house and I've been on the search for a Santa Claus to model our line of Santa regalia for a new catalogue. I knew the moment I saw you that you were perfect. And to find my Santa in a toy store! Wow."

So began our journey into all things Santa Claus, and what a fantastic adventure it's been. As my husband took on the persona of the man in red, children began to flock to him, no matter where we were or what we were doing. Even in shorts and a T-shirt or playing the fiddle in a country band they thought he was the real deal.

Often, in a restaurant, we have heard "Santa" and a child will make a beeline for him. He puts on his glasses, tilts his head, and with a twinkle in his eye, chuckles a hearty ho-ho-ho. "You found me," he says, "but I'm in disguise. I can't fool you, though!"

"Are you the real Santa?"

"Are you the real you?" he replies. "What does the real Santa look like? Does he have a white beard?"

"Yes."

"Well, I have a white beard. Does he wear glasses and laugh ho-ho-ho?"

"Yes," chorus the children.

"I wear glasses and laugh ho-ho-ho. Let's see. How can we tell if I'm the real guy? I know. There's an official test to solve the question. If I were really him, I would know all the names of the reindeer. Right? Okay, let's see if I know them. There's the famous guy with the green nose."

"No," the children shout. "He has a red nose."

By this time, the whole restaurant is tuned into the conversation.

"Right. I can't fool you. That's Rudolph. Who are the others? There's Sleepy, Bashful and Doc."

The children giggle. "No, Santa, those are the seven dwarfs!"

Santa chuckles. "You're right again! Let's see, there's Dasher, Dancer, Prancer, Vixen, Comet, Cupid, Donner and Blitzen. I know them all. I guess I must be Santa!"

From there, the conversation goes anywhere from "Where are the reindeer?" to "We've moved. Will you be able to find me this year?" Santa always answers their questions with gentleness and warmth. Often adults stop by our table to say, "You've got me believing you're the real Santa."

One of my husband's favourite memories is of the time that our granddaughter phoned and asked for her grandfather.

"Bucka," she said. "Will you come to my school in your Santa suit for show and tell?"

He was blown away. Never in all his life did he expect to be the subject of show and tell for a kindergarten class.

"I would love to come," he said. "Let me call your teacher and make arrangements."

Donning his Santa suit, he walked into her class with a hearty ho-ho-ho. Some of the children squealed and rushed to him for hugs. Some had never seen Santa up close before and were shy and anxious. He shared songs and told stories. He listened, really listened, to each and every child. Those who were scared soon learned there was nothing to fear. The children and adults all left the school happy and laughing. Once again, his fun and gentle demeanour brought the magic of Christmas to a small corner of the world.

Another time, at a company's children's Christmas party, Santa was giving out gifts to the children and laughing with them. A small girl had jumped to her feet as soon as he entered the room. She tugged on her mother's hand and pulled her away from Santa and out the door. As she was leaving she looked back and glanced at Santa from under her lowered eyelids. Her face had gone white and she wore a frown.

I followed them. She was shaking and crying. I approached her mom and asked if I could speak with her. Her mom told me her name was Maddy and that she didn't want to go into the room as long as Santa was in it.

"Are you afraid of Santa?"

"Yes."

"Do you know why you're afraid of Santa?"

"No."

"Is it because of the big red suit or the loud ho-ho-ho?"

"No."

"Is it his beard?"

"Yes."

"Well, Santa is my very best friend. He's very gentle and won't hurt you, I promise. The beard can make him look a little scary, but it's really quite soft. I'm sure he'll let you touch it if you'd like. Would that help you to not be afraid?"

"No, I don't want to go in there."

"Okay. You can come and meet him when you're ready."

"Okay."

I left Maddy and her mom and returned to the party. A short while later, I noticed them enter the room. Cautiously, Maddy moved closer to where the children were sitting. Her name was called to receive her present. Taking her mom's hand, she guardedly approached his chair. She stood so that her mom was between her and Santa. He sensed her fear and gently began to talk to her.

"What would you like to do?"

"I would like to sing 'Feliz Navidad'."

"Do you know that song?" asked Santa. "I know that song too! Let's sing it together."

They began to sing and she started to smile. When they were finished, Maddy's mom said, "Wasn't there something you wanted to ask Santa?"

"Oh, yes," replied Maddy. "Santa, can I touch your beard?"

"Of course."

Maddy moved closer to him, reached out her small hand and gently touched his beard. Santa lifted his hand and softly touched her hair.

"See, it's just like your hair, only yours is brown and mine is white," whispered Santa.

Maddy's eyes widened and she started to giggle. She and Santa smiled at each other for a long time. Then they laughed and she gave him a big hug. Maddy's mom gave him a hug also and whispered, "Thank you so much for helping my girl."

Being Santa is magical. My husband loves to make the children laugh and smile. To think it all started because a young woman found him in a toy store! He is grateful for that day and the circumstances that brought them together. Coincidence? He doesn't think so.

"I love keeping the dream alive for the little ones," says Santa. "That's what being Santa is all about, not just at Christmas but throughout the year. To be able to share hope, laughter and joy with people is awesome. I'm a lucky man."

— Maighread MacKay —

95

Holy Night

A bit of fragrance always clings to the hand
that gives roses.
~Chinese Proverb

Sometimes the magic and miracles of Christmas come to us in ways we don't expect. A number of years ago, when my husband, Larry, and I were newly married, we took off for a two-year adventure in Asia. We left behind family, friends and jobs to work for a charity in Hong Kong.

Two months after we arrived in our new home, it was Christmastime. But there were no frosted windowpanes or sleigh rides or holly branches in Hong Kong. I had never spent a Christmas away from home before, and I found myself desperately homesick for my family and for our traditions — Christmas Eve with friends, singing carols at the piano, crowds of people coming and going, and a big tree loaded with gifts.

Instead, we found ourselves living in a tiny flat on the thirtieth floor of a high rise. We did our best to decorate. Our tree was a pathetic thing that we had inherited: green plastic, about eighteen inches tall with little white presents glued onto its branches. We didn't have two cents to rub together for anything better, so we strung popcorn and wound it around. And under the tree went a few small presents.

As Christmas got closer, I felt ready to throw in the towel on this whole idea of working for a charity. All the warm fuzzies about spending two years to help change the world didn't seem all that glamorous anymore.

When a British family invited us to share the day in their lovely home, I thought we had hit the jackpot. But my excitement soon dissipated when Larry suggested we decline the invitation.

"We've met so many people here who don't have anywhere to go for Christmas," he said. "I think we need to cook a turkey and open our door to whoever wants to come."

So we declined the invitation, and got the word out to our new friends: "We're cooking a turkey. If you need a place to spend Christmas, come and join us."

Of course, now we know all about the rules of Christmas entertaining. If you're going to have people in, the tree should be beautiful, the table should be set with candles and good china, there should be a fire blazing in the hearth and a big wreath on the door.

But then, we didn't know any better. We didn't know that paper plates were not enough, that a plastic tree didn't make a good focal point, that a living room the size of a sandbox wasn't big enough for a crowd.

In the days leading up to Christmas, our guest list started growing. Even on Christmas morning, the phone rang several times — new acquaintances, people we had met in passing — "I heard you were having Christmas dinner today. Is there room for a few more?"

When they arrived, they introduced themselves to us and to one another, loaded their plates with food and found a place on the floor. The room buzzed as twenty people shared their stories — some were traveling through Asia, some were volunteers in China or Hong Kong, some were just lonely and had no one else to spend the day with.

When the meal was finished, we sat around the living room, enjoying the conversation. In a quiet moment, someone started singing: "Silent night, holy night, all is calm, all is bright...." And everyone joined in. When the song ended, it was quiet. And then someone started to sing again: "Away in a manger, no crib for a bed, the little Lord Jesus lay down his sweet head...."

And there we were — like Mary and Joseph and Jesus, we were all uprooted from our families and friends. Like them, we were vagabonds a long way from home. They were being asked to do something big to change the world. We were all trying to do our small part to change the world too.

And in that tiny living room on the thirtieth floor of a high rise in the bustling city of Hong Kong, we found a Christmas that none of us had planned. It was simply a gift to us all. For the vagabonds and volunteers around that little tree, it was a holy night.

—Marla Stewart Konrad—

96

Dr. Christmas

Miracles don't just happen, people make them happen.
~Misato Katsuragi

"Angie, you have to understand," my mother pleaded, tears in her eyes. She reached for my hand, which I promptly pulled away.

Oh, I understood all right. My very own mother was a murderer. I stared at her in disbelief as she tried to justify her reasons for killing my best friend. It was too much for my nine-year-old brain to comprehend.

"Angie, please don't look at me like that," she said softly, her voice breaking up, "Teeger was very sick. He had a bad bladder infection. The operation was too expensive and the veterinarian couldn't guarantee that it would work anyway. I had no choice but to have him put to sleep. It's better this way. He's not in pain anymore."

Teeger was a big, fat, roly-poly, orange cat who I loved like no other. And now he was gone. I wanted to close my eyes and make it all go away. This would be the worst Christmas ever.

"You didn't even let me say goodbye," I finally choked out.

Teeger had come into my life at a time when I really needed a friend. It was shortly after my dad had moved out for good. I was the only kid in my class whose parents weren't together, so there was no one I could talk to who would really understand what I was going through. I had a hard time making friends as it was, since I was painfully shy. Moving once a year didn't help. Being overweight also didn't help. My mother saw how much I was struggling, but she didn't know how to make it better. She did, however, know how to cheer me up. Enter Teeger.

Teeger and I had bonded instantly. He was a lot like me, actually. Shy... chubby... loved Cheezies. He had a playful side — but only when no one was looking. If you caught him chasing his tail, for example, he would stop and pretend that he was just cleaning himself or doing something equally sensible. What I loved most about Teeger, though, was how special he made me feel. He preferred me over everyone else he knew and he wasn't afraid to show it. He made me feel like the most important person in the world.

As the years went on, my bond with Teeger grew even stronger. When I was home, he followed me wherever I went. He sat beside me on the piano bench as I practiced for my upcoming lesson, occasionally putting a paw on the piano keys to remind me that he was there. He slept at my feet every night. He licked away my tears when I told him about the kids at school who made fun of me or about how much I missed my dad. He was my best friend.

One fateful morning, I woke to find that Teeger was not beside me and I immediately knew that something was wrong. I jumped out of bed and ran from room to room, frantically calling his name. I checked every nook and cranny in our little farmhouse, but Teeger was nowhere to be found. For two more days I searched like this, refusing to accept the possibility that he might actually be gone. On the third day of searching I was in the basement, looking for the hundredth time, when I heard a faint "meow" coming from up above. I looked up and suddenly saw those familiar green eyes and orange fur. Teeger was in the furnace duct!

I called for my mom, who ran down the stairs as fast as she could, and I pointed out the unlikely hiding spot where Teeger had been this whole time. We instantly got to work. It took a while, but I finally got him down. And then panic set in. He didn't look like the Teeger I knew. His fur was matted, his stomach bloated, and his eyes seemed quietly desperate.

"Angie," Mom said quietly, "I think Teeger is very sick. Sometimes cats go off into hiding when they know they are going to die."

I could not accept this. I had already decided long ago that Teeger was a miracle cat and he would live forever.

"He's not going to die," I said firmly. I held him close, comforting him as he had done for me so many times. "You're going to be okay, buddy," I told him over and over. "You'll get better, I just know it. You can't leave me yet."

Mom looked at me sadly and promised to take him to the vet right away.

Looking back, I understand why my mother didn't talk to me before making the decision to have Teeger put to sleep. How could she possibly have said no to a teary-eyed, inconsolable girl begging her to save her best friend? I likely would have told her to keep my allowance and to take back my Christmas presents so we could afford the operation. She might have taken a third job just to pay for it, even though she was exhausted working the two jobs she already had just to make ends meet. No, she really didn't have much of a choice at all. I understand that now.

In the weeks that followed, my mother did her best to try to cheer me up. She sang. She baked. She decorated the house for Christmas, going "all out" like she always did. But this time there was no cheering me up. I didn't want to get into the Christmas spirit. And besides, I wouldn't get what I wanted for Christmas anyway... my best friend back. No one could give me that. Or so I thought.

And then I got a phone call that I would never forget.

"Angie, the phone's for you," my mom said, handing it over to me with a puzzled expression on her face. "It's the veterinarian. He asked specifically for you."

"The veterinarian?" I echoed, equally puzzled. I had never even met him before. Why would he ask for me? Hesitantly, I picked up the phone.

"Hello?"

"Hello, Angie," a deep voice greeted me. "I... well... I wanted you to be the first to hear what I have to say. Your mom told me that Teeger was very special to you. So... in the spirit of Christmas... I gave Teeger the operation for free."

Could it really be true? Was Teeger alive this whole time? It was a miracle! A Christmas miracle!

"I'm sorry that I didn't call sooner," the veterinarian continued, "but I wanted to make sure that Teeger was completely better and stabilized before I called you to let you know. He's ready for you to pick him up now. I think he misses you."

It seemed an eternity before I was able to blurt out the words, "Thank you! Thank you so much!" Tears of joy streamed down my face and I had my shoes on before I could even explain to my mother what was going on.

When we got to the animal clinic, the veterinarian was waiting for us. I immediately ran over and hugged him, thanking him over and over again. He looked over at my mother and blushed, unsure of how to handle my display of emotion. He brought out Teeger, who immediately began purring so loudly you'd swear that a car with a bad muffler had just driven through the office. My heart felt like it was about to burst with happiness.

Thanks to that wonderful man, I got to spend twelve more years with Teeger by my side. And I got to learn at an early age that the true spirit of Christmas has nothing to do with spending money or getting gifts; it's about giving to others from the kindness of your heart with no expectation of getting anything in return. And I learned that sometimes... just sometimes... angels come disguised as veterinarians who make Christmas miracles happen and little girls' wishes come true.

— Angela Rolleman —

97

Christmas Connections

This time of year means being kind to everyone we
meet, to share a smile with strangers
we may pass along the street.
~Betty Black

"T he eighteenth bus was delayed a bit, but don't worry, the police are waving it through." It was December, dark and raining. I was a very new coordinator of volunteers in a large hospital for children with mental or physical problems. I had some experience with people issues — fleets of buses were another matter entirely. But this was the evening of the Christmas lights tour.

The head of recreation, his suit covered by a bright yellow slicker, consulted his sheet and directed bus after bus — full-size city buses — to different entrances where the drivers whipped them around in impossibly small spaces so that patients could get aboard without getting wet. Besides the transit buses, we had a fleet of wheelchair buses — they had arrived earlier because they took longer to load.

Most of the drivers were dressed as Santa Claus; some had brought their wives along dressed as Mrs. Claus, carrying baskets of candy. As we loaded patients, bright-eyed and eager, I noticed that the drivers were all mature men. When I asked about that they said, "You need a lot of seniority to get this volunteer spot."

When every last person was on board and settled down we were waved on our way. The lead bus bore a large sign with the name of the hospital and "Christmas Lights Tour" on it. I had wondered, with so many buses, if we might get separated at traffic lights. No worries! At every traffic light in this busy urban area police were stationed. Our entire convoy was waved through together.

I was on a bus with young boys, and having cops wave them through red lights was the highlight of their evening. Never had they imagined a privilege as great as that. Life could get no better. They eagerly looked forward at each intersection, hoping the light would be red, cheering as the cop on duty waved us through.

When we came to the brightly decorated houses, we saw that the owners had been alerted. Street after street had organized for the evening. Our patients might have been rock stars based on the way the groups of homeowners cheered our arrival. Neighbours, family and friends had been roped in to help bring every young person hot chocolate, nuts, and candy.

Smiles and hugs were the currency of the evening. We arrived at one street after another to see people smiling and waving. Once in a while I spotted someone a little uncertain about greeting young people with handicaps. It took only a little encouragement to bring them onto the bus, where they connected and made friends.

We left to more vigorous waving and to wider smiles, to mums and dads and grandpas holding up their little ones to wave or knock on bus windows to say goodbye up close and personal. Every barrier had been broken, smashed by the Christmas connection.

On our return we sang carols on the bus. We had all learned something that night. The boys counted their loot as if it were Halloween. Back at the hospital we collected candy wrappers and hot drink cups and told the lads to make sure to say "thank you" to the driver.

When we got back the drivers spun the great buses into place before the hospital entrances as if they were driving toy cars. The boys appreciated their skill. Their "Wow! Cool! Can you do that again?" was an even better reward than the "thank you."

It was part of my job to send letters of thanks to all the drivers, police, and homeowners. The transit dispatcher phoned me back two days before Christmas. "I thought I'd let you know. All the drivers have signed up to volunteer for this shift again next year."

—Valerie Fletcher Adolph—

98

The Light of the Carolers

Healing requires from us to stop struggling,
but to enjoy life more and endure it less.
~Darina Stoyanova

As I drove into the garage on a snowy winter's day, Bing Crosby was crooning "I'll Be Home for Christmas" on the radio. The lyrics stung, as it would be our first Christmas season without our eldest son, Davis, who had been killed in a traffic accident six months earlier.

Decorating the tree was one of our favourite family traditions. I thought about the carols that would be playing as we untangled the tree lights and laid out our collection of ornaments. Each ornament had a history and a story. How would we get through Christmas without Davis?

Our friends, Jim and Fiona, knew how difficult this "first" would be for us. They, too, were facing their own Goliath. Jim had been diagnosed with a cancerous brain tumour the year before and was in full battle mode. He and Fiona understood how precious life was. Yet they were determined to brighten our home by bringing over a home-cooked meal and spending an evening with us.

As I looked out the window into the neighbourhood, I noticed our neighbours' homes outlined in coloured lights and festive displays. Our house was usually one of the earliest to be decorated. Not this year; we were the hurting house. I went back into my kitchen to put the finishing touches on the appetizers I was preparing.

The doorbell rang a little earlier than I expected. My husband and I met at the entrance, ready to greet the Prestons. To our amazement, our snow-covered yard was filled with flickering candles and familiar faces singing, "We Wish You a Merry Christmas." There were carolers as far as the eye could see. The sound was angelic. One carol followed another in beautiful harmony, with faces aglow in the candlelight. As tears flooded my eyes, I felt such gratitude for this meaningful gesture of love. All was calm, all was bright.

Several of our neighbours opened their doors to the songs of the carolers and joined in. After another carol had been sung on this cold winter's night, someone piped up with, "Well, can we come in now?" The initial dinner plan had been a ruse to gather together our friends and colleagues in a Christmas experience we would never forget, one that we needed so desperately. Within minutes, a potluck of Christmas dishes appeared from the back seats of cars or from their hidden places under bushes.

We stoked the fireplace, brought out the eggnog, and filled our home to capacity with the large group that had gathered. Christmas would never be the same as it had been during our eighteen years with Davis, but I realized something that night. Joy can trump sorrow. Love came down and gathered on our doorstep. Jim and Fiona had given us the wondrous gift of community to fill the gap. It set the tone for the Christmas season that followed. Even though Davis wouldn't be home with us, God compensated for our loss with a love so evident in this gesture of friendship and support. Each caroller had taken a piece of our heartache from us. As I looked around at the smiling faces in our crowded house, I knew I wanted to decorate the tree tomorrow, assured that Davis would be present with me in a different but meaningful way. He'd be home for Christmas — if only in my heart.

— Sally Walls —

99

Just Tell Us You Love Us

Silent gratitude isn't much use to anyone.
~G.B. Stern

Most of my life I've been the type of person who listened to the opinion of others and if they said something couldn't be done, I accepted their decision and went about what I needed to get done that day. That was before an event that happened last year just before Christmas. At the time I was standing at the counter in a gift shop signing a copy of my latest book, *Christmas in the Maritimes,* when I overheard a lady say, "I'm sending this to my nephew in Afghanistan and I know he'll love it. When he's finished, he'll pass it around to the other Maritimers in his unit."

"Other Maritimers in his unit," her words kept repeating themselves over and over in my mind. Gradually an idea began to take shape. I shared my idea with a friend but she said, "You'd have to raise the money. You'd have to know where to ship the books. You'd... forget it, there's no way!" But this time I wasn't about to take "no" for an answer. The news last year was full of stories about the conditions our troops were serving under and I thought if this little book would mean something to the members serving our country, then I was going to at least try to find a way to send some copies to them.

My first step was to write to Roger Cyr, a friend who had been in the Air Force before his retirement. I asked him if he thought the book would be welcomed. He wrote back right away encouraging me to pursue this idea. He also said, "I spent four years in Europe during the Cold War serving with our NATO troops plus a tour as a peacekeeper in Africa (Congo). One of the things we treasured the most was a Canadian newspaper or a word from home."

The more I thought on it, the more I was convinced stories from home would be such a morale booster. I began investigating the possibilities and started by making phone calls, doing web searches and writing e-mails. However, the results from my inquiries only served to add to my earlier doubts. It was fast becoming evident that it wasn't a workable project. My major stumbling block was the fact that I'd never done anything like this before, so I was unfamiliar with all the rules and considerations involved in sending something to our troops. I discovered parcels could only be sent if you knew the specific name and address of the unit and the name and number of the person receiving the gift. My friend was right. This idea might have been a good idea but it was fast becoming a dream that would never be fulfilled.

Somewhere along the way I read an article about another Elaine who was able to help the troops through her project "Operation Wish." She didn't listen to the "no's" and her story encouraged me to press on.

Finally, on a Wednesday, November 15th I made contact with Margaret Reid, Coordinator of Deployment Services of 14 Wing Greenwood. Her response was immediate. She wrote, "Great idea! Definitely possible from my perspective anyway. We're doing our packages to the troops on Nov 21st. I guess the question now for you is if you can make the Christmas miracles happen by next Tuesday?"

I called Nimbus, my publisher. "Do you have 140 books in stock?" (They were waiting for more books from the printers and I wasn't sure if they had enough to fill their immediate orders.) The managing editor assured me they could fill my order if I could raise the funds needed to purchase the books by Friday at 3:00 PM. I needed to meet that deadline in order to leave enough time for the books to be delivered from Nimbus' warehouse to Greenwood in time to be packed with the parcels on Tuesday.

I wrote back, "Dear Ms. Reid, I believe this Christmas miracle will happen!"

My idea was to ask the community (through contacts with the media) to get involved and sponsor the books as a way of showing the men and women serving our country they were being remembered. Two reporters agreed to help, but before the afternoon was over I ran into another snag. I didn't have a business address where people could drop off the money and my telephone inquiries to this point suggested setting up an account for this purpose would take some time. The deadline for getting the story out in Thursday's papers was fast approaching. Around four o'clock I remember thinking that Ms. Reid said I needed a Christmas miracle, so why not ask God? I did. Within minutes I had an unexpected phone call from someone I'd talked to earlier in the day.

"Elaine, I was touched by what you want to do. You're going to get your Christmas miracle. I'll cover the cost!"

Two days later the books arrived in Greenwood in time to be packed in the Christmas parcels being made up for 140 troop members of 14 Wing Greenwood who were serving our great country, Canada, in various places throughout the world.

As I wrote my Christmas letters last year I thought of a poem I'd received from a friend. In the poem, the author asked a young soldier who had left a wife and child at home to serve his country, what he could give him for Christmas — money or a feast? The young soldier's answer was, "Just tell us you love us." When I sent the books it was my prayer that the small gift of stories and memories from home would do just that — tell 140 soldiers who were serving their country that I loved them.

— Elaine Ingalls Hogg —

The Christmas Lesson

The human spirit is stronger than
anything that can happen to it.
~C.C. Scott

"**W**e'll get you to do Emma's treatment tonight," the charge nurse said to me as she was doing her workload assignment. "It's difficult and takes time, but Emma will put you at ease with it."

It was Christmas Eve, and I was looking forward to the morning, when my children would see what Santa had brought them. Christmas is a hectic time for young, working mothers, and I was no exception. I was totally fatigued. There had been so many Christmas concerts and parties, and shopping, baking, and all that we do at Christmastime.

During the holidays, to accommodate the vacation schedules of the employees, our hospital reassigned nurses to where the need was greatest. I had already worked a day shift on this particular unit, and had heard about Emma, a frail little eighty-year-old lady who suffered in silence. Advanced carcinoma was gradually destroying Emma's face, exposing blood vessels and leaving her prone to hemorrhage.

Emma was on a progressive care unit, and many of its patients would be going home the next day, Christmas, to spend time with their families. I read Emma's chart and realized that going home was not an option for her. She required too much care to be eligible for a nursing home, so she stayed where she was on the unit, the place she now thought of as home.

I went to her room and introduced myself.

"Do you like my tree, dear?" she asked.

Yes, I told her. Though she could barely see it, Emma had a wonderful tree with twinkling lights, and ornaments donated by her nurses. Her tape player quietly played Christmas music, and before I started her treatment, Emma asked me to change the music. I chose a tape, put it in the player, and "Silent Night," my favourite Christmas carol, started softly playing. I glanced out the window at the glistening snow which was reflecting the Christmas lights that were part of the hospital's effort to make it feel more like home for those who could not go home for Christmas.

I started to remove the huge bandages that covered Emma's head and face. I was ill-prepared for how disfigured she was from the carcinoma, how involved her treatment was, and tried hard not to let her see my shock and disbelief. I had never, ever, seen facial deformity so severe. I found myself sweating, and my heart racing.

Emma could barely see, and spoke in a whisper. "You're not scared, are you dear?" she asked in a whisper. I assured her I was not. Tiny, frail and ill, she endured her treatments without complaint, often reassuring me that she was okay, and not to be upset for her because it wasn't too painful if her treatment was done gently.

"You're new though, and very young. Do you have children, dear?" she queried. (To Emma everyone was "dear.") I told her about my little children and how excited they were about Santa.

Then I felt her hands on my face. Emma said she wanted to know what I looked like, and remarked that I had my hair pulled up under my nurse's cap. She asked if she could touch my long hair. I stopped the treatment, removed the gloves, took off my cap and let my hair fall loose. She ran her hands through my hair, and told me about the long hair she had as a young woman, how her husband had loved it, how he would tell her how attractive she was and how proud he was of her and their children. She told me about the Christmas traditions they kept, how she loved him, and how she was relieved that, having predeceased her years ago, he did not have to see her like this.

Emma's care took over an hour, and she talked in her whispering voice as I did her treatment with a lump in my throat, and listened to the soft sounds of the Christmas carols filling the room.

When I was through, Emma asked me to sit for a moment. The night was quiet so I sat beside her as she held my hands. She continued to talk, and give me advice, which overwhelmed me. She told me she thought I was tired, and she remembered being tired when her children were small and Christmas so demanding. From under those heavy bandages, she advised me to never take my health for granted, to be thankful I could see and hear, that I could dance around my house with my baby girl in my arms as I told her I did, that I could drive a car, read a book, laugh and sing, and do all the things that make up a life, things I had never thought about to any degree. She felt my wide wedding band, and expressed how she wished she could see it.

A tear fell from my face unto her hand from the tears I could no longer hold back.

She told me not to cry, that she had accepted her fate, and I should too. Emma made me promise to live life fully while I was able, thanked me for my tenderness with her painful treatment, and wished me a Merry Christmas. The music was still softly playing.

When I left her room that night, I knew that my experience with Emma was exceptional. A weak, elderly woman, clinging to life, understood the angst of a young nurse, wanted to touch my hair, wanted to talk, and to give advice to a young nurse and mother. She made me aware of just how much I took for granted, and reminded me to remember the reason for the season.

Because I was then off for the holidays and after that I returned to work in the operating room, I never saw Emma again. That Christmas Eve with Emma was thirty years ago, but I recall it with amazing clarity. I believe our paths crossed for a reason.

Emma reminded me that I should slow down and treasure all that I had in spite of my busy life. This is especially true at Christmas, when amidst the tumult, frenzied activity and hurried preparations, the true meaning of Christmas is often lost. It was an unforgettable lesson.

— Bonnie Jarvis-Lowe —

A New Tradition

*Mankind is a great, an immense, family. This is proved
by what we feel in our hearts at Christmas.*
~Pope John XXIII

A s I walked into the Fifth Street Bar and Grill my aunt
stood up from a table in the corner, beside a window
that spilled winter sunlight.

As usual, it had taken weeks to agree on a time for
our semi-annual lunch. She worked as a psychologist and ran her
own bustling private practice, and she also owned a couple of vacation
properties that she always seemed to be in the process of selling,
renting or redecorating. I hadn't seen her in months.

"Hi," I exclaimed. "You look great." And she did: she wore her
dark, straight hair down to her lower back in glimmering waves. An
assortment of fashionable jewellery sparkled on her skin. While we
hugged, I worried that I might wrinkle the fabric of her tailored white
blouse, which smelled of Chanel No. 5.

"So it's been a while! How are you? You must be almost done
with your classes," she said in a rush of enthusiasm as we sat down.

"Yes, this is my last semester."

We talked for a while about my imminent graduation from university,
and then I asked her about her properties. Her eyes narrowed
and she became even more animated, waving her hand through the air
as she talked so her gold bracelet caught the light. Apparently, she had
set her sights on a condo in an exclusive new development beside a

golf course, where prices were sky-high. It was the epitome of luxury.

"We're just waiting to hear back about our offer," she said.

"Wow."

"Yes, fingers crossed."

My aunt loved everything about real estate and luxury living. She'd worked hard to earn her wealth, and I admired her cutthroat attitude to business. I felt as if some of her adrenaline rubbed off on me as she regaled me with stories about her investment successes. I'd even begun looking at condos for myself — albeit cheap ones — and she was the first person I wanted to tell if I ever bought my own place.

On that sparkling, winter day we had an even more successful lunch than usual. I measured success by whether or not she ordered tea or dessert so we could continue to chat. She ordered both, and we were on our second cup of Earl Grey when she proposed a new idea.

"I wonder if maybe… this has been so much fun, maybe you wanted to carry on and do something else together?" she asked.

"Sure, that'd be fun."

"Okay, great." She paused, tapped a French-tipped fingernail against her lips. "To tell the truth, I was thinking it might help us get into the holiday spirit and, well, I wonder if maybe we could start a new tradition."

"What?" I asked, suddenly full of anticipation. From her face, I could tell she felt excited — and if she was excited, it meant there must be at least some degree of risk involved in her plan.

"I have this one-hundred-dollar bill burning a hole in my pocket, and I was thinking maybe we could find a homeless person and give it to him or her."

I couldn't have been more shocked if she'd told me she wanted to go swimming in the restaurant's fish tank.

I swallowed down a gulp of tea and tried not to look as surprised as I felt. It's not that I'd thought she was uncharitable — although we'd never talked about charity before. Mostly I was surprised that she either didn't know, or didn't care, that giving money directly to a homeless person in our city was thought by some people to be less-than-ideal because the money, some said, could be swiftly exchanged for booze or drugs.

"Sure," I said. "I think that's a great idea. It's very generous of you."

"I was thinking that we could walk around until we find somebody who we really want to give it to. And say 'Happy Holidays.' What do you think?"

"Yes, that sounds good."

"Okay." She grinned. "And maybe we can do this again next year. It could be our holiday tradition."

"Absolutely."

Off we went, squinting in the harsh winter light on the main street of downtown and searching for someone who appeared most in need of my aunt's one hundred dollars. As we walked, she continued to talk in rushed, excited tones as she had done during lunch. Her boots made a staccato clicking sound along the sidewalk. I was becoming tired just trying to keep up with her: her quick, constantly churning mind and her fast walking were almost too much for me. Luckily she found her prospect almost immediately. The fabric of his coat had faded to a pale, greyish green. I saw dirt on his cheeks and vagueness in his eyes as we approached. He was slouched against a building, and parts of his scalp showed through his white hair.

I lingered a step behind my aunt as she neared him, strutting in the brisk no-nonsense way of hers and smiling widely.

"Hello." She rustled in her purse, producing the one-hundred-dollar bill. She held it out toward him. "Here, I want you to have this. Happy Holidays."

He extended a rough hand and hesitated, staring at the money. Then he raised his face to look at her. She nodded encouragingly.

Shaking, he folded his fingers around the bill. His gaze was steady as he looked at my aunt, eyes filling with a youthful kind of light.

"Miss, thank you." He took her hand in his, and kissed it once. I smiled at them both, but I wasn't involved in this interaction: it was private, and existed only for the two of them.

On the walk back to the car, my aunt remained silent for a while. Her steps were slower.

"He seemed happy, didn't he?" she said thoughtfully.

"Yes, he did," I agreed. "You made his day."

I felt that I'd just witnessed something spectacular, but I couldn't quite define why.

It wasn't until later that I realized: not only did the man look genuinely joyful when he accepted the money—which in my mind made the event worth it no matter how he invested that bill—but I had the impression he had given my aunt a gift as well.

And the fleeting, magical exchange they shared had an effect on me, too: I learned that the good energy of any gift can spread outward, touching those who are simply spectators and creating a memory that sticks and shines for years. Never again will I even consider believing that certain forms of giving are "lesser" than others.

—Jessica Lampard—

Meet Our Contributors

We are pleased to introduce you to the writers whose stories were selected from our library to create this special Canadian kindness collection. All bios were current as of the time the stories were originally published by Chicken Soup for the Soul.

This is **Val Fletcher Adolph's** third story published in the *Chicken Soup for the Soul* series. She writes historical fiction based on the lives of women in gold rush times. Her first novel, *Bride Ship Three*, is about three women arriving on a bride ship. Val worked in a large institution for many years, appreciating vastly different realities.

Heidi Allen began her journey as a successful wedding photographer, but knew she was supposed to be doing something bigger. Determined to make her mark, she has had many careers. Yet, it was working as a TV makeover producer where she realized she was meant to motivate and inspire, and the "Positive People Army" movement began.

Mary M. Alward has been writing professionally since 1989 and has been published in both print and online venues. She enjoys spending time with her grandsons, reading and gardening. Currently, Mary is taking a course with the Institute of Children's Literature and hopes to one day write children's books.

Nancy Barter-Billard is a journalism graduate who works as a marketing professional in Brantford, ON, Canada. In addition to spending time with her three grown children and volunteering in her community, Nancy enjoys golfing, gardening, playing online *Scrabble*, and watching *MasterChef* with her daughter, Olivia.

A former English teacher, **Irene R. Bastian** loves to write and paint, and recently began drawing. Gardening and working the family tree nursery near the foothills of Alberta allow her to appreciate the great outdoors. Her two yellow Labradors love keeping her company, especially if she is driving the RTV. E-mail her at ibastian@platinum.ca.

Emily Bednarz received her Bachelor of Arts, with honours, from Wilfrid Laurier University in 2012. She completed her Master's degree in English at the University of Western Ontario, and is currently pursuing her Ph.D. at Wilfrid Laurier. She resides in Kitchener, Ontario, but loves visiting Cape Breton, Nova Scotia whenever she can.

Glynis M. Belec celebrates life after cancer with her family in Ontario, Canada and counts her blessings daily. She is a freelance writer, a children's author and a tutor to some fabulous students. Check out her webpage at www.glynisbelec.com.

Juan Bendana is a youth motivational speaker and best-selling author. He has dedicated his life to helping young people find out what they want to do with their lives. He is also a snowboard instructor, sushi fanatic, and has a passion for travel.

Nancy Bennett is an avid pet lover, whose pets include several rescue cats, Tim Tim, Nina, Maya and Scraps as well as Kali the dog. She lives on a two-acre farm on Vancouver Island, where she raises heirloom vegetables, and small rare bantam chickens.

Susan Blakeney is a writer of fiction for children and young adults with several novels on the go at various stages of development. Her works include historical fiction as well as speculative fiction/fantasy. Susan enjoys cooking and baking, and time with her "hairy boys" — Rudy and Barrett — and her supportive husband, Henry.

Cynthia Lynn Blatchford is the author of several stories published in numerous Chicken Soup for the Soul books. As a former foster child success story, she aspires to help others to both heal and succeed using the written word based on her own life experiences. E-mail her at cindy_700@hotmail.com.

Jennifer Bly is a freelance writer and blogger at *The Deliberate Mom*. Mother of two girls and wife to one amazing husband, she spends her days homeschooling and living life fully. Jennifer regularly writes about parenting, homeschooling, blogging and her Christian faith. Her writing has been featured on *The Huffington Post*.

Barbara Bondy-Pare has four children from her first loving husband, Ronald M. Bondy. Since he passed away from lung cancer, she has married a high school classmate, Eddie Pare. Their twelve adorable grandchildren keep them young, active and entertained. Barbara is all about love, family and hugs.

Family is key to happiness, says **Ellie Braun-Haley**. She continues to write/talk on miracles and goodness. She's a regular contributor to the *Chicken Soup for the Soul* series and the author of books, two on creative movement for children, one on miracles, and a co-author on a book about spousal abuse with husband, Shawn.

Tim Brewster is an outdoor enthusiast in Alberta, Canada. He loves skiing, cycling, hiking, and fishing with his two daughters and wife Cindy. Someday he hopes to turn the tales he made up for his kids into children's books.

Nathan Burgoine grew up reading and studied literature in university while working at a bookstore. His first novel, *Light*, was a finalist for a Lambda Literary Award. His second novel, *Triad Blood*, is available now from Bold Strokes Books. He lives in Ottawa, Canada with his husband, Dan, and his Husky, Coach.

Kimberley Campbell lives in Centreville, NB, with her husband, two cats and two retired racing Greyhounds. She enjoys skating, biking and walking with her husband and hounds, as well as reading, writing and spending time with her three young nieces.

Niki Card, B.Ed, M.Ed, lives with her husband and her two children, Nolan and Ainslee, in Winnipeg, Manitoba. She is a teacher-librarian and a life-long learner. Niki enjoys reading, running, working with children, and food trucks.

Joseph Civitella, MscD, is an ordained minister of spiritual metaphysics. He founded the School of LifeWork, has written the book, *Turning your Passion into a Profession* and the novel *Shadows of Tomorrow*, and recorded the CD "Soulace." He is currently working on a new book, *The Sacred and the Profane*.

Harriet Cooper is a freelance writer and instructor. She specializes in writing creative nonfiction and articles. Her work has appeared in several *Chicken Soup for the Soul* anthologies, as well as in newspapers, magazines, newsletters and websites. She often writes about health, nutrition, family, cats and the environment.

Elizabeth Creith raised sheep for ten years in Northern Ontario. She has written humour, how-to and short fiction as well as a children's book, *Erik the Viking Sheep*. She divides her time between writing and working in her pet store with her Australian Shepherd, Sky. Contact her at hedgehog.ceramics@sympatico.ca.

Jo Yuill Darlington is a writer of short stories and poetry. This is her second story published by Chicken Soup for the Soul.

Bruce Davidsen began his career in the 1960s as a bass player in Montreal. He went on to become a concert and theatre producer and personal manager who has travelled the world and worked with the biggest names in the entertainment business. His first love... Hockey! Les Canadiens! E-mail him at brucedavidsen@gmail.com.

Connie I. Davidson is a wife, mother and grandma. She received her Social Service Worker diploma with honours from Fanshawe College and lives in Southern Ontario, Canada. This is Connie's first story submitted for publication. Connie enjoys writing poetry as well. E-mail her at cdavidson001@amtelecom.net.

Manpreet Dhillon is a freedom catalyst for women. Manpreet is a certified personal and business coach, Heal Your Money Story Certified Coach, and a certified human resources professional with a master's degree in Organizational Management.

Donna Fawcett is a retired creative writing instructor for Fanshawe College in ON, Canada. Donna writes in the freelance magazine market and her novels *Rescued* and *Vengeance* (Donna Dawson) won Best Contemporary Novel in Canada's largest Christian writing awards, The Word Awards. Learn more at www.donnafawcett.com.

Trish Featherstone is a retired RN living in the Interior of British Columbia. Her nom de plume is an acknowledgement to her mother, who gave her the gift of loving books.

June Rogers Flahie is an editor and writer for a variety of Canadian news, travel, health and women's publications. She loves playing the ukulele, dancing the samba and writing poetry.

Linda Gabris has instructed writing workshops and international cooking courses for over sixteen years. She has written a book, *Cooking Wild*, and hopes to have another book finished soon. Linda writes outdoor cooking columns and articles for magazines in Canada and the USA. You can reach her at inkserv@telus.net.

James A. Gemmell is a married father of two children. Most summers he can be found hiking across Spain on the Camino de Santiago. His other hobbies include writing, playing guitar and collecting art.

Robyn Gerland is the author of *All These Long Years Later*, a book of short stories; the past editor of the internationally distributed glossy, *Hysteria*; a frequent contributor to the *Chicken Soup for the Soul* series; and a contributor and columnist for several magazines and newspapers. She is also a member of The Federation of British Columbia Writers.

Kristin Goff is a retired journalist, grandmother of five, plodding runner and slow triathlete. She enjoys travelling, trying new things and is grateful for the love and support of friends and family, who may laugh with her but not at her.

Pamela Goldstein has followed her passion for writing for more than twenty years. She has completed three manuscripts and four plays, and has several short stories published, many in the *Chicken Soup for the Soul* series. Pamela is honoured to be part of the Chicken Soup for the Soul family. E-mail her at boker_tov2002@yahoo.ca.

Charmaine Hammond received her Master's Degree in Conflict Analysis & Management from Royal Roads University, BC, Canada and is owner and president of Hammond International Inc. A professional speaker, facilitator and consultant, Charmaine is passionate about helping individuals and businesses reach and exceed their potential. Please contact Charmaine at charmaine@hammondgroup.biz.

Rob Harshman has been in education for over forty years. He is married with two daughters and two grandchildren. Rob enjoys travel and photography and is planning to continue writing stories, both fiction and nonfiction.

Between and during writing and filmmaking projects, **Harley Hay** has worked as a professional drummer, a paralegal, a high school English teacher, a photographer and a TV videographer. He lives in Red Deer, Alberta, Canada with his wife Nina, their children Jesse and Jenna Lee, and Scamp, their slightly deranged Shih Tzu.

Colleen Stewart Haynes completed an MA degree at fifty-something through Royal Roads University, then retired from nursing, having worked in emergency, home care, psych/mental health, and academia. She lives in Edmonton, Canada with her husband Michael and works as a freelance writer, editor, and recipe blogger. E-mail her at cls03@shaw.ca.

Elaine Ingalls Hogg is an award-winning author and the editor of *Christmas in the Maritimes* (Nimbus Publishing), a book which became a Canadian bestseller in 2006. Elaine shares her office with two Ragdoll cats, Angus and Alex, enjoys writing, music and travel. Please contact her through her website: http://elainehogg.com.

Janelle In't Veldt, of Ontario, Canada, wrote this story at the age of sixteen, and owes this success to everyone who cheered her on. In her spare time, Janelle loves to edit videos and perform in musical theatre. She would like to thank her mom for being such an amazing role model.

Tanya Janke has worked in three schools, two shopping malls, a theatre, a market research company, and a berry patch. She now spends her days writing. Her first play, an adaptation of *The Little Prince*, was produced in Toronto in 2010.

Phyllis M. Jardine, a retired nurse and grandmother, writes from the Annapolis Valley, Nova Scotia, where she lives with her husband Bud. Her inspirational essays and poems have been widely published and heard on national radio. This is Phyllis's fourth story in the Chicken Soup for the Soul series.

Bonnie Jarvis-Lowe is a retired Registered Nurse who spends much of her time now working with animals at the SPCA in her town. She just celebrated her fortieth wedding anniversary and is the mother of two and the grandmother of one little girl.

Tom Knight is a husband and father who lives and works in Toronto, Canada. After reading *Chicken Soup for the Soul* he realized he had his own stories to share and he hopes that his first published story will not be his last. He is eternally grateful for the love and support of his wife and children, without whom none of his dreams would ever have been realized.

Marla Stewart Konrad is the author of several books for children, including the award-winning picture book, *Just Like You.* She lives with her family near Toronto, Canada.

Teresa Kruze is a broadcaster and journalist. She got her start in television as one of the first female sports reporters and anchors in Canada. Teresa currently hosts and produces a weekly television talk show and writes a national newspaper column called "The In-Credibility Factor." Visit her website at www.teresakruze.com.

Danielle Kuhn is a full-time mother who lives in St. Thomas, Ontario with her husband, five children and two parrots. She is a sarcoidosis warrior and advocate for her exceptional children. She draws on these experiences when sharing her lifelong passion for writing. In her leisure time she enjoys crochet and nature.

Jessica Lampard studied writing at the University of Victoria, where she graduated with a Bachelor of Arts degree. She enjoys hiking with her dog, playing tennis, and inventing recipes. She is currently working on a novel.

Lisa McManus Lange is a frequent contributor to Chicken Soup for the Soul, this being her fourth book. She likes cats, writing, her kids, and peace and tranquility — but not in that order. Visit her at www.

lisamcmanuslange.blogspot.com or e-mail her at lisamc2010@yahoo.ca.

Deborah Lean is a retired nurse, mother of two, and grandmother of seven. She enjoys painting, crochet, and a variety of crafts. Writing is an ongoing interest, with two blogs and a number of ebooks online.

Foxglove Lee specializes in LGBTQ fiction for teens and young adults. Her books include *Tiffany and Tiger's Eye* and *Truth and Other Lies*. Find out more at foxglovelee.blogspot.com and follow her on Twitter @FoxgloveLee.

Emily Linegar is a student at Brandon University. She hopes to become a teacher one day, but will keep writing on the side.

Jennifer Litke is happily married to her husband of fifteen years. Together they have three sons and they live and play in the small town community of Prince Edward County. Jennifer is the author of *Conceived: Encouragement and Hope for Young Single Moms*. Learn more at www.conceived.weebly.com.

Maighread MacKay is an author from Toronto, ON. She has published three books for children: *Bedtime Treasures*, *The Mysterious Door* and *The Crystal Grove* under the name Margaret Hefferman. Her novel *Stone Cottage* is her first foray into adult literature, to be published in 2015 by Solstice Shadows Publishing.

Gail MacMillan is an award-winning author of twenty-seven published books and numerous short stories both in North America and Western Europe. She is a graduate of Queen's University and lives in NB, Canada with her husband and two dogs.

Laurie Ann Mangru completed a double major program at the University of Toronto in English literature and Spanish. After, she moved to Japan where she has taught English for nine years. Laurie is a world traveler and has enjoyed writing short stories and poems since she was a child.

E-mail her at laurieloveswriting@gmail.com.

In 2001, **Miriam Mas** started Canines with a Cause, a charity dedicated to training assistance dogs for people with disabilities. She left the high-tech world to better focus on helping others. By sharing this story, she hopes others will also take the time to share hope with others in need. You can reach Miriam at miriam.mas@gmail.com.

Dennis McCloskey has a journalism degree from Ryerson University in Toronto. He has been a full-time freelance writer since 1980 and is the author of several books, including the 2008 award-winning biography, *My Favorite American*. He lives in Richmond Hill, ON, with his wife Kris. E-mail his at dmcclos@rogers.com.

Avril McIntyre is a showroom manager and lives on a mountain. She enjoys traveling, friends and is passionate about animals. Her plans are to continue writing inspirational animal stories and finishing her book.

Heidi McLaughlin is an international speaker and author of five books. She inspires women to become beautiful from the inside out. Heidi lives with her husband Jack among the beautiful vineyards of Kelowna, British Columbia. She loves her eclectic family of five children and nine grandchildren. Learn more at www.heartconnection.ca.

Chris Mikalson is a retired bookkeeper, who is now enjoying camping with her husband, as well as pursuing the creative "loves of her life" — writing and painting. Chris is a Reiki Master and finds great joy in helping others heal with the aid of this beautiful energy. E-mail her at chris_mikalson@yahoo.ca.

Mary Anne Molcan is currently a fine arts student at North Island College on Vancouver Island. She has published poetry in a local magazine and plans to continue sharing her words and artwork so that others can learn about themselves. Mary Anne can be contacted at faerie.artiste@gmail.com.

Like most people who tell their story about singing from the day they were born, **Samantha Molinaro's** passion for writing was seeded at birth. The bottom line remains that for Samantha, writing is an escape and mode of expression in which she hopes others can be inspired to laugh, cry, or even write themselves.

Marya Morin is a freelance writer. Her stories have appeared in publications such as *Woman's World* and Hallmark. Marya also penned a weekly humorous column for an online newsletter, and writes custom poetry on request. She lives in the country with her husband. E-mail her at Akushla514@hotmail.com.

Lauren Murray is a writer and knitting aficionado who lives in the Rocky Mountains of Alberta, Canada. She's older than she looks — really — and younger than she feels — most of the time — and she loves to explore women's journeys in her stories. Visit her at www.laurenhawkeye.com.

Shirley Neal is a freelance writer and photographer who lives in Ontario, Canada. She teaches travel, writing, and photography. Shirley is an accomplished playwright and screenwriter, and recently sold her screenplay to a film production company. Introducing people to the world beyond their doorstep through words and pictures is a dream realized. Contact her at sneal@interhop.net.

Diane C. Nicholson is a writer and professional photographer/photo-artist, specializing in companion animals and special needs children. A long-time vegan, her affinity and respect for animals and her patient understanding of children with special needs are reflected in her art. Diane has eight stories published by Chicken Soup for the Soul.

Born and raised in Port Alberni, BC, among friends **Louise Nyce** is jokingly referred to as the crazy cat lady. She has always had a love of the written word, finding comfort and a place to hide in the magic that all stories, be they fact or fiction, can provide.

Christine Pincombe-DeCaen previously worked as a chef. Now she takes care of her young daughter full-time. Christine enjoys writing, painting, making and selling her jewellery. She is working on her first fiction novel. E-mail her at sarahkayday@hotmail.ca.

Wendy Poole is now a retired Early Childhood Educator. She worked in both staff and management positions within the ECE field as well as teaching part-time at a community college. Wendy also wrote/piloted a literacy program for preschoolers and also wrote/piloted a parenting information program for newcomers to Canada.

Jeannette Richter lives on a farm on the short-grass prairie of Alberta with her husband John. She is currently working on a novel about the loss of language rights and confessional schools in Manitoba after the Riel Uprising of 1870.

Rachael Robitaille is a high school student who enjoys reading, writing, soccer, hockey, curling and dramatic arts. She hopes to someday publish a novel. E-mail her at rrobitaille3579@gmail.com.

Heather Rae Rodin serves as Executive Director for Hope Grows Haiti. An award-winning writer and author of *Prince of Vodou: Breaking the Chains*, Heather has always had a passion for a story. Heather and her husband Gord live in Ontario, Canada. When not in Haiti, she enjoys time spent with their large and growing family.

Angela Rolleman is a social worker, writer, speaker, trainer, entrepreneur, wife, daughter, aunt, sister and friend. She is founder of Mission: Empowerment, a company that provides personal and professional development seminars and events. Angela loves animals, travelling, reading and spending time in nature. To learn more, visit www.angelarolleman.com or www.missionempowerment.ca.

Catherine Rossi adds creative flair to everything she touches. She loves cooking, floral arranging and cake decorating. This is her first writing adventure. She has also just illustrated her first children's book called *Katie's Smile*.

Leigh Anne Saxe's passion is to inspire others to be happier and healthier. She is an independent consultant with Arbonne International and is a happiness coach and inspirational speaker. Leigh Anne loves to downhill ski and spend time up north with her family. Learn more at www.leighannesaxe.myarbonne.ca.

Cassie Silva has her social work degree and works with youth and children near Vancouver, British Columbia. She has been volunteering with Make-A-Wish British Columbia and Yukon since December 2008. She was previously published in *Chicken Soup for the Soul: The Cancer Book* (2009). E-mail her at cassiesilva@ymail.com.

Shirley K. Stevenson earned her B.Ed. from University of Alberta. She is a retired teacher and widow with two grown children. She is very active as a volunteer with seniors in care and in teaching and helping at senior centers in Edmonton, AB. Shirley enjoys writing up her own memories and helping others do so.

Kim Tendland-Frenette is a graduate of the Institute of Children's Literature. She received her Bachelor of Education in 2009 and now works as an elementary teacher in British Columbia where she lives with her husband and two kids. Kim's current projects include kids' books and articles. E-mail her at kimtf.writer@gmail.com.

Nancy Thorne lives just outside of Toronto with her husband, two sons and a yellow Labrador. Her stories have recently appeared in *Canadian Tales of the Mysterious* and *Canadian Tales of the Heart*. She hopes her writing, reflecting the unpredictability of life and new beginnings, inspires others.

Lynne Turner received a Journalism degree from Ryerson University in Toronto and spent the next nearly forty years as a reporter, editor and manager at the *Mount Forest Confederate* newspaper in Ontario. She enjoys writing, reading, walking and spending time with her family. Her mother is an inspiration to all who know her.

Sirena Van Schaik is an honours graduate from Mohawk College in Early Childhood Education. She has been published in several anthologies and magazines and has found her passion in writing. She enjoys reading, spending time with her husband, two children and curling up with her cat Lobo. E-mail her at sirena.van@sympatico.ca.

Rachel Wallace-Oberle has an education in journalism and broadcasting and is working on a degree in communications. She is senior marketing writer for a software company and her work has been featured in *Reader's Digest*, *Homemakers*, *Canadian Living*, *Woman's World*, *Today's Parent*, and numerous other publications.

Even as a young child, **Sally Walls** loved to write. She has a passion for encouragement and a heart for people. Other short stories she has written have been published in *Chicken Soup for the Soul: O Canada* and in *Chicken Soup for the Soul: Devotional Stories for Tough Times*. Learn more at www.sallywall.com.

Laura Whitman is a storyteller, social innovator, inspiration chaser and proud Nova Scotian who leads with empathy and believes in better. When she's not writing, creating or making ideas happen, Laura loves relaxing with her family, getting fresh air and exercise, and sharing experiences and laughs with her girlfriends.

Leslie Anne Wibberley loves the written word almost as much as her family. Her creative nonfiction essays are published in several literary journals, and her short story, "That Damn Pumpkin," in *Devolution Z*. She has won 6th place and an Honorable Mention in Writer's Digest's Annual Competitions. E-mail her at wibberleythewordsmith@gmail.com. **Crysta Windsor** has retreated to her journals to find release, through writing, since she was small. Her other hobbies include painting and baking. She is currently finishing a Bachelor of Arts (Honours) degree at Mount Royal University. She is an English major and plans to continue onto a master's degree in 2014.

Julie Winn is a musician and freelance writer/editor living in the Toronto area with her husband and three children. Her hobbies include singing with the Amadeus Choir, composing music, studying French and German, and working on her blog, found at winnwords1.wordpress.com.

Angela Wolthuis lives in the woods of Alberta with her husband and three boys. She finds inspiration for her writing in everything around her, and loves to quilt, craft and be active. Last year she published her first book. E-mail Angela at angwolthuis@me.com.

After receiving a Master of Education degree at UBC, **Sarah Wun** traveled to the Middle East to begin her career as an ESL teacher. She currently resides in Shanghai, China where she teaches sixth and seventh grade English and Sexual Health Education. She enjoys writing, often about her experiences overseas.

Melissa Yuan-Innes dedicates this essay to her father, James Yuan. She would like to thank the doctors and nurses at The Ottawa Hospital and Saint-Vincent Hospital for their care. Melissa is an emergency physician who writes and cares for her family outside of Montreal, Canada. Learn more at www.melissayuaninnes.net.

Karen Vincent Zizzo, MA, is an author and inspirational speaker whose passion is to inspire people to overcome obstacles in their lives. She generously shares very personal messages of faith, hope, love and the power of prayer through her *Ask and You Shall Receive* series of books, CDs and workbooks at karenzizzo.com.

Meet Amy Newmark

Amy Newmark is the bestselling author, editor-in-chief, and publisher of the *Chicken Soup for the Soul* book series. Since 2008, she has published more than 150 new books, most of them national bestsellers in the U.S. and Canada, more than doubling the number of Chicken Soup for the Soul titles in print today. She is also the author of *Simply Happy*, a crash course in Chicken Soup for the Soul advice and wisdom that is filled with easy-to-implement, practical tips for enjoying a better life.

Amy is credited with revitalizing the Chicken Soup for the Soul brand, which has been a publishing industry phenomenon since the first book came out in 1993. By compiling inspirational and aspirational true stories curated from ordinary people who have had extraordinary experiences, Amy has kept the twenty-five-year-old Chicken Soup for the Soul brand fresh and relevant.

Amy graduated *magna cum laude* from Harvard University where she majored in Portuguese and minored in French. She then embarked on a three-decade career as a Wall Street analyst, a hedge fund manager, and a corporate executive in the technology field. She is a Chartered Financial Analyst.

Her return to literary pursuits was inevitable, as her honours thesis in college involved traveling throughout Brazil's impoverished northeast region, collecting stories from regular people. She is delighted to have come full circle in her writing career — from collecting stories "from the people" in Brazil as a twenty-year-old to, three decades later, collecting stories "from the people" for Chicken Soup for the Soul.

When Amy and her husband Bill, the CEO of Chicken Soup for the Soul, are not working, they are visiting their four grown children and their first grandchild.

Follow Amy on Twitter @amynewmark. Listen to her free podcast, "Chicken Soup for the Soul with Amy Newmark," on Apple Podcasts, Google Play, the Podcasts app on iPhone, or by using your favourite podcast app on other devices.

About United Way Centraide Canada

United Way Centraide Canada is a federated network of over eighty-seven local United Way offices, serving more than 5,000 communities, each registered as its own nonprofit organization and governed by an independent volunteer-led local Board of Directors. Each United Way works locally to raise funds and invest in improving lives in its community.

United Way has a long history in Canada, dating back almost a century. Over the years, it has been known by many names — among them Community Chest, United Appeal and Red Feather. In  French, both in Quebec and across Canada, the organization is known as Centraide, but the organization often uses the United Way and Centraide names together, recognizing the bilingual nature of Canada's culture and people.

United Way Centraide Canada is the national office and provides leadership, guidance and support to local United Ways across the country. Together, local United Ways and United Way Centraide Canada form the United Way Movement, with a mission to improve lives and build community by engaging individuals and mobilizing collective action.

Thank You

We owe huge thanks to all of our Canadian contributors and fans. We had a wonderful time poring over all the stories in our library that were written by Canadians and were not already published in books that were specific to Canada. We want to thank the Canadian writers who welcomed the chance to be in this special collection that benefits United Way Centraide Canada.

Ronelle Frankel and D'ette Corona did the bulk of the work on choosing the stories and they both said they would like to take a vacation in Canada now... which they need. Our fabulous team of Associate Publisher D'ette Corona, Senior Editor Barbara LoMonaco, and editors Kristiana Pastir and Elaine Kimbler jumped in at the end to proof, proof, proof. And yes, there will always be typos anyway, so please feel free to let us know about them at webmaster@ chickensoupforthesoul.com and we will correct them in future printings. We tried hard to use Canadian spelling!

The whole publishing team deserves a hand, including our Senior Director of Marketing Maureen Peltier, our Senior Director of Production Victor Cataldo, Executive Assistant Mary Fisher, and our graphic designer Daniel Zaccari, who turned our manuscript into this beautiful book.

Sharing Happiness, Inspiration, and Hope

Real people sharing real stories, every day, all over the world. In 2007, *USA Today* named *Chicken Soup for the Soul* one of the five most memorable books in the last quarter-century. With over 100 million books sold to date in the U.S. and Canada alone, more than 250 titles in print, and translations into nearly fifty languages, "chicken soup for the soul®" is one of the world's best-known phrases.

Today, twenty-five years after we first began sharing happiness, inspiration and hope through our books, we continue to delight our readers with new titles, but have also evolved beyond the bookstore with super premium pet food, television shows, podcasts, positive journalism from aplus.com, movies and TV shows on the Popcornflix app, and licensed products, all revolving around true stories, as we continue "changing the world one story at a time®." Thanks for reading!

Share with Us

We all have had Chicken Soup for the Soul moments in our lives. If you would like to share your story or poem with millions of people around the world, go to chickensoup.com and click on "Submit Your Story." You may be able to help another reader and become a published author at the same time. Some of our past contributors have launched writing and speaking careers from the publication of their stories in our books!

We only accept story submissions via our website. They are no longer accepted via mail or fax. Visit our website, www.chickensoup. com, and click on Submit Your Story for our writing guidelines and a list of topics we are working on.

To contact us regarding other matters, please send us an e-mail through webmaster@chickensoupforthesoul.com, or fax or write us at:

Chicken Soup for the Soul
P.O. Box 700
Cos Cob, CT 06807-0700
Fax: 203-861-7194

One more note from your friends at Chicken Soup for the Soul: Occasionally, we receive an unsolicited book manuscript from one of our readers, and we would like to respectfully inform you that we do not accept unsolicited manuscripts and we must discard the ones that appear.

Chicken Soup for the Soul.

Christmas in Canada

101 Stories about the Joy
and Wonder of the Holidays

Amy Newmark
& Janet Matthews

Paperback: 978-1-61159-943-5
eBook: 978-1-61159-245-0

More winter joy

Chicken Soup for the Soul®

O Canada The Wonders of Winter

101 Stories about Bad Weather, Good Times, and Great Sports

Jack Canfield,
Mark Victor Hansen,
Amy Newmark & Janet Matthews

Paperback: 978-1-61159-931-2
eBook: 978-1-61159-231-3

and Canadian kindness

Changing the world one story at a time®
www.chickensoup.com